T0065361

About the Author

From 1965 to 1971, John Densmore was the drummer in the Doors. Since 1971, Densmore has been involved in theater—both acting and writing plays—and in dance, playing percussion for avant-garde productions. He has codirected and produced several long-form Doors videos, and was a consultant to Oliver Stone's film biography of the band. He lives in Los Angeles with his wife, daughter, two dogs, one cat, and three chickens.

My Life with Jim Morrison and The Doors

John Densmore

Delta
Trade Paperbacks

Published by
Dell Publishing
a division of
Penguin Random House LLC
New York, New York

The trademark Delta® is registered in the U.S. Patent and Trademark Office.

ISBN 978-0-385-30447-4

Reprinted by arrangement with Delacorte Press

Published simultaneously in Canada

October 1991

BVG

146122000

To John Lennon
who inspired me to put
my personal life on the line

ACKNOWLEDGMENTS

I want to thank Bob Miller from Delacorte Press for believing in my writing very early on, and finally buying the book and editing it with care. I could tell that it wasn't just a job. Thanks to Bernie Schwartz for early encouragement and editing. Finally, hugs to Leslie Neale for all the support, and thanks to Robby Krieger, Ray Manzarek, Sam Joseph, Michael Ventura, Danny Sugerman, Amy Ephron, Abe Somer, Bill Siddons, Debbie Berman, Paul Rothchild, Bruce Botnick, Leslie Werner, Lanette Phillipson, and Robert Bly. And beneath the weight of this project, I wish to thank those whom I have carelessly omitted.

Finally, I want to thank all the fans, old and new, who have responded to my venture into a new avenue of creativity: the printed word. It has inspired me to continue.

There would be no book without Phil Cousineau. His help with the structure, editing, and writing was invaluable. Not to mention his friendship, guidance, and work as benevolent taskmaster.

PREFACE

It seems that whoever met Jim Morrison walked away with a different impression: Southern gentleman, prick, poet, brute, charmer, etc.

I lived with Jim for six years on the road and in the recording studio. This book is my truth. It may not be the whole truth, but it is the way I saw it. From the drum stool.

CONTENTS

1

BREAK ON THROUGH

Paris, 1975

It smelled like rain. I had hoped it would storm. Then we wouldn't have had to see his grave. My heartbeat was increasing. I looked over at Robby, Danny, and Hervé in the car as we approached the cemetery. They all seemed to be nervously anticipating what was to come. The high thick walls looked ominous, as if they protected something ancient and mysterious inside.

As we rounded the entrance, a Chaplin-like gendarme waddled up to us and asked where we were headed.

"Do you know where Jim Morrison's grave is?" I asked with trepidation.

"Ah, *mais oui,*" he answered in a thick accent. "Monsieur Morrison's grave is up that cobblestone lane. The graffiti will guide you there. It was removed recently, but as you will see, plenty more has been added. So don't contribute, *d'accord?*"

"*D'accord.*" Let's get this over with, I mumbled to myself as we walked past his guardhouse.

The lane got steeper and steeper as we ascended past moss-covered gravestones. A cold, damp mist began to surround us. Several mangy cats scurried across our path into dark holes that were graves. Besides many famous European corpses, Père Lachaise Cemetery is home to hundreds of stray felines.

Strange that a good ole boy from Florida is there. Jim would've

1

liked the company, though. Have to wonder if he didn't plan it that way.

The massive, baroque markers along the cemetery road led the way to Oscar Wilde, Balzac, Edith Piaf, and Chopin. And then the graffiti: "Morrison—this way," carved into a tombstone probably over a hundred years old; then, painted crudely over one old ornate marker after another: "Acid Rules," "This Is Not The End," "Jim Was a Junkie." As the desecration got more and more outrageous, I sensed that the gravesite was getting nearer.

"Over here," Hervé, the French journalist, said wearily. He was standing behind some large granite crypts. We shuffled along the side of the lane, then began to climb over several tumbledown stones to a small rectangle of cement in the ground.

I stared at it incredulously. This is it? I cried to myself. This is the end of the Electric Shaman, the Acid King, Oedipus Rex himself?

Shit. *Merde.*

I looked over at Danny Sugerman and my eyes welled up with tears. My stomach knotted, my legs began to itch with the old maddening rash. I wanted to run away. "Do you understand *now?*" I said to Danny under my breath.

He nodded, then turned to me. "My God, I had no idea," he said, noticing my grief, as if for the first time.

"Of course not. You weren't in the band. You were the publicist," I snapped, feeling a need to lash out.

Robby straggled alongside, quiet as ever, keeping a lid on his feelings, as usual. Our guitarist was introverted, but he was my best friend.

"How could he fit in there?" I asked, feeling slightly ludicrous. "He *was* six feet tall—wasn't he?"

Maybe it's true, I thought. Maybe he isn't dead. Maybe he is in Africa trying to live out one more myth. First Dionysus, then Nietzsche, then Rimbaud?

Wait a minute. He's dead, you asshole. You watched him destroy himself, I hissed at myself as I stared at the grave. And you didn't do anything about it. *Couldn't* do anything about it. You saw it coming for years, but . . .

Nietzsche killed Jim Morrison, I had once said rather melodramatically to some startled friends in Berkeley. Morrison the Superman, the Dionysian madman, the Birth of Tragedy himself. But who knows who or what killed him? God knows, a million people have come to me hoping I had the answer.

I shoved my hands into my coat pockets and sighed with deep despair. This is a beautiful place to be buried, Jim, but your plot seems so small and cold and dirty and—unworthy.

All our lives we sweat and save
Building for a shallow grave
Must be something else we say
Somehow to defend this place.

"The Soft Parade," remember, Jim?

The gravesite was silent. Defiantly silent. I felt the cold rain creeping down my neck. Chills. Hervé and Robby milled around nervously. A young rock-'n'-roll pilgrim nearby strummed a Doors song on his guitar in homage. On his backpack was a Doors sticker. There's no escape.

٪

Jim, I'm still in the labyrinth, trying to find answers to questions I don't even know how to phrase. Sure, Ray, Robby, and I talked about your self-destruction, but Robby and I rationalized that you'd probably live till you were eighty, like a tough old Irish drunk. My body knew better, though. I got year-long headaches, rashes, phobias. And still I hung in there. Robby said that one thing that made the band powerful was the psychic strength we had to tolerate your excesses. If this were still the sixties I'd accept that, but I need more than that now so I can move on.

I turned back to the surreally decorated tombstone. What were you saying in your songs that could possibly defend your courting of insanity and nearly dragging us down with you? What *was* your

3

fucking message, Jim? Anarchy? Why did I put up with it all those years? For the money? The fame? The girls? All these years later I feel like I betrayed myself, compromised, that I was never man enough to stand up to you and really quit. Oh, I stormed out once —in Michigan—remember? But I came back.

You knew I would, didn't you—how?

"C'mon, John, we gotta go," said Danny.

I waved them on. "I just need another minute."

After they'd gone: silence. Then the rain started pattering on the moss, filling up a corner of the dirt inside the plain gravesite. A couple of flowers floated limp in the mud.

Jim, I'm real proud of what we did, I whispered to my old friend's burial plot, but I'm weary of only being known as your drummer. I don't know who I am. I'm thirty-one years old, I know that. Outlived you by four years, you son of a bitch. I realize now that I wasn't very conscious about my path in life at the time. At least you fulfilled your prophecy, even if you had to die to propagate the Doors' precious myth. Our secret death pact. Nonverbal, of course.

Or am I hallucinating? You had started out for the void and Ray, Robby, and I, your Feast of Friends, supported you. To a point. We had no idea that you meant to do it literally. Now I wonder if I could have done anything to stop you, even while watching old footage and old interviews where we say, Well, somebody has to go out on the edge for the rest of us.

Did I compromise myself? I have to know.

A freezing gust of wind shook me out of my reverie. I spun around quickly and ran to catch up with the others. At the gate I put my arm around Danny's shoulder as we headed down the cobblestones to Hervé's car. Robby shook his head in deep despair. He had gone pale. He couldn't even look at me. He just stared numbly out the foggy car window as we slowly pulled out of the cemetery.

*

Later, at the Regency period desk of my Paris hotel room, I gazed out the window over the city rooftops. The sun was trying (in vain) to break through the misty gray morning. I ate the chocolate mint left on my pillow by the maid the night before and laughed quietly at my L-shaped room. Another eccentric European hotel room.

My eyes moved from the window with its view of the blue-gray Paris rooftops to the hotel stationery staring at me from the desk.

I picked up the hotel pen and began a letter.

Paris, 1975

Dear Jim,

Well, we finally visited your grave. I can't speak for the others, but I suppose I didn't come to your funeral because I was so mad and disappointed in you the last few years the band was together. But you knew that. It took me three years to pay my respects, I'm ashamed to say, but I'm here.

It wasn't hard to find your plot with all the graffiti leading up to it. But I was shocked that there wasn't any marker. It seems Pam, your girlfriend (or were you married?), ran off with the money we gave her. There were rumors that it went into her arm. Did you know she was into the brown powder?

Hey, that's a low blow. I don't know why I'm writing this to you. Proves how much you possessed all of us—me, at least. You're supposed to be fucking dead, and here I am brooding over a letter to you in a hotel.

But I don't care. I'm still pissed off and hurting. I wish I would have had the balls to say some things to you back in the sixties, but you were incredibly powerful, and intimidating. I'm extremely proud of our music, but there's some things I've got to get off my chest. It's too late—for you. But it's not too late for me, and maybe some others, like the young kids who still idolize you.

One of the newly carved quotes from your fans implies that you were into smack. I didn't know that. How could I? I didn't know you very well at all during your last days. I didn't want to. It's ironic how the parasites who met you at the end of your life, no matter how briefly, are now trying to

5

cash in on your friendship. While I couldn't even look into your eyes. Those demonic eyes. I had to protect myself. Don't ask me from what.

If anyone could have pulled you out of your nosedive, it was Pam, only she started to slide into drugs, casual affairs, and general decadence along with you. I don't know who encouraged whom, and blaming doesn't do any good.

What was that big black Morrison cloud that hovered over your head? Anyone who came into close contact with you found himself under the fringes of that darkness. You were the fucking Prince of Darkness, Jimbo. At some point the myth we were building overtook us and started running things instead of the other way around. You'd think we could've torn it down or at least backed off a little. Or not underestimated the power of a myth.

But it was a Game Called Insane, as you say, and you were its Poet-Priest, as they say; I say it became a freak show. When did it get out of hand, Jim? What was the point of no return? I need to know because I'm still carrying a shitload of guilt around.

✷

Los Angeles, 1971

The phone rang on a Thursday morning.

"Hey, man, how ya doin'?" said the voice I knew only too well, the whiskeyed voice that struck terror in me.

"Hi, Jim," I replied tentatively, thinking that he was the last person in the world I wanted to talk to. "How is it over there?" I added. "How's France?"

"Okay. Not bad," Jim said noncommittally. "How's *L.A. Woman* doing?"

He didn't sound loaded. Too early in the morning? Wait a minute, I thought. It's early evening there.

"Great! It's really doing great," I said enthusiastically. " 'Love Her Madly' is a hit and everyone really likes the album." What I was not going to tell him was that we had already started rehearsing. Without him. We'd done it before, but this time I had an eye for going on without him. As hard as it was to admit it, I couldn't

6

bear the thought of going through another recording session with the rock-'n'-roll world's Dr. Jekyll.

"Yeah, everything's great." I wondered if he could pick up the subtext.

"Well, maybe we should do another one?"

"Sure, Jim, good idea."

Bad idea, I thought as I fumbled with the receiver and cleared my throat uncomfortably. I hope I never find myself cooped up in a recording studio with you again. It's nice that you want to rock 'n' roll again, especially with us, but I think it's for the wrong reasons. You never did anything because you thought it was going to sell. But maybe you've realized that the four of us *are* a great team. You must not be writing the Great American Novel over there as you had hoped to. Probably *drinking* the Great American Novel.

"When do you think you might come back?" I asked him, while hoping it wouldn't be for a long time because I wanted to take him up on his suggestion that Ray, Robby, and I should do some instrumentals.

Betrayal? Of Jim—or the fans? Of ourselves?

Fuck it! It's a relief to play without Morrison.

"Oh, a few months."

"Elektra wants 'Riders on the Storm' as a second single off the album, so you've got plenty of time."

"A second single . . . wow. . . . It *must* be doing great."

"Yeah."

But I knew we were going on without him. And I was relieved. I just hoped Ray and Robby would go for it. He can't come back, I thought. He would just want to play the blues, the slow, soulful, monotonous blues, which is great for a singer like him, but boring for a drummer like me.

I cursed to myself as Jim carried on about life in Paris. If he came back I knew the other band members would give in. Even I wouldn't be able to say no. If he reappeared, I saw us spending the rest of our lives in dumpy clubs and in grumpy recording sessions. The down side of a great peak. I thought I would die.

Or could I quit? Yes. We're not going down to the Golden Bear kind of dives with the old blues man. No way, José. Fuck it, I resolved as we spoke.

I can quit. I can really quit this time.

"All right, well . . . see ya later."

"Yeah, thanks for callin'."

I hung up, shaking, relieved. Then I thought, Jesus Christ! Wait a minute. Ray and Robby and I have already rehearsed some great instrumentals tracks. Maybe there is no going back. We're committed. Wait till I tell the others. They won't believe he wants to make another record . . . in his alcohol-drenched condition. I knew his sobriety was temporary.

"God," I said with a sigh.

٪

"Jim's dead," Robby said to me as I entered the Doors' office in West Hollywood. It was three weeks after Jim's Paris phone call to me. There had been dozens of death rumors and even threats, but by the seriousness and sadness on Robby's face, I knew this was finally it.

I was the last band member to speak with him. Now, in July of 1971, just six years after we had met, he was gone—my mentor, my nemesis, my friend.

I sat down on the nearest chair and let out a big sigh.

"I got a call from Bill last night," Ray said as he sat down next to me. "He said the European branch of the record company called and said Jim had died. He doesn't have any details."

In his most avuncular manner, Ray went on to say that he had taken the liberty of telling Bill Siddons, our manager, to get on the next plane to Paris to check it out and call the minute he had more information.

I felt numb. As I heard the side musicians arriving downstairs for our scheduled rehearsal, I thought, He's finally gotten what he wanted. Broken on through. To the other side.

The three of us trudged down the cement steps to the studio. I remember how cold the steel railing felt on my hand and how light-headed I was and how it might be good to play some music.

I looked at Ray before going through the rehearsal room doors. "Stupid, stupid," he said angrily. "No different from Jimi and Janis. No originality." He paused, lit a cigarette nervously. "Lousy timing, huh? He just had to be number three, didn't he?" Ray was obviously covering up his grief with anger.

"I'm glad," Robby mumbled with a white face. "He's finally achieved peace."

Once inside, the studio musicians sensed the gloom.

"Our old singer just died," I said. The words ricocheted around in my head as I picked up my drumsticks.

We began rehearsing. It felt a little better to lose ourselves in our music for a while. We forgot for a few moments, if you can ever forget.

Later we took a dinner break and went to the Old World restaurant up on Sunset Boulevard. The loudspeaker was playing rock radio. Twenty minutes into our meal the deejay interrupted the programming with a news flash.

"The rock singer Jim Morrison, of the Doors, is dead at twenty-seven. No further details are available at this time."

The words razored through me. Hot flashes ran up and down my body. I gazed around to see if any of the other patrons in the restaurant recognized us. They didn't for a change, thank God.

Back at our studio, where only months before we had recorded our "comeback album" as the critics were already calling it, where Jim had recorded his vocals from the funky bathroom, the evening session for what eventually became the *Other Voices* album was lifeless.

I flailed madly at my drums but my heart wasn't in it. My mind kept going back to the early days. The cruising days with Jim around the canals of Venice, with the radio blaring out the hot hits of the summer of '66 while we discovered psychedelics and girls and meditation and it looked like we were gonna change the world and change it—NOOOWWW! ! !

2

WILD CHILD

I've always loved music. As an eight-year-old, I never understood the constant genuflecting up and down at St. Timothy's Catholic Church, but the organ player got to me. The stained-glass windows were pretty, but the smell of that incense and all the mumbling was weird. And those twelve pictures of people hammering that guy's wrists and feet to a wooden cross were disgusting.

My mother insisted that I go to church with her and my older sister, Ann, every Sunday. How did Dad get out of it, anyway? I wondered. At least Mom let me go up to the balcony where I sat in the back pew next to the organ pipes that were the loudest (the low notes). Mr. K never smiled, but when he played the low notes with his feet, the walls of the church shook. Especially my seat. I was usually alone up there and I could see Mom and Sis downstairs. No one sat up there except on Easter and Christmas when the church was full. Too loud. Mom said Mr. K got too carried away with the volume pedal. Mr. K also had a red nose on Sunday morning. Maybe he got too carried away with the bottle the night before.

When he played "Ave Maria" I seemed to leave my body. I imagined Mr. K playing so loud that all the windows in the church would break and everyone downstairs would turn around and look up at the two of us and we would be smiling. I just knew that would make Mr. K smile.

At home I enjoyed my parents' Glenn Miller records, and their classical collection as well. Music hypnotized me and transported me out of my little suburban bedroom into fantasyland. At eight and a half years old I asked my parents for a piano and lessons. They obliged and rented an old upright. I took to the instrument immediately. My parents never forced me to practice, although sometimes they gave me subtle prodding. "Your lesson is the day after tomorrow!" Mom would say. I enjoyed playing a piece after I had learned it, especially for an audience.

Even as a kid I knew that what made the difference between a great musician and a mediocre one was what was played in between the notes: the feeling you gave the silences as well as the sounds. I preferred fooling around on a few chords I had learned rather than learning new pieces. It put me into a trance to take a section of an old warhorse tune like "Love Is a Many Splendored Thing" and make it my own with some crude syncopation.

By the time I got to Daniel Webster Junior High School in West L.A., I wanted to join the band and play any instrument. It didn't matter. I thought of the clarinet, but my dentist said it would screw up my teeth (I already had braces). The band director, Mr. Armour, suggested drums. I was afraid I wouldn't be able to practice because of all the noise.

But Mr. Armour was persistent. He showed me a drum practice pad made out of rubber and wood. It didn't seem very exciting, but I could get started at home as soon as possible and worry later about talking my parents into having the real thing.

Eventually they agreed, but in the meantime I had to take private lessons. My greedy little eyes nearly popped out of my head when I first entered Mr. Muir's Drum Shop in West L.A. I had passed by the shop several times before, practically drooling on the windows as I lusted after a gleaming set of new drums. Mr. Armour said I would advance quickly if I took private lessons, so again my parents obliged. It was terribly frustrating having to be taught the nine essential drum rudiments on a silly piece of rubber while being surrounded by sparkling drums of every color.

But Mr. Muir insisted that I wasn't quite ready for the big, loud drum set—or his ears weren't ready to hear my earnest pounding. I was eager to impress him because my lesson followed Hyle King's, a weird fourteen-year-old kid with greasy sculptured hair. But he was a hot drummer and an even hotter piano player. A musician at fourteen.

I suspected my parents of paying Mr. Muir off to keep me away from those cacophonous drums until the last possible moment. It was for the best. Those damned nine essential rudiments gave me my touch. It made the difference later on between a tree-trunk-slamming, heavy-metal technique and a subtler jazz-rock style.

A year later, as an eighth grader, I became the bass drummer of the symphonic band at school and the tympanist with the orchestra. In orchestras, tympani (kettle drum) players spend a lot of time counting bars of music until it is time to come in and play. However, the tympani are usually called for at the end of symphonies, where dramatic drum rolls accentuate the crescendos. I enjoyed providing the dramatic climax of "The Great Gate of Kiev," the final movement of *Pictures at an Exhibition* by Moussorgsky. (They were simplified classical compositions, of course.)

In high school, I graduated to the marching band. With our horrible plumed hats and gaudy, rigid uniforms, I felt like I had joined the army. In those days, playing in the marching band ranked next to having leprosy, but I loved the feeling of power one got when playing with forty other musicians.

I worked my way up from bass drummer to cymbal player and, finally, first snare drummer. To develop a solid sense of time, learning the basic drum beats first (called the "grandfather beat" in Native American cultures) is of primary importance. I was earning the right to play the complicated rhythmic nuances of the snare parts. When playing trap drums or the entire drum set, you put it all together and play all the percussion instruments at once: snare, bass, tom-toms, and cymbals. I was fortunate to learn the drum instruments separately, so that I had a thorough understanding when I put them all together.

⅄.

It was 1960. Kennedy was debating Nixon. The Pirates were beating the Yankees in the World Series. *Wyatt Earp* was the most popular show on television, and *The Apartment* won the Oscar for best motion picture. Singers like Pat Boone and Fabian were at the top of the pop charts.

It was not yet cool to be a musician. If you were a football player, you were definitely the coolest. Basketball was second in "cool," then baseball, track, and finally tennis. The jocks with their lettermen sweaters got the girls. If you were on the tennis team, you might be considered gay—no, back then they were called faggots.

I was last man on the tennis team and, to top it off, in the marching band. Looking back, music was my salvation through those lonely adolescent years, as it would prove to be for years to come.

Luckily, in my second year of high school I was asked to join a pop band. My mother painted our logo on the front of my bass drum—"Terry and the Twilighters." All the other guys in the band were from Catholic families like me, but they went to parochial schools. After I threw up in the first grade of our local Catholic school, my parents thought public school might offer less pressure. So I ended up attending University High School, or Uni, as we called it, but I couldn't get out of catechism classes on Saturdays. The Twilighters started playing the Catholic school circuit around L.A.—Marymount, Loyola, Notre Dame—and I found I could impress the girls with my drumming, or maybe I was just the new kid in town. Whatever it was, I noticed that I was being watched, which made me show off a little. I could feel everybody's eyes on me, and I milked the attention with melodramatic self-importance. I thought I was a pretty good drummer, and with an audience I was inspired to concentrate even more.

Now I had my own clique. At one of the Catholic parties, I got real friendly with a girl named Heidi. Her skin was olive and she had a great smile. She had been dating Terry, the leader of the

14

band, so when she danced with me and put her arms around me so tight, I couldn't believe it. That night I dreamed of taking off her Hawaiian muumuu and running my hands and lips over her soft, round body. In the morning my sheets were damp.

We started dating and I tried to get her to "go all the way," but she had been warned for many years by the nuns at her school about the eternal damnation of sexual desire. In addition, she had promised her mother to remain a virgin until marriage, so the best I could get was some serious petting. I remember attending Marymount dances with Heidi, and the nuns, the little penguins in my dreams, not only frowned at her low-cut dresses, but they came around to make sure there was daylight between our bodies on the slow dances. Terry didn't say anything about Heidi and me, but I felt some guilt over stealing my best friend's girlfriend. Rehearsals were impossible afterward, and the band folded.

After a couple of years of playing casuals (weddings, school dances, bar mitzvahs) as a drummer-for-hire, I graduated from high school.

My grades had been average in all my classes other than music and sports, and no major universities were seeking a snare drum player for their marching bands.

So by the fall of 1963, it was off to Santa Monica City College, where I majored in apathy and changing majors. First it was music, but I thought I could never make a living at it. Therefore, I switched to business. After getting a D in accounting—the second time around—I thought someone was trying to tell me something. Maybe college wasn't for me.

But music was in my blood. I didn't have time for studies because I was hanging out at the music building jamming with the cats. The head of the department used to storm across the hallway.

"Could you guys please turn it down?" he would plead. "I'm trying to rehearse the junior orchestra."

Despite all the hassling, we were doing something right. We were the foundation of a mutha of a marching band. By the middle of my second semester, our SMCC band had been accepted in the citywide competition at the Rose Bowl.

※

"Bbbbbbbrrrrrrrr! Bbrr!" the whistle sounded. I kept my head locked straight ahead as we marched through the streets of Pasadena on our way to the stadium. Peripherally, I could just pick up the groove coming from the ultra-cool black band from L.A. City College. I didn't think it was possible for a marching band to swing, but these dudes did it.

We had no sooner sat down inside the mammoth stadium than the results were announced. The judges, who had been placed surreptitiously along the route, called the winners up to the stage.

I don't remember the third-place winner, but I'll never forget the runner-up.

"Placing second in the 1964 All-California Junior College Marching Band Competition—Los Angeles City College!"

A roar went up from the stands.

"And the number-one band in the state . . . and the winner of a national TV appearance . . . Santa Monica City College!"

We won! Best band in the city!

A month later we were in the L.A. Coliseum for the Pro Bowl. My most vivid memory is of standing in the tunnel about to go out to the field when Big Daddy Lipscomb, old number 33, passed by as the teams came in for half time. He was the most colossal guy I had ever seen. Or ever hoped to see.

※

In the summer of 1964 something amazing started happening to the music scene in L.A. New clubs were opening up and down the Sunset Strip: Fred C. Dobbs, the Trip, Bedo Ledo's, and the Brave New World. The bands that played there weren't into top 40 music. They played their own stuff, at deafening volume. Every night I could, I would go to Hollywood with a high school friend, Grant, and hang out at the clubs until two or three in the morning. There was no age limit because they didn't serve alcohol. My parents were sure I was going to end up in the gutter.

My parents. Mom was a native Californian from a good Catholic family with five children: the Walsh clan. Margaret Mary went to Beverly Hills High during the Depression and became a librarian. When she was sixteen, Ray Blaisdale Densmore moved in next door. He had driven his family across the country from York, Maine, to the suburbs of Los Angeles when he was only twelve. At twenty-three, Ray attended USC in pursuit of a degree in architecture and moonlighted as an actor with the Santa Monica Players. Mom was also making money as a commercial artist. They dated for several years before he proposed. She agreed to marriage if he agreed to having their offspring raised Catholics. He wasn't about to convert, a hesitation possibly rooted in the fact that his father had told his four sons that no matter what they did, they shouldn't marry a Catholic!

As it turned out, they all did.

I was raised with my older sister, Ann, and my younger brother, Jim, in a middle-class home in West L.A. It was the *Ozzie & Harriet* show and I was Ricky. I identified with his droll sense of humor in the face of such well-meaning but ultimately square parents. I grew up restless and anxious to get away from home, but when the notification arrived from the State of California Transportation Department that a freeway was going to be built right through our property, I remember being devastated. My roots were being paved over. Now there is a freeway on-ramp where "home" was. It reads "San Diego Freeway North."

Maybe that instability is why my parents wanted me to grow up so conservatively. By the time I was in high school, the pressure was on for me to cut my growing, shoulder-length hair and concentrate on my studies like a normal kid.

The breakaway had begun. I was feeling a pull from suburban L.A. into the clubs of Hollywood.

I was in junior college now, but I sensed there was a whole scene out there that I knew nothing about. I began by scouring the unknown streets of Venice and Westwood, and eventually

17

made my way into Hollywood. It didn't take long to be seduced by the bright lights and dark corners of Sunset Boulevard.

I was discovering a new world of music and people. Grant and I were nineteen-year-old jazz buffs and very condescending toward rock 'n' roll, but we sensed that something special was beginning in the rock scene. The popular bands emerging in L.A. at this time were the Byrds, Love, and the Rising Sons, with Ry Cooder. I dreamed that if someday I could just be in a band like Love, I'd be happy. They had so many chicks hanging around! The first couple of times I saw Love I was somewhat shocked. They were bizarre, even for 1964. Arthur Lee, the black lead singer, wore rose-tinted granny glasses, and they had a guitar player whose pants were so tight it looked like he had a sock stuffed inside his crotch. They were a racially mixed group and seemed to be friends. After experiencing Love, I knew I had a ways to go before being hip. They wore bright colors, leather vests, and suede jackets with fringe everywhere. I wondered if they went out on the street like that.

The audiences were composed of nonconformists, to say the least. It was a fashion show for freaks: long hair and beads, leather capes and pinstriped pants, suede moccasins, paisley shirts, and Nehru jackets. Pretty tame by today's punk standards, but outrageous for a West L.A. suburban kid of the mid-sixties. Those cats were hip. Hippies. Flamboyant and free-spirited characters. Their uninhibitedness was infectious. I did belong somewhere! It sure wasn't with the Tab Hunter crowd at college.

After the clubs closed at 2 A.M., everyone went to Canter's on Fairfax, probably the best deli on the West Coast. How Canter's survived those years is a tribute to tolerance. What a scene. Food was hurled across the room as often as it was eaten. It was fun to let loose and act outrageous and loud, usually just up to the point before being hassled by the waitress and thrown out. When celebrities like record producer Phil Spector or the Byrds would come in, the place would erupt in applause. Twenty years later Canter's became a night hangout once again, for the punk crowd. Musical styles can change, but lox and bagels endure.

In order to support my Hollywood habit, I needed a car, and I was desperate to stay away from home as much as possible. So I went to work in a Chinese laundry folding shirts in a room that never dipped below ninety-eight degrees. And that was in winter. It was like taking a sauna every day. I drank gallons of Orange Crush and ate Twinkies by the box while singing the Sweatshop Blues, and somehow saved enough money to buy a '57 Ford convertible. Hot damn! It was painted silver. Weeeeuuhh! When I got it home I stepped into the backseat and my foot went clear through the floorboard to the pavement beneath.

Undaunted, Grant and I were sure that because of the tuck-n-roll dashboard and the glass pack mufflers, we could pick up all sorts of girls. So we cruised Westwood, the movie theater and slick shopping district of L.A. near the UCLA campus. And we cruised. And cruised. Listening to Henry Lewy on KNOB, "the jazz knob." And coming down with the "Summertime Blues" because the chicks would hear the weird be-bop and wouldn't get in the car. Hey, does anybody actually pick up girls in cars, anyway? Even the handsome types? The beach bums? The G.Q. crowd? I don't believe it! It was the first of many precious myths to be exploded.

In addition to the Hollywood scene, Grant and I frequented several jazz clubs. The best were the Lighthouse, Shelley's Manne Hole, the Bit, the Renaissance, and Melody Lane down on Adams Boulevard where no honkies ventured. The convertible wasn't scoring, so we had plenty of time to hear new music.

Like many other white jazz buffs, my first exposure was to Dave Brubeck records. In the old days the record stores still had listening booths, so Grant and I expanded our musical knowledge without having to buy anything. We turned on to Les McCann, the black piano player whose style was a funky-gospel type of soulful jazz. In those glass booths you could monopolize the turntables and headphones for about twenty minutes before the sales-conscious management would prod you into a purchase.

Some kids went to the movies for escape. We found it with jazz. Coltrane and Miles seemed to us to be the culmination of twenty years of jazz. This is where we got religion. It was a kind of raw spiritual anarchy. Grant and I would talk in passionate riffs about how these jazz geniuses were "out there," playing in the cracks between the chords, searching for the unknowns beyond chord structure. Grant's father described Coltrane's music as sounding like someone stepping on a cat's tail. People who thought it was noise hadn't followed jazz through its evolution from be-bop to cool to free form. How could they possibly understand? We were elitists without knowing what the word meant. It was our secret society.

Any time I would drop the needle on *Live at the Village Vanguard* to hear "Chasin' the Trane," the bellowing, driving energy would make me imagine I was actually inside drummer Elvin Jones's body. The tempo pulsed in my veins.

I've spent the last twenty-five years trying to recapture that— dreamtime?—through music, acid, sex, books, travel, anything to Stop the World, as Don Juan tells Carlos Castaneda.

But mainly music.

Grant and I went to see Les McCann play live at the Renaissance Club, where Lenny Bruce had performed. It was our first time in a jazz club. We were ushered to a table in the back behind a pole. Sheepishly we ordered our soft drinks, knowing we would be carded if we tried for beer. We were the only white people in the joint. The Renaissance was intimidatingly cool. It had an attitude. We hadn't cultivated one yet.

This comedian came on. His shtick was to snap his fingers once, wait about ten seconds, then do it again. This went on for about five minutes, culminating with beatnik-cool "All right"s and "Hey, baby"s. I didn't understand what he was trying to do, but his personality was infectious. He seemed crazy and I loved that. I identified with nonconformists. Years later the finger-snap-per—Hugh Romney, a.k.a. Wavy Gravy of the Hog Farm Commune—would be the host at Woodstock.

We ventured down to Redondo Beach to hear Cannonball Adderley at Howard Rumsey's Lighthouse. Waving his right arm in a circular motion, Cannonball would start snapping his fingers, counting off an extremely fast tempo. While keeping up the count-off (he snapped on the off beats, two and four in a 4/4 tempo, a difficult thing to do—you have to feel the one and three beats in your head or take slight breaths on one and three to keep the count-off steady), Cannonball would do some jive-talk with the audience and the band.

"Snap-snap-snap—Are you ready, Joe (Zawinul)—snap-snap?"

Nods his head affirmatively.

"Snap-snap—Are you ready brother Nat—snap—snap?"

"Yeah . . . uh-huh."

"Snap-snap—*ladies and gentlemen*—snap—BROTHER NAT IS READY!—snap-snap—ONE-snap-TWO-snap-ONE-TWO-THREE-snap . . ."

Then they would roar into "Jive-Samba" or "Dis Here," and my mouth would hang open in disbelief at the fast, tight groove.

Shelley's Manne Hole was *the* jazz club. It was very expensive, but we scrounged up the money somehow. Though we were obsessed with meeting girls, jazz was our substitute. Grant, being a keyboard player, dragged me to see Bill Evans five or six times. At first I didn't get it. He was so subtle. Then I realized what incredible touch he had. It was not cocktail music, as some critics suggested. I sat right next to the stage when Art Blakey, king of the press drum roll, grunted his way through smoldering Afro-jazz rhythms. He was in his late forties then, but his playing still had energy; more energy than my own drumming, and I was only nineteen.

Kerouac and Cassidy saw Charlie Parker in his prime. We saw John Coltrane. Several times. He was unbelievable. Everyone in the club would make a path as he walked by, out of respect. When he picked up the tenor or soprano sax and started the old Johnny

Mercer song "Out of This World," Trane indeed left this world. With his eyes closed for his solo, he would go into a fifteen-minute trance. On "Chasin' the Trane," they would play for about half an hour, and sometimes McCoy Tyner, the piano player, would get up and walk off in the middle of the song and Coltrane would turn his back to the audience, facing Elvin Jones, my favorite drummer, and they would battle it out. It was so primitive! Totally in the jungle. After the last set, Grant and I lurked around the back of the Manne Hole as Elvin used a hammer to pull out the two nails he'd nailed into the stage floor to keep his bass drum from sliding. We heard Coltrane say "Hotel" to Elvin, and for the next few days all we could say to each other was "Hotel, hotel."

My own musical career was still in its caterpillar stage, but Grant and I jammed for hours, imitating McCoy and Elvin. Once in a while we found work at UCLA fraternity dances, where we played top 40 hits. Five sets at forty-five minutes each for fifteen dollars apiece a night—pretty good money for those days. We threw a band together with a guitar player, Jerry Jennings, who was six feet five inches tall and had perfect pitch. If a factory whistle blew somewhere, Jerry would say "E flat." The group was rounded out with a bass player who was terrible, but he played acoustic, so he wasn't heard much.

Playing frat parties was radically different from being at jazz clubs in Hollywood, or even rock clubs. The volume of small talk was much louder, and there was an aggressive feeling that was compounded by the quantity of beer being consumed.

One night Grant and I pulled a fast one. We had made some homemade John Cage-like avant-garde recordings. The tapes sounded like freeway traffic and toilets flushing. We turned them on in the middle of songs like "Louie, Louie." The frats looked real confused, but they kept right on dancin' and drinkin'.

In order to be able to play in bars, you needed to be twenty-one, and as we were nineteen, Grant and I drove down to Tijuana in his VW van to get fake identification cards. I was also hoping I might lose my burdensome virginity. Grant had been getting it on with his thirteen-year-old neighbor, so he wasn't as desperate as I was. He would let me and a couple of friends hang around the outside of his parents' garage and listen to him and the neighbor go at it. (After twenty years of living together and two kids, Grant and his neighbor got married.)

I was a jangle of nerves standing on the corner of Tenth and Avenida de Revolución, the main dirt drag in T.J. A Mexican guy came up to me and said, "Hey, surfer, you want bennies, Spanish fly, fake I.D., my sister?" I didn't have blond hair, but I didn't have dark skin either, so I guess to him I was a surfer. Maybe it was just a joke on the gringo. But six dollars later I had a draft card that said I was the ripe old age of twenty-two.

Now to try to get laid. The same guy took us down a narrow passage between two stores, behind which were dirt lots with old mattresses thrown on the ground. Milling around in dark corners were several giggling Mexican women, who, from what I could see, looked six to eight months pregnant. This wasn't how my initiation was supposed to be.

We panicked because we didn't want to go through with it. Some of the women started grabbing our arms and several men started moving in behind them. We threw the money down on the mattresses and ran.

Driving back, we were stopped at the immigration check a few miles north of San Diego. Our tailight on the VW van was out.

"Coming back from Tijuana and you ain't got no tail!" the guard said jokingly.

٪

By the fall of 1964, armed with our fake IDs, Grant and I moved out of our parents' homes into the developing hippie community of Topanga Canyon. My parents agreed to pay half of the $70-a-month rent as long as I was going to college.

I transferred to San Fernando Valley State College at Northridge just over the hill from Topanga, the beautiful tree-filled mountainous area forty minutes from Hollywood. So there I was, finally, in a legitimate school, not just another junior college. Fulfilling the American Dream. En route to a nine-to-five job downtown.

The problem was it wasn't *my* dream. From somewhere in my deep subconscious a voice called out: "LSD!"

Soon I was dropping units along with acid.

Grant and I would go to jam sessions where local musicians would get together and play jazz. At first I was afraid to sit in myself. There were always a couple of other drummers in attendance, which was intimidating. Actually, I was dying to show them my Elvin Jones licks. After a few tries my confidence grew because I received some positive feedback on my performances, and these guys were "players"! This wasn't no frat party. This was some serious jammin'. A nod, or a "Nice playing, man; you were really in the pocket," made my night. I thought about it for days if I really played well.

One of the musicians at these sessions was a sax player, Bud, who was confined to a wheelchair. His body was twisted, but he could play like Coltrane himself. He was full of interesting stories, one of which was about how he used to gig at the Gaslight Club in Venice Beach, where Allen Ginsberg and other Beat poets read.

One time the place was raided and everybody gave their pot to Bud before the police got inside. He stuck it in his wheelchair, knowing that the narcs would never have the nerve to frisk him.

He was a warm, friendly guy, but I was uncomfortable looking at him when he was really "into it." He would contort his body while playing, and it was painful just to watch him. He had great chops, technique-wise, but the anger in his solos was relentless. There was no breathing room, never any release from the rage.

Once he told me that he had a friend who would bring him over to our house with some acid. His eyes lit up for a moment.

"You can see colors in the air, man," he said euphorically.

Drugs were not in my repertoire. I was intrigued but a little confused. Lysergic acid sounded more like something that would burn my arm than give me a high.

"Well, we'll try it . . ." I replied coolly. Inside I was trembling. I hadn't even smoked grass yet. But here's this guy, I thought, who can't go out and take a walk so he travels in his mind with hallucinogens. The more he described his trips, the better it sounded.

Bud appeared at our house a few days later. He was carried up the stairs in the arms of an athletic black man with an acid-induced glow on his face.

Once inside, we all sat around the food-stained coffee table, while Grant and I proudly showed off our jazz collection.

Finally Bud pulled out a sandwich bag that contained something that looked like tooth powder.

"Divide it in half," Bud said. Ed, the black panther of a man, gestured that it was okay. "You have to start out with smaller doses so you don't freak out."

Ed nodded benevolently. He had a genuine love vibe. I needed the reassurance.

After they split, we opened up the bag. The acid was in powder form. We divided it into two mounds, me taking a little less than half, and wet our fingertips and stuck some into our mouths. Five minutes passed and nothing cosmic happened. Impatiently Grant and I decided to take the rest of it. We licked it up off the kitchen counter, laughing nervously.

I went into the living room and lay down on the couch. Grant followed and sat down in slow motion on the armchair.

Take me on a trip upon your magic swirling ship
My senses have been stripped, my hands can't feel to grip
My toes too numb to step,
Wait only for my boot heels to be wandering

I slowly scanned the room, looking earnestly at the black-hole artwork on the wall. We had hung an enormous piece of canvas at which we had invited all our musician friends to hurl great gobs of paint, a tribute to Jackson Pollock, I suppose.

Hey Mr. Tambourine Man play a song for me
I'm not sleepy and there is no place I'm going to

I began taking deep breaths of the incense Grant had lit. By now all of twenty minutes had passed. I looked down over the frayed edge of the couch at the floor between us and saw a dark pit a thousand feet deep. I was a child again, afraid of the monsters outside my crib. Helplessly I began slipping off the couch into the bottomless abyss. I started getting scared, and shouted to Grant that I was falling into the void.

Take me disappearing thru the smoke rings of my mind
Down the foggy ruins of time
Past the frozen leaves
The haunted frightened trees
Out to the windy beach
Far past the twisted reach
Of crazy Sorrow

His reaction was to laugh. The more frightened I got, the more he laughed. His laughter was so absurd I was suddenly yanked out of my first—and only—bummer. Grant was trying to make me see the humor in the situation. The whole episode took only about two or three minutes, but it seemed to last forever.

Hey Mr. Tambourine Man play a song for me
In the jingle jangle morning I'll come followin' you

We had an acacia tree with bright-yellow flowers outside the house, and I urged Grant to come outside and see the unbelievable pulsating colors and blossoms. Our footsteps sounded like loud crunches as we walked on the grass. I felt the breezes on my skin as if for the first time. The distant sound of mufflers sounded like a freight train was about to come roaring through the house. It was like Fellini's movie 8½, an outrageous surreal comedy. We doubled over with laughter at the intensity of it all. Somehow we managed to make it back into the house to see what playing music would be like while tripping.

I started pounding on the piano keys with my fists, trying to imitate an avant-garde composer. Grant couldn't stand it; he got a side ache from laughing.

Later, when Grant became totally absorbed by a Charlie Mingus album cover, I disappeared into the bedroom and masturbated. I took my time and my fantasies were very detailed. It seemed again like hours passed. Psychedelic jacking off—that was the sixties for you.

Acid had more of a kick than the stale wafer I swallowed on my first holy communion. LSD was a *direct* experience with God that I felt, or at least something otherworldly, or mystical.

A couple of days after our trip I still felt a little high, or at least different. I knew that the drug had worn off, that I was back into more or less my previous state of mind, but the sense that there were other ways of experiencing things was a powerful new awareness that is still present to this day.

A crack had appeared in the facade of reality and I had peered through. My adolescent initiation had taken place.

Nothing had changed, yet everything had.

MOONLIGHT DRIVE

Do you know how pale and wanton thrillful comes death
on a strange hour, unannounced, unplanned for

Like a scaring overfriendly guest you've
brought to bed

Death makes angels of us all and gives us wings
where we had shoulders smooth as ravens' claws

No more money, no more fancy dress

This other Kingdom seems by far the best

Until it's other jaw reveals incest and
loose obedience to a vegetable law

I will not go

Prefer a Feast of Friends

To the Giant Family

Dear Jim,
Those last lines of "American Prayer" remind me of the constant argu-
ments you and Ray used to have about man's evolution. Ray wanted the
golden race to come out of blending, and you argued against the loss of
individual characteristics. In retrospect, I think your early lyrics are the

28

great poetry. Back then I didn't really understand your words. But I knew there was a fluidity and rhythm there.

> Let's swim to the moon, let's climb thru the tide
> Penetrate the evening that the city sleeps to hide
> Let's swim out tonight, love, it's our turn to try
> Parked beside the ocean on our moonlight drive

I started thinking right away about how I could complement your lyrics with my drumming. The lyrics seemed like an acid trip in themselves. I was hypnotized.

> Let's swim to the moon, let's climb thru the tide
> Surrender to the waiting worlds that lap against our side
> Nothing left open and no time to decide
> We've stepped into a river on our moonlight drive

When we first started out your voice was weak, and you were so painfully introverted. I thought, This is the next Mick Jagger? But there was something fascinating about you: your love of words. Your fierce conviction that you were a poet. I had never heard of anyone trying to put poetry to rock 'n' roll before. To me, "Moonlight Drive" was revolutionary. A psychedelic love song.

> Let's swim to the moon, let's climb thru the tide
> You reach a hand to hold me but I can't be your guide
> It's easy to love you as I watch you glide
> We're falling through wet forests on our moonlight drive

And you were so incredible-looking. You reminded me of Michelangelo's David. I could sense you were unique, but you didn't act like the typical cocky lead singer I was used to working with at the parties, weddings, and bars I started out in. When I first saw you fooling with the mike cord in those early rehearsals, I mused, "How's this guy going to work up an audience when he's so preoccupied with the stupid cord?" I just hadn't *realized you were finding your own way, totally, and that eventually when you faced the audience, the cord would transform into a snake. They became mesmerized with your every move. . . . But by then, so were we.*

⁊.

Los Angeles, 1965

A few weeks after the "electric Kool-Aid acid test" with Grant, I reconnected with another musician, Robby Krieger, a frizzy-haired guitar player.

One of the first times I'd met him, back in high school, he was recklessly driving his parents' fancy Plymouth and using a credit card to buy gas. This was a bit much for me, living south of the railroad tracks that ran along Olympic Boulevard. Robby said he had gotten kicked out of Menlow, a private school in northern California, so now he was going to Uni Hi. I thought he was a rich kid with an attitude. He was also very quiet. It didn't take long for me to realize that Robby's shyness was due to sensitivity and gentleness, not snobbery. As I got to know him better I also realized that in his solitude, ideas were always spinning in his head. While everyone else was listening to top 40, Robby was digging Paul Butterfield, Robert Johnson, and Jimmy Reed. Plus playing flamenco guitar.

Over the next six months Robby started turning me on to Bob Dylan, the Jim Kweskin Jug Band, and Robert Johnson, so I reciprocated with my new secret: acid.

I told him that Grant and I had dropped. He could hardly wait to take it himself after I described the intensity of the experience.

Soon Robby was the one bringing the acid to our friends.

In April of 1965 there was a party and Robby, as usual, came with his stash. A couple of friends, Bill and Tommy, were along with him. I found out that Robby had been busted for grass (I was never popped—contrary to what was reported in the other Doors bio). He was riding in his car, smoking a marijuana cigarette, and got pulled over. I wondered if Robby was a little too wild to become my friend. We took acid at the party. Robby gave Tommy a little speed (Methedrine) to make sure he got a running start before dropping the acid. I felt it was unnecessary, for Tommy was such an introverted guy, but Robby encouraged the "appetizer." Robby was only a year younger than I, but sometimes he had an edge. Sadistic stubbornness was Robby's Achilles heel.

We went outside and talked to the flowers, everyone put the make on Grant's girlfriend, to no avail, and then Tommy started to freak out. His face went from happiness to terror every few minutes as he said, "I'm enlightened . . . Oh, no! I'm dying!" After the drug wore off, Tommy cooled out, but he never seemed to stabilize completely.

Bill Wolf was a local guitar player with a great sense of humor, and he and I hit it off real well. We had a discussion about the universe and God and nothingness, and we laughed a lot. He told me that there was some kind of wild animal—he thought it was a tiger—just behind his neck and he had to concentrate real hard to keep from being devoured.

At the end of the evening Robby, Grant, Bill, and I decided to form a band and call it the Psychedelic Rangers.

By the spring of 1965, the Beach Boys were sweeping the charts with their surfer songs, and there were mumblings about our boys fighting in a far-off country called Vietnam. It seemed light-years away from sunny southern California.

Our first rehearsal was held in the living room of Robby's parents' house. We wrote a song called "Paranoia" in a folk-rock style, with absurd lyrics by Grant like "that black-and-white fever has got you uptight," referring to the cops. It was fun rehearsing and we weren't too serious about "making it," although if Barry McGuire could have a hit with "Eve of Destruction," we could with "Paranoia."

A friend of Grant's had an eight-millimeter home movie camera, so we decided to make a little movie of our potential hit song. Going downtown to Chinatown to get brightly colored kimonos for our wardrobe was Wolf's idea. The film began with a shot of me jumping off a ledge, kimono flying behind me, landing on my drum stool and starting the first beats of the song. By the time it was over, Grant had tipped his electric piano over, and we had wrecked our equipment and were laughing hysterically (before we'd even seen the Who!).

The band was crumbling from lack of gigs, but we still hung out together. We were convinced we were turning on to more than just drugs—it was another reality. "The Rangers" would walk into liquor stores, record shops, or coffee shops like Uncle John's Pancake House and be amazed at how serious everyone else was. On the outside we probably looked like just a bunch of giggling teenagers, but to us we had our own cult.

That spring Robby got Bill Wolf, Tommy, and me interested in taking a meditation course. I liked the "separate reality" perspective that acid had given me, but I knew I couldn't take it all the time. I knew I was onto something, but I also knew that it shouldn't be abused because of how powerful it was. My intuition told me to plan my environment (going to the mountains or the beach) before taking a trip, which helped eliminate fear from my experience. A couple of years later my thoughts were confirmed by Carlos Castaneda in his book *The Teachings of Don Juan.* As Don Juan, the Yaqui Indian who was an expert in hallucinogenic plants, said to Castaneda, "You must be ready first. This is not a joke. Mescalito requires a very serious intent."

Meditation sounded like a less shattering route. We went to some preliminary meetings in L.A.'s Wilshire district and listened to a mellow man in a business suit. His name was Jerry Jarvis, and his eyes seemed to express a remarkable inner contentment.

After completing the series of meetings, we were on our way to being initiated into Maharishi Mahesh Yogi's Transcendental Meditation. We joked while driving over about how we'd stumbled onto instant nirvana for only thirty-five dollars. Tommy, who was never quite the same since his acid trip, seemed to think meditating was going to be the answer to all his problems in life. I was worried about him once again, and also curious about what meditating would be like. They asked us to bring flowers, fruit, and a white handkerchief. We would each receive an individual mantra, an Indian Sanskrit word that we were supposed to repeat mentally. Our teachers instructed us not to speak it aloud or write it down; it could lose its power if we did.

I got dizzy during my first meditation, so I was anxious to go to the follow-up meeting the night after our initiation into TM. Everyone was sharing his experiences of calm and serenity while Jarvis explained what goes on when one meditates, to make sure we were doing it correctly.

He talked about how the mind's nature was to have one thought after another. Mind-chatter. He said that the mantra was a vehicle to take a thought from the surface of our mind down to the source of thought below. Still, not too much happened when I meditated. There were no colored lights or explosions. Though I was expecting the same quick, startling effect as my LSD experiences, in the back of my mind I knew that most Eastern religions spoke of years of rigorous meditation before illumination or enlightenment, if then. I did notice that the sounds of the cars rushing by outside—in fact, all noise—seemed to disappear for the fifteen or twenty minutes I was meditating.

I must have been somewhere—but where?

At least it was more interesting than communion at church.

During the follow-up meeting, a blond guy with a Japanese girlfriend by his side kept raising his hand and saying to Jarvis, "No bliss, no bliss!"

It was very embarrassing. He acted as if he had been ripped off. I think he expected to become Buddha on the first day. We had all hoped it wouldn't take too long, but he was especially impatient.

After the meeting the same guy came up to me and said, "I hear you're a drummer. Want to put a band together?"

"Sure," I said. "Why not?" I was already in a couple of other bands, but I wouldn't pass up a chance to play. Jamming was a natural high and I was hooked.

"My brothers and I are in a bar band down at the Turkey Joint

West in Santa Monica. We want to try something new. The time's not quite right yet, but give me your number and in a few months I'll call you."

The time's not quite right yet? What is this guy—into astrology, or something? Interesting dude. Definitely off the wall. His name was Ray Manczarek (that's how he spelled it then).

⁊.

That spring I changed my major several times at Valley State. I knew I was going to hate business, but I had taken it because I figured you had to know it if you were going to eat. I wouldn't listen to my real feelings. I was letting other people influence me. So this time I made my own absurd decision.

I liked people. I wanted to help people. Maybe sociology was for me.

But I hated that too.

I next declared myself an anthropology major because of two of the department's professors. Fred Katz was an ethnological music instructor and cello player for the Chico Hamilton jazz quintet. Professor Katz automatically gave everyone in the course an A, and there was no term paper or final exam. Class was popular not only because it was an easy A, but because Katz was so interesting. I got the sense that he had been out in the world and knew about life. He would have fellow musicians come in and perform for the class, so one actually got a glimpse of the real world. Of course, the administrators "voluntarily" let him go a couple of years after I left. Too far out!

Edmund Carpenter was more of a legitimate professor and a great storyteller. He'd reminisce about how he once lived in an igloo while studying the Eskimo culture. Then he would spice up the lecture with anecdotes about how it is an insult not to have sex with the wife of your host if you're visiting an Eskimo's pad.

I was the only long-haired male on campus, and in the spring of '65, long hair meant rebellion. Carpenter was the only person over thirty I had met who understood this. After the final class, Carpenter told me that he was sorry the semester was over because he was curious to see how long I was going to let my hair grow. He knew that my hair was a metaphor for my rebellion. How far out toward the edge was I going to go?

Later I heard that San Fernando Valley State College "voluntarily" let Carpenter go, too, just before the campus erupted in student protests.

My other classes were not as compelling, and I knew I had to take a gamble on what I was best at—playing music. And it was then that Ray Manczarek happened to give me a call. He invited me down to his parents' place in Manhattan Beach to play. I entered by the beach house just in time to hear his parents make several unkind remarks about their son living with a Japanese girl. I exited quickly and went out to the garage/rehearsal room. Out came Ray with his beach thongs on and a daisy in his shirt. This time he seemed warm and friendly. Good-natured. I liked his frameless glasses, which to me looked groovy. Intellectuallike. He introduced me to his two brothers, Rick, the guitarist, and Jim, the harmonica player. Their band was called Rick and the Ravens.

They seemed like your basic hippie types to me, with Jim wearing those corny granny glasses. No originality. They were playing a few riffs I recognized from "Money," "Louie, Louie," and "Hootchie Cootchie Man." Rick was an adequate rhythm guitarist, but something was lacking. I thought they needed a good lead guitar player. Ray played some nice blues licks, coming from his Chicago roots. Growing up back there, he listened to the all-blues radio station, all day and all night.

Lurking in the corner of the garage, meanwhile, was this guy wearing standard collegiate brown cords, a brown T-shirt, and bare feet. Ray introduced him as "Jim, the singer." They had met at UCLA film school. Ray was moonlighting while pursuing his master's degree in film, after a BS in economics, and Jim was finishing up a four-year degree in film. He was in an accelerated two-and-a-half-year program. Smart guy. They had played together once when Ray was stuck with a union obligation for a sixth member of the band, and he convinced Jim to stand off to the side of the stage with a guitar that wasn't plugged in. They were backing up Sonny and Cher. It was Jim's first paying gig, and he didn't play or sing a note of music.

The twenty-one-year-old Morrison was shy. He said hello to me and went back to the corner. I suspected he felt uncomfortable around musicians, since he didn't play an instrument. While Morrison moped around the garage looking for a beer, Ray grinned like a proud older brother as he handed me a crumpled piece of paper.

"Take a look at some of Jim's lyrics," Ray said to me.

You know the day destroys the night
Night divides the day
Tried to run, tried to hide
Break on through to the other side

Made the scene, week to week, day to day, hour to hour
Gate is straight, deep and wide
Break on through to the other side

"They sound very percussive."

"I've got a bass line, wanna try something?" Ray said.

"Yeah, let's do it."

Ray began and I used a knock sound on my snare, putting the stick sideways. Jim Manczarek joined us with some funky harp playing. Morrison, after a long wait, finally started singing the first verse. He was very tentative, not looking anyone in the eyes, but he had a moody kind of sound, as if he were trying to sound surreal. I couldn't stop looking at him. His self-consciousness drew me in. Rick was playing very soft rhythm guitar, but Ray had nice energy coming from the keyboards. Then we played a couple of Jimmy Reed songs and Morrison's energy picked up. I agreed to come down for some more rehearsals, as I loved to play. I knew they wanted me, and I thought I'd follow this lead for a while.

The next few rehearsals went about the same, but I was getting more and more interested in the originals. We eked out the arrangements together, and I felt I was with kindred spirits, Ray especially. Ray remembers: "We'd listen to Jim chant-sing the words over and over and the sound that should go with them would slowly emerge. We were all kindred souls—acidheads who were looking for some other way to get high. We knew that if we continued the drugs we'd burn out, so we went for it in the music!"

Also, Morrison was mysterious. I dug that.

4

SOUL KITCHEN

Los Angeles, 1965

On a Tuesday morning in June, I hurried up the driveway to Ray's Ocean Park garage apartment, where Jim was staying. I paused on the landing at the top of the stairs and looked out over the palm trees and Victorian rooftops of Venice.

Mom and Dad had stopped the rent on my Topanga pad after I had dropped most of my classes, so it was back living at home again. I kept the brown shutters closed most of the time in my old bedroom, which now had an inch-thick foam rubber pad under imitation Oriental rugs. On a tabletop I had a shrine that consisted of pictures of Maharishi, *Autobiography of a Yogi* author Paramahansa Yogananda, and Krishna. Candles burned continuously. I slipped in and out of the back door at all hours of the day or night. If hunger knocked, I raided the fridge or tolerated the bad vibes at the dinner table. I had a secret world and my parents' homemaking routine seemed mundane compared to what I saw in Topanga Canyon.

Now, why can't I get out from under their wing and get a place like Ray's? Westwood is so lame. Sneaking up to the Mormon Temple at midnight for my meditation walks is the only cool thing to do. If I lived in Venice I could hang out with Jim. He's fascinating; he questions everything. Hell, Ray's place is only seventy-five dollars a month for a two-room Victorian with an ocean view.

38

Venice, man. . . . This ain't no surfer territory. This is beat-nik vibes with artists and musicians. Groovy.

"Listen to this," Jim said as he let me in. His hair was still wet from the shower, and he ran his hands through it affectedly while leading me into the apartment. The lion's mane fell perfectly into place.

"How do you get your hair to go like that?" I asked him as he hustled over to the stereo.

"Wash it and don't comb it," he replied, putting Ray's John Lee Hooker album on. He was already on his way to looking like a rock star. I hadn't seen him for a few weeks and there had been a change in him. Was he posing?

The blues filled the room. Jim walked over to the window and opened it. The sun spilled in. We both marveled at the ocean view.

"Play 'Crawling King Snake,' " I demanded. "I love the groove on 'Crawling King Snake.' When we're on about our second or third album, I think we should record that. After we've done a lot of originals. Of course, we have to get a record deal first."

I was brimming with anticipation about the future. These peo-ple—Ray; his girlfriend, Dorothy; Jim; and their film school friends—were independent, creative students, and I wanted to be around them. We had all gone to see Louis Malle's *Phantom India* at UCLA a couple of weeks back, and Ray and Jim had been talking about the French "new-wave" in cinema.

"You should see *400 Blows*, John," Ray had prodded. I knew it was a film by a French director (Truffaut) and the title turned me on. I thought it meant *400 Blow Jobs*.

Looking around Ray's place, I felt a college buzz and an Orien-tal flair. Books, film magazines, Oriental rugs, Indian bedspreads, erotic photos. Whole new worlds were opening up to me in this room.

I was twenty, and everything was possible.

"It'll happen," Jim retorted with cool confidence. "Just listen to this guy's pipes, man." His voice was almost reverential. Considering Jim's Southern background, it made sense. He was obsessed with the way black blues singers sounded. The raw feeling of pain expressed in their voices seemed to reverberate in him. He listened intently, lost in his own world.

After several more cuts, Jim suggested Olivia's for lunch.

I jumped to my feet. My mouth watered at the thought of Southern home cookin'. Mashed potatoes and gravy. "Okay, but we shouldn't have dinner there too!" I teased, rubbing my stomach.

"I know, I know. Several meals in a row there and you get the runs. But it reminds me of Florida home cookin'!"

"And it's *cheap!*" I exclaimed.

Jim curled that slow smile that you could hang on forever.

⅄

Olivia's. A small soul food restaurant at the corner of Ocean Park and Main. A roadside diner that belonged in Biloxi, Mississippi. The place was packed, as usual. The restaurant that Jim later memorialized as the "Soul Kitchen" was full of UCLA film students. It looked like an Amtrak dining car that got stranded at the beach.

A young girl with big brown eyes and long black hair strolled in.

"Hey, Jim, there's that singer, Linda Ronstadt, who lives on Hart Street."

"Yeah. What's the name of her group?"

"The Stone Poneys."

"I hate folk music, but she's cute." He gave her the once-over twice.

The food arrived and we scarfed it down, mumbling about the local music scene in between mouthfuls of chicken-fried steak. My eyes darted around the diner while Jim talked. It was hard to hear him over the buzz of college students and local patrons.

Half an hour later Olivia bellowed, "Lunch is over!" She wore the traditional print apron over a full skirt and had a slight limp in her right leg. Her vibe was warm, but the big black woman whose name was synonymous with soul never let any patrons in at closing time, and she always tried to hustle out the ones who were there. She didn't care about a few extra dollars when she could have some peace. You knew she loved to cook for the people, though.

Her restaurant may be long gone, but the legend lives on in Jim's words:

Well, the clock says it's time to close, now,
I know I have to go, now,
Really like to stay here, all night

Let me sleep all night in your soul kitchen,
Warm my mind near your gentle stove,
Turn me out and I'll wander, baby,
Stumblin in the neon grove.

"Let's go to the Venice West Café tonight," Morrison suggested as we got up to leave. He took one long last pull on his Carta Blanca and I stared out the window at some passing girls.

"Sure," I said, preoccupied with the girls outside. "Never been there." When I couldn't see them anymore I continued, "They still have poetry?"

"I don't know, but we can check it out."

Early that July, I was back driving Jim around Venice in my Singer Gazelle, the European car I'd traded for the Ford. The Gazelle looked exactly like a Hillman Minx, and it got much better gas mileage. With gas selling for thirty-five cents a gallon, a dollar's worth of regular would get me all over town. My dad went with me to make the trade, because I'd never driven a stick. After we lurched out of the used car lot, Dad asked me again if I wanted him to drive.

I coughed up twenty-nine dollars for an Earl Scheib paint job and chose the color black after the Stones' song "Paint It Black."

The job was so sloppy they even sprayed the tires, but I loved that high-gloss shine.

Jim didn't have a car, but he had interesting friends. They were all a year or two older, and I looked up to them. We went over to Felix Venable's house in the Canals, a sloppy version of Venice, Italy, that had seen its heyday in the 1920s, complete with ducks waddling around. They're still waddling today. Felix looked like an aging surfer who had spent too much time in Mexico, but he was real friendly, loved to party, and the woman he lived with turned me on. She was older—pretty face and nice figure.

After a few hours we paid a visit to Dennis Jacobs, another film student. Dennis lived in a rooftop apartment on Brooks Street, half a block from the ocean. He loved to talk about Friedrich Nietzsche, the German philosopher. I picked up one of Nietzsche's books, *The Birth of Tragedy*, while Jim and Dennis were talking, and read a couple of paragraphs. I couldn't figure out why anyone would want to read a whole book of such double-talk. Dennis seemed crazy, but his zest for life was contagious.

On the outside, Jim seemed to be a relatively normal college student. He was infused with an aggressiveness toward life and women. He also wanted to learn everything there was to know about getting our band on the road and making records.

After a few hours with him when he'd been chain-smoking dope and rapping philosophy, however, another side emerged. Sometimes I was frightened. I'd ask myself, Goddamn, how far down does this guy go? Morrison knew something about life I didn't. His curiosity was insatiable and his reading voracious. I didn't get half of his references, but the passion always came through.

"John, did you ever really think about what's on the other side?" he would ask with a strange gleam in his eye.

"What do you mean exactly by 'the other side'?"

"You know . . . the void, the abyss."

"Sure, I've thought about it, but I don't dwell on it." I would laugh sheepishly, trying to defuse the tension.

Then he would be off again on a dark monologue, quoting from poets like Rimbaud and Blake.

"The road of excess leads to the palace of wisdom," he echoed over and over.

Meeting Jim was the death of my innocence.

Fortunately, music was the great equalizer for us. I could tell he admired my ability as a musician and I, his intelligence.

"What did you mean the other night when you said the guitarist was playing outside?" Jim asked as we drove to Hollywood one night.

"He was as far out as you could go without getting outside the chord structure. In other words, he was real loose. You want to get out there where it sounds real free, but not so far that it sounds like you don't know the changes. You can dance over the edge a little. Like Coltrane and Miles. They have a right to go way out there because they have paid their dues; they've made many beautiful mainstream records." Jim acted as if he understood. When I would rap on about Coltrane's music as stream of consciousness "sheets of sound," Jim would listen intently and make literary connections.

"Yeah, *right*. Like Rimbaud and the 'derangement of the senses'! Hey, would you take me to the Trip tonight? Allen Ginsberg is supposed to show up."

"All right. You know . . . if jazz and poetry are supposed to blend . . . I think we're it!"

"You wanna bet on it?" Jim snapped.

"What?"

Jim pulled a quarter out of his pocket, flipped it up in the air, and then popped it into his mouth.

"Did you swallow that?"

"Yup."

"You're crazy."

"Yup. Uh-huh."

LIGHT MY FIRE

Ojai, 1977

The sun was setting in the west and the famous Ojai "pink moment" was about to happen in the east end of the valley against the Topa Topa ridge behind my barn. The afterglow was stunning. As far as the eye could see were orange groves, acres and acres of orange groves. I got down off my horse, Metchen, and walked her to the edge of the field at Thatcher School. Forty years ago, Ronald Colman trudged up to this same precipice on a similar foggy afternoon and looked down over Shangri-La in the movie classic *Lost Horizon*. It made sense to me that the movie people had chosen this valley to shoot. I fell in love with it at first glance when I was searching for a home for my two horses.

Metchen scuffed the ground with her hoof, neighing loudly to her compatriots back at the corral. She was barn sour, always wanting to go home, but I'd wrestled with her for ten years already and she was family.

It had been ten years since Jac Holzman, president of Elektra Records, had given her to me as a gift for the outrageous success of "Light My Fire."

Jim had chosen his car, a Mustang Cobra, Ray and Robby had asked for tape recorders, and I had asked for a horse. We joked about it then. The deluge had just begun.

⁊

It was in July 1965. Ray was owed three hours of recording time from his friend Dick Bock, owner of World Pacific Recording Studios in Hollywood, and decided to use it to finally get some songs down on acetate so we could hear what we sounded like.

I arrived at the studio a half hour early to set up my three-piece Gretsch drum set. My anticipation was peaking on the drive over, but when I saw Ravi Shankar's group packing up in the large recording room, my pulse quickened even more. I felt strangely giddy at that moment. Here I was, in the same space with musicians I had been admiring from a distance.

I watched Alla Rakha, Ravi's drummer, pack up his little Indian drums. They looked much simpler to mike than my drums, but I knew they were much more complex to play.

Dick Bock said good-bye to the Indian musicians leaving in their colorful saris. He asked what he could do to help.

"I want to be close to the piano," I said with slight trepidation. This was my first recording session. Who was I to tell the producer where to set up?

He shrugged "no problem" and pointed to an area in the curve of the grand piano. In the pocket. That way I was nearer to Ray. I was pleasantly surprised that Ray and I had a lot of the same favorite jazz musicians, and he was the one I wanted to connect to.

I looked around at the acoustic walls of the businesslike room as I set up my kit. Acoustic tiles with millions of little holes in them to absorb the sound. You didn't want echo in the recording room. You could add that later. I knew that much.

Ray and Dorothy arrived with Jim, and shortly thereafter, Rick and Jim Manczarek walked in. Within hours, using only one or two takes, we had cut six sides: "Moonlight Drive," "End of the Night," "Summer's Almost Gone," "Hello, I Love You," "Go Insane," and "My Eyes Have Seen You."

It was done very quickly. Everything live. Bock was a low-key character who had produced West Coast jazz, and you don't tell jazz musicians how to play, so he hardly said anything. Before we knew it the session was over and we were back on the street.

We had our own acetate with six songs. Ray took it under his arm and he, Dorothy, and Jim slipped into their yellow bug. Ray shouted through the window that he would start shopping it around to the record companies over the next few days. Jim, having heard his voice on tape for the first time, was beaming from the backseat.

The reactions from the record companies were amusing. Ray later remembered, "It was funny; in Los Angeles we walked the streets with these demos, went to record companies and said, 'Here are six songs, we have many more; listen to these.' And everyone, but everyone, said, 'No! You can't—that's terrible—I hate it—no, no.' I especially remember the guy at Liberty. He listened, then said, 'You can't, you can't do that kind of stuff!' He threw us out of his office!"

When I heard the stories later I was disappointed but also a little surprised Ray would even play the bizarre "A Little Game" after being turned down for our less threatening songs: "Once I had a little game, I like to crawl inside my brain, I think you know, the game I mean, I mean the game, called go insane."

I did dig his other anecdote, though. Apparently Lou Adler, the record producer for the Mamas and Papas, literally dropped the needle onto the first few notes of each of the cuts and said, "Nothing here, nothing I can use here!"

Incredible, I thought. They just don't understand our vision. They don't get it!

⅄

After our demo was rejected, we resumed rehearsals halfheartedly. An hour into our practice, Morrison disappeared on a break. Jim and Rick Manczarek took the opportunity to take Ray and me aside and say that they were quitting the band to go back to school.

I knew that Rick and Jim Manczarek, like Ray, had played a substantial number of club gigs and that they didn't enjoy working with someone as unprofessional as Morrison. But I thought they were making a huge mistake.

Morrison walked back into the garage, the picture of innocence.

The others shifted uncomfortably, and I suggested that we play a few songs. It was futile. We played lackadaisically, and I knew Ray's brothers had already quit. Ray had a long face, but I tried to reassure him with a few casual glances that it might be for the best. I was hoping we might replace them with a guitarist who could solo.

*

My romantic life at this time was nonexistent. I went back to visit Heidi at her parents' house in Beverly Hills, after not seeing her for eight months. After my initiation into meditation and the counterculture, however, she seemed naive. I suspected she was looking for a husband, two kids, and a house. I went home immediately and put on one of my favorite Bob Dylan songs.

> Go away from my window, leave at your own chosen speed
> I'm not the one you want, babe, I'm not the one you need
> You say you're lookin' for someone
> Who's never weak but always strong
> To protect you and defend you,
> Whether you are right or wrong,
> Someone to open each and every door . . .
> But it ain't me, babe, no, no, no it ain't me, babe,
> It ain't me you're lookin' for, babe.

Heidi in the past, fantasies of groupies longing for me in the future, and me and Lefty goin' to bed together in the present. I fell in love several times a day just driving around town. Well, maybe in heat. Actually, I was so scared of women, I rarely struck up a conversation with one.

I knew I was likable and could be "sensitive" with a girl, but the fear of rejection was too great, so I just fantasized. When the group gets somewhere, I figured, we'll have girls crawling all over us!

Meanwhile, the hope that our songs were good enough was something to live for.

⁊

I leaned back and balanced my weight on the two rear legs of my parents' dining room chairs. I'd done this since I was a kid, and the flak culminated at thirteen, when I broke a chair. Here I was, doing it again. But I was nervous and it made me feel more comfortable. It was a relief that the spaghetti dinner my mother cooked for the band was going smoothly. I was worried about Jim in this family situation, but he was being a Southern gentleman, and rather quiet at that. I guess his stomach was happy. Everyone seemed to be starved, appreciating a home-cooked meal; "home" was back in Chicago for Ray and Florida for Jim.

Dorothy, Ray's girlfriend, was her usual quiet self, but Ray was talking up a storm with my mother. The eternal optimists. My younger brother, Jim, who was twelve, was preoccupied with how to roll the spaghetti onto his fork and get it into his mouth. Dad, of course, was lost in his own world, so I tried to break the ice.

"I think if we get a hit album, a gold *album* as well as a single, then we'll be set. When you sell a million singles the money comes rolling in, but the record company takes a huge percentage for manufacturing and profit and the artist gets like five percent, so you have to get a hit album and then you've made it."

"Sounds right to me," Dad responded. "Do you have a name?"

"Not yet."

"More spaghetti?" Mom interjected. "There's plenty!"

"I'll have some," Ray responded. He looked at Dorothy and she gave him her plate, which he also handed to Mom for another helping.

Nice evening. Everyone went home with a full stomach that would hold for a few days.

After Rick and Jim Manczarek quit, I brought Bill Wolf over to a rehearsal. He was a good solo guitarist, but Ray didn't think he seemed to fit, musically or visually. Jim didn't have much to say about it; he seemed to leave the musical decisions up to Ray and me.

Ray didn't know any other guitar players, so he patronized me and let another former member of the Psychedelic Rangers, Robby Krieger, come down. He was worried about Robby's shyness, because Robby's playing was the antithesis of loud electric guitar, which seemed to be the hallmark of rock 'n' roll. He had a unique style of picking, though. Instead of a pick, Robby used his long fingernails, the same way he played folk and flamenco music.

Robby also had a fundamental understanding of chord structure that I was hoping could help us with our songs. And another addition: Robby played a bottleneck on his electric guitar, something he picked up from old blues records. Traditionally, a blues guitarist would break a wine bottle off at the neck and stick his little finger inside the opening. Then he would strum a chord and slide the bottleneck across the fretboard, producing a funky, eerie howl. I had heard it on a few records that Robby had turned me on to, but never on an electric guitar.

It blew me away. I was fairly sure that Robby's sliding liquid sound would knock Ray and Jim out.

"I think you passed the audition," I cracked to Robby as we drove back to his parents' house in the Palisades. "I was nervous until you picked up the bottleneck for 'Moonlight Drive.' Shit, it looked like Ray saw God when he heard you!"

Robby stopped nervously twisting his frizzy hair with his finger and adjusted his glasses. "Aw, I guess it was okay. But remember that Robert Johnson song I played you: 'Squeeze my lemons till the juice runs down my—beeerrrrrwwwwwwwuuuuuuuuuu'— now *that's* bottleneck!"

"There aren't many electric players, though," I said.

"Mike Bloomfield occasionally plays it with Butterfield." He smiled for a moment, stared out the window as we approached his house. "How did you get that place to rehearse, anyway?"

"A film school buddy of Ray and Jim's rents it. Hank. He said it was cool to rehearse there in the afternoons. It's weird, isn't it, a little house hidden behind all those Santa Monica stores?"

"Yeah, it's great. But Jim . . . the singer. He's pretty intense. The way he yelled at his friend who came in and sat at the kitchen table with the mound of dope, rolling joints—Felix? Was that his name? Whew, strange crowd."

"Aren't they? And we could easily be busted because of all the noise we're making. I was hanging out with Jim a month ago and we went to the Venice West Café and he started hassling this guy who was real loaded. Jim asked him over to Ray's to hear some records and when we got there, Jim started flipping the lights on and off, on and off, freaking the guy out. We played a Chet Baker record—the one where he sings—and this dude just gets up and says he's going to split. Morrison looked pleased with himself. He said he just wanted to test him."

"Doesn't surprise me," Robby said nonchalantly.

Test him, I thought. What was this—school? What are we studying—*fear*?

"Yeah, well, I'm never going to take acid with him," I murmured, "I'll tell ya that. Do you think he's too crazy?"

"Yeah . . . he could also be a big star. Don't the two go together sometimes?"

"Ha, I think you're right."

I pulled into the driveway. Robby hesitated before getting out.

"So you like the band?" I coaxed.

"Yeah, I'd like to be in it. I have to see what's happening with this other band, but yeah." He opened the door, slammed it shut, and leaned in through the window. "Hey, wait a minute. I'm already in one other band and you're still in two others."

"So?" As I started to back the car up, I yelled out the passenger window, "You quit your band and I'll quit both mine."

Late that night I got back to my parents' and called Ray. "Hi, it's John. What'd ya think of Robby?"

"I like the bottleneck a lot," he replied. "Maybe he can play it on every song!" Ray was stoked.

"Well, let's not go overboard."

"But he's not very aggressive. I'm worried about what he'd be like onstage. He doesn't exactly milk every note. A guitar player has got to be half showman."

"We can't all be show-offs like me," I countered.

"Well, let's rehearse with him again and see how it goes."

He was as good as in. Now I knew the band was coming together.

٪

Rehearsals now were a joy. The respect that each of us had for each other's craft made for a free-flowing democracy. We all had played our instruments for years, Jim had read voraciously, and everyone was expected to put his two cents in when an idea came.

Getting a bass player proved more difficult than finding a guitarist. It wasn't just finding a good one, it was finding someone who fit. One day we had this girl come down (which we thought would be different), and we played "Unhappy Girl," "Break On Through," and a couple more originals. We tried some blues—our cover of "Back Door Man," inspired by John Hammond, and a recently worked up version of "Little Red Rooster" by Howlin' Wolf. Still, we sounded too traditional. Adding a bass made us sound like every other rock-'n'-roll band. Too much like the Rolling Stones. Although we loved them and talked endlessly about their new record, *Aftermath*, we were determined to do almost anything to sound different.

I enjoyed rehearsing with just two other instruments and Jim's voice. The sound was so open. My first job was to keep the tempo, not to let anybody rush or drag, but there was a lot of room for all four of us to express our individuality, which seemed to result in a unique group sound. With my jazz, Ray's early classical training and then exposure to blues, Robby's folk and flamenco, and Jim's obsession with old black blues singers, we were slowly forming the Doors' sound.

Eventually Ray found a Fender Rhodes keyboard bass, so we didn't need a bass player. It completed the sound. Because he

51

played the bass with his left hand and the organ with his right, it forced Ray to play simple bass lines while he concentrated on his right hand playing the organ. The Rhodes sounded a little mushy but gave us the bottom we needed and made us even more different.

The lack of a real bass player left room for me to fill, and I enjoyed adding percussive comments to Jim's singing. For some reason, sometimes when there was a real quiet musical section, such as the one that later evolved into "The End," I blasted through with one or two drum shots, breaking the tension. I also knew it was scary in those silences, and I wanted to make it more scary.

"We never doubted we were going to make it," Robby now remembers. "We knew immediately that we had the best material of any group; we knew that we had the best-looking singer of any group. What could go wrong?" We felt complete.

By now all we lacked was a name. At the time most American groups had long psychedelic names, like the Strawberry Alarm Clock, Jefferson Airplane, or Velvet Underground.

It was orange blossom time, the summer of 1965, T-shirt weather, and I was sitting in the backseat of Ray's yellow VW bug as he headed south on the San Diego Freeway. Jim was in the passenger seat, dressed in jeans, T-shirt, and bare feet. He never seemed to wear shoes. He lit up a number.

"What do you think of the name 'the Doors'?" Jim asked while turning around and handing me the joint.

"Hmm . . . it's short and simple," I responded, taking it from him. "Aren't you paranoid about smoking in the car?"

Jim shrugged his shoulders. I took a short drag and handed it back in a hurry.

"Keep that roach down, would you guys?" Ray chimed in. "And give me a hit." Morrison held the joint up to Ray's lips and he took a huge toke. "Jim got the idea for the name from the Huxley book, *The Doors of Perception.*"

"The Doors." I ran it over in my mind. "I like it. It's different.

It sounds odd." Huxley, I thought to myself, I've heard of him. Better read that book.

Morrison explained that Huxley had gotten the phrase from William Blake. "If the doors of perception were cleansed everything would appear to man as it is, infinite." When I heard that, I was convinced we had a legitimate poet in the band.

The Doors. I liked the bluntness of it.

"What do you think we should wear?" Jim continued with a straight face. "How about wearing suits?"

"I don't know . . . let's see what evolves," I muttered, thinking to myself that Jim's wardrobe suggestion was the worst ever.

Sometimes Jim was so naive, I thought. Some of his Jacksonville, Florida, roots were showing through. Not too hip. More hick.

⁊.

The last thing that stood in our way was the army draft. The idea of learning how to kill made me sick. Just as worrisome was the fear that the group would be destroyed if someone was drafted. Vietnam was heating up fast. Several friends had already been called up. I couldn't figure how our government came to the conclusion that our national security was threatened by communists going into some Far Eastern country on the other side of the world.

Ray had already been in the service a few years before. He didn't have to sweat it. I remembered the story from his student film, *Induction*, which was fairly autobiographical. Depressed over a lost girlfriend, Ray had enlisted. (Must have been really down. Must have been some girl!) A year after turning on to grass for the first time and smoking Thai sticks in Asia Ray wanted out.

Ray swallowed a small ball of aluminum foil, which showed up in his X rays as an ulcer. Then he told them he was homosexual and they said go home.

That summer, Jim, Robby, and I received our notices to report for our army physicals. Robby's well-to-do family hired a psychiatrist to write up a letter saying he was unfit. Then they sent him to the draft board in Tucson, Arizona, where the local antidraft movement hadn't yet made them immune to excuses.

I had to go down to the induction center in L.A.; Jim was to follow the next week.

The physical was one of the low points of my life. The headlines in the *Los Angeles Times* told of the first draft dodger sent to jail. He was a friend of a friend whom I had met once. With that in mind, I had been up for days taking Methedrine that Robby had thoughtfully provided and reading Kenneth Patchen's *Journal of Albion Moonlight* for inspiration. With pacifist rhetoric under my belt and Bob Dylan's lonesome harmonica playing "God on Our Side" in the background, I tried to convince myself I had the courage of a Quaker. By the time my parents dropped me off downtown at the induction center I was a nervous wreck. Wearing a blue and pink striped shirt and brown cords that hadn't been laundered in weeks, I pushed open the swinging doors into the large, noisy army headquarters to await my fate. My clothes smelled so bad I couldn't stand it myself.

"All right, you guys," the recruiters barked at us as if we were already in the service. "Fill out these forms and then go upstairs for your physical."

I filled out the test forms as sloppily as I could, worrying that I would lose my mind if I didn't get a deferment. With acid, I'd found sanity in an insane world. With the army, I felt on the edge of madness already. My musical career seemed to be disappearing before my eyes.

As I finished up the forms, an old high school buddy, Ed Workman, boldly walked across the recruiting room toward me. Shit, I thought. He could blow my cover. I tried to hide my face.

"Hey, John. Watcha know? Guess I'll see you in Nam, man."

I wasn't amused at his macho humor. I grimaced, embarrassed even to look at him, since he would know I wasn't as messed up as I appeared. Fortunately, he took one look at my pitiful disguise, shook his head, and walked the other way.

When he had gone, I bolted upstairs for more tests. As I walked

It was the *Ozzie & Harriet* show and I was Ricky.

Me and Heidi.

right
The carousel, Santa Monica Pier, 1966.
(PHOTO CREDIT: BOBBY KLEIN)

"I hate folk music, but
she's cute."
(PHOTO CREDIT: BOBBY KLEIN)

Robby, 1965.
(PHOTO CREDIT: JOEL BRODSKY)

Me in 1965.
(PHOTO CREDIT: PAUL FARRARA)

Ray, 1965.
(PHOTO CREDIT: JOEL BRODSKY)

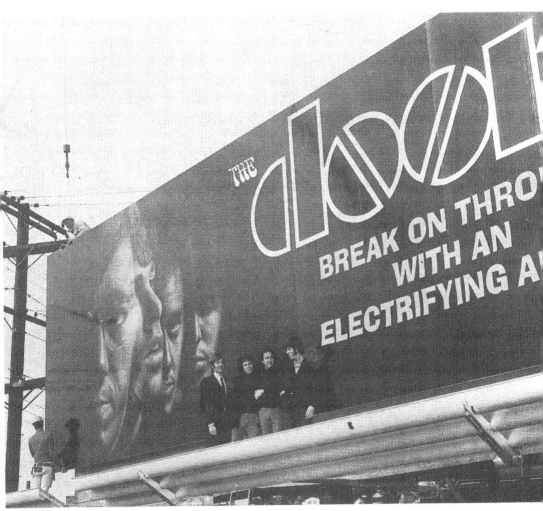

The first rock billboard. (PHOTO CREDIT: BOBBY KLEIN)

down the hallway toward the urine test area I realized I could have spiked my sample—if I'd thought of bringing something.

But all I found was office after office. I was getting frantic by the time I was directed to get into line for the interview with the army psychiatrist. It was getting down to the wire and I was running out of ideas fast. If they had simply checked my heartbeat right then and there I could've flunked the physical fair and square.

I noticed an effeminate black dude in front of me as we awaited our turn with the shrink. The dude was loud and impatient and very swishy. I would've bet a hundred dollars he'd get his deferment.

He was just the inspiration I'd been waiting for.

I was petrified as I walked into the psychiatrist's office. With my head spinning, my heart exploding, my knees turning to jelly, I minced my way up to the psychiatrist's desk. Avoiding any eye contact with him, I pulled the chair out from in front of his desk and dragged it over into the empty corner of the room, right under photos of President Johnson and a B-52.

I sat facing the wall.

"GET BACK HERE, YOU ASSHOLE!" the psychiatrist yelled.

Trembling with fear but determined to carry out my improvised plan, I pulled the chair back as daintily as I could. Then I leaned across his neurotically neat desk until I was inches from his face. My breath could have downed one of those jets up on the wall. I hadn't showered in a week.

"Do you want to be in the army?" he inquired, leaning back away from me and catching his breath.

"No, sir, I really don't think I can take it," I responded earnestly, oozing sincerity. My eyes started welling up with crocodile tears. I was auditioning for the first time in my life and didn't even know it.

"It'll do you good!" he said, shaking his head in disgust. He stamped my papers, oblivious to my Olivier theatrics.

He returned my forms to me and directed me to the next office. I staggered to my feet and left in great despair.

I soon found myself in front of a long table where the completed forms were being collected. A black woman volunteer put
out her hand to file my papers. Around fifty years old and bursting out of the seams of her uniform, hers was the first warm face I
had seen all day. As I handed her my forms, she sensed my dejec-
tion and took me aside. Pointing suggestively to the "homosexual
tendencies" box on the form, she asked, "Is there anything else
you want to check?"

I looked at her, first startled, then hopefully, and she nodded
toward the papers as if to say "Check it." I don't know whether
she honestly thought I was gay or just too brittle for the army.
The look in those maternal eyes assured me that if I checked that
box I would be spared.

A few hours later I got my classification: 1Y. The clerk told me
I was supposed to return in a year, but meanwhile I was FREE! I
had wanted a 4F, which meant a permanent deferment, but I
wasn't about to hang around and argue with them.

My mother picked me up outside at the corner of MacArthur
Park. I was embarrassed by my stench when I got in the car, but
when I finally explained my ruse, she was as relieved as I was
about my getting out.

Dad didn't let me know how he felt about it.

One more army rejection and the Doors would be unencum-
bered.

٪

On July 14, Bastille Day, I took Jim downtown for his physical.
There was a long line outside the induction center this time, so
Jim nonchalantly told me to just come back in a couple of hours.
He would be all through by then. I tried to tell him that it had
been an all-day affair for me, but he just gave me that wolf grin of
his, so I agreed to get something to eat and at least check back. I
didn't want to hang around anyway. I felt nervous just being in a
military area.

At high noon I returned and sure enough, there he was standing in front of the entrance looking cool as ever, leaning against the wall, one leg bent, brushing his hair back on the sides with his hands.

I pulled to the curb and stepped out of the car as he came strolling over casually. "Well? What happened?" I shouted over the traffic. "Are you done? C'mon, give."

Morrison shrugged his shoulders and said, "No sweat. All finished. They gave me a 'Z' classification." He slipped into the car.

I shook my head in confusion and got into the driver's seat. "What the hell is a 'Z' classification?"

"I don't know," he said, baiting me.

I started up the Gazelle, ground it into first, and headed toward Hollywood. "C'mon, Jim, what did you do in there?"

He just flashed his mischievous grin. Goddamn, I thought. This guy's too much. He's transcending a trauma that nearly gave me a heart attack. I kept prodding him as we drove across town, but he basked in the mystery. How had he bluffed his way past this one? I wondered.

While heading west on the Santa Monica Freeway toward the Allouette Coffee Shop in Venice, the Stones' version of "King Bee" came crackling on my old radio.

Jim perked up immediately and began keeping bad time with his hands, pounding on the dashboard.

"Ya know, I love this song but I get embarrassed when Ray—the 'old blues man'—sings it," he said with a weird expression.

"Why?" I asked. "It's a change of pace and besides, Robby gets to play bottleneck." Jim just shrugged and kept on trying to keep time on the dashboard.

"I don't know . . . I kinda like the way Ray does it," I added. Still no reply.

"It's just corny," Jim said finally.

I changed the subject. "You're not going to believe this, but last weekend when I took acid I thought I was God!"

"No kidding," Jim replied sarcastically.

"Yeah, I went out to Malibu with Bill Wolf, that girl Georgie who used to hang around Robby, and my piano-playing friend Grant, and we were tramping around in this dried-up streambed. I went up on this little hill overlooking the riverbed where Grant and Bill were poking around. Georgie had hiked over to the Sierra Retreat monastery nearby and we could see her in the distance climbing up on the huge wooden cross overlooking the ocean!"

"Ha ha ha!"

"Anyway, from the dried-up moss, I could see exactly the way the water went during a rainstorm, and I got a sense that nature goes on forever, unless we nuke ourselves. I started saying to Grant and Bill down in the stream, 'Carry on, carry on with the things that are necessary, everything in its place.' They were laughing 'cause I was acting like I was directing them with their choirs. I felt like God directing the universe."

"Pretty heavy. Sounds like a big ego trip to me!"

"Come on! It didn't feel that way. I felt benevolent!"

"Ray had the opposite experience last weekend."

"You guys took acid?"

"Yeah, and Ray went on a bummer."

"Really? What happened?"

"Nothing . . . it's just that he complained all the time."

"I wonder why."

"I don't know, but it was kind of a drag 'cause we had to concentrate on helping him instead of enjoying our own trip."

"Yeah, I know what you mean."

"Hey, John, do you think we could be as big as the Stones?" Jim asked, changing the subject quickly as he loved to do.

I arched my eyebrows, as if to say of course!

Jim nodded his head up and down in time to "King Bee," tapping his foot.

As I pulled down the alley behind the Venice boardwalk, I felt that with the draft out from around our necks, an acetate under our arm, and the brotherhood that was forming alongside the music in the band, there was nothing that was going to stop us.

Jim never did tell me what the hell a "Z" classification was.

During the winter rehearsals, Jim began singing with more authority. Every week or so he would bring in a few crumpled pieces of paper or coffee-stained napkins that had the most incredible lyrics on them; he reminded me of Dylan Thomas with his matchbook-cover poems.

Jim was a guy with a natural *instinct* for melody but no knowledge of chords to hang it on.

"Sometimes I make up words just so I can remember the melody I hear." He had the gift of hearing the melody in his head, and then it was up to us to walk him through it, telling him which notes he was actually singing.

"Jim wasn't that musical, but he could pound around on the piano pretty good," Robby commented in an interview. "That's about it. He really wasn't musical. You couldn't say, 'Okay, Jim, hit a B flat.' He was not like a Frank Sinatra, who could read a chart and sing. He didn't have a lot of input on the arrangements."

"It sounds like a G," Ray would guess as Jim sang a verse. Robby might play a few notes, then a chord on the guitar, then I would chime in with a comment on the beat. "It sounds like a 4/4 feel to me. A shuffle." Then we would get Jim to sing another verse or chorus on top of the three instruments.

These group sessions where we were honing down our style were a great thrill for me. The combination of Robby, Ray, and me was perfect for orchestrating Jim's words.

She holds her head so high, like a statue in the sky
Her arms are wicked and her legs are long,
When she moves my brain screams out this song

Hello, I love you. Won't you tell me your name?
Hello, I love you, let me jump in your game

Sidewalk crouches at her feet
Like a dog that begs for somethin' sweet
Do ya hope to make her, see you, fool,
Do ya hope to pluck this dusky jewel
Hello, hello, hello

"Could you take me over to Rosanna's apartment in Beverly Hills? I gotta get out of here for a couple of days," Jim begged.

"Who's Rosanna?" I asked as we walked to my car.

"This girl. A UCLA art student."

"Uh-huh!" I teased.

I made a left on Ocean Avenue as we split from Ray and Dorothy's digs.

"It's off Charlieville, in one of those Spanish duplexes."

"Right."

Jim rang the doorbell.

"Oh, it's you, come in." The attractive long-haired blonde sounded surprised. Apparently Jim hadn't called.

"This is John."

"Hi."

"Hi."

Jim went straight to the kitchen table, took out a bag of grass, and started rolling joints. He acted like he lived there.

Rosanna responded with loaded sarcasm. "Help yourself, Jim." Maybe Jim had met his match? She seemed to enjoy the verbal bantering.

"I'll be back in a little while," I said, feeling claustrophobic from the mounting tension.

I drove around the shopping district and stopped at a liquor store for some apple juice. Was Jim going to sleep there? I decided to check on the way home.

The door opened as I knocked, not having been shut completely. I pushed it open the rest of the way and saw Jim standing in the living room holding a large kitchen knife to Rosanna's stomach. A couple of buttons popped on her blouse as Jim twisted her arm behind her back.

My pulse tripled.

"What do we have here?" I exclaimed, trying to defuse the situation. "Quite an unusual way of seducing someone, Jim."

Jim looked at me with surprise and let Rosanna go. "Just having a little fun."

Rosanna's expression changed from fear and rage to relief. Jim put the knife down.

I'm in a band with a psychotic. I'M IN A BAND WITH A PSYCHOTIC!

I'm in a room with a psychotic.

"Well, I've gotta go. . . . Do you wanna ride?"

"Naw."

I made a hasty exit. I was worried about Rosanna but I was more worried about myself. There was definitely sexual tension in the room as well as violent tension. That's how I rationalized leaving. I drove to my parents' house in a daze. Why was I in a band with a crazy person? I wanted to tell someone, my parents, anyone . . . but I knew I couldn't. "The Doors" was my only ticket out of my family and a possible career in something I loved, and if whoever I related the incident to reacted by saying I should quit, I would have no options. School offered me no options, there was nothing else I was interested in. I tried to forget the knife incident. But problems come back one way or another when not dealt with. A rash that itched constantly developed on my legs.

Something's wrong, something's not quite right,
Touch me, baby, all through the night.

⁊

"We need more material," Jim said at a December '65 rehearsal. "Everyone go home and write a song tonight. Use universal imagery instead of specifics. Earth, air, fire, water."

Nothing great came at the next day's rehearsal, but just after the New Year something happened at Robby's parents' house out in Pacific Palisades. We arrived there one afternoon when we weren't able to use Hank's for rehearsal.

Robby greeted us at the door with unusual enthusiasm. "I've got a new song, my first song, and I think it's a hit," he said, leading us into the living room where we rehearsed.

Jim said, "I've got one too." Ray and I were silent.

After picking up his guitar, Robby squeezed out a few catchy chords and sang the opening lines, which immediately sounded like a hit single to me. It had a hook. It stuck in your memory the moment you heard it.

Everyone nodded. "Yeah, yeah, nice, nice, Robby."

Then Jim sang his new one *a cappella*.

This is the end, beautiful friend,
This is the end, my only friend
The end, of our elaborate plan
The end, of everything that stands
The end, No safety or surprise
The end, I'll never look into your eyes,
Again . . .

A chill ran up my spine. These weren't lyrics, they were an epitaph. He may be a poet, I thought, but he sure is hung up on death. Beautiful lyrics . . . but they make me sad.

Robby had been trying out a few licks behind Jim, but shook his head. "I'll have to tune my guitar different for that one," he said. "I've been wanting to try this Eastern way of tuning that I've heard in sitar music."

"Let's work on yours first," Ray suggested to Robby. "You can change your tuning after that."

The energy picked back up in the room. I started playing a Latin beat on my drums. "How about a jazzy feel to it?" I suggested.

Ray and Robby nodded together. Ray leaned over his organ for a moment, working on an intro.

"Da-dada-da-da— Shit. Da-dada-da-da-da— Shit. Da-dada-da-da-da-da. Damn."

For the next ten minutes Ray labored over the intro while the rest of us took a break. I went into the kitchen, made sure nobody was around, and grabbed a handful of Pepperidge Farm's Bordeaux cookies from the cupboard. Robby's mother knew I was addicted to them and didn't come down too heavy on me.

"My dad said 'The Doors' was the worst name he ever heard for a band," I blurted out as I sat back down on my drum stool. "I told him that his reaction meant we were on the right track!"

With crumbs at the corner of my mouth, we went at the new song again. The chorus seemed to warrant a heavier rock feel, while the jazzy feel was right for the verses. Damn, I thought to myself, this chorus is sooo catchy I could play it all day.

We kept at it for an hour before taking a beer break.

Jim popped open a Dos Equis and slumped onto the dark-green leather couch. "I think we should divide up all the money evenly, including the songwriting money," he said out of nowhere. We were surprised. It was a generous offer, but also shrewd in terms of keeping peace within the ranks of a band. It turned out that he and Robby wrote most of the songs, but we were all sharing in the arranging. I had been thinking that I was only the drummer, but suddenly it appeared as if Jim really did respect my and Ray's talent. From the moment Robby started bringing in his own songs, his talent was obvious. I hadn't been quite so sure about mine.

"Yeah, all right," Robby agreed. Ray and I made it unanimous. Now, with the money issue behind us, we felt more than ever like family.

"You know the groove on 'Dis Here,' by Cannonball?" I asked Ray.

"Yeah, it's really tight."

63

"Isn't it! It's in three. Let's play something in three . . . like 'All Blues.' " I started a 3/4 jazz tempo using my brushes. Ray and Robby picked up the cue and we jammed on "All Blues" by Miles. Ray had taught Robby the turnaround at the last rehearsal and he had it down now. Jim carefully crept in with a single maraca beat, and I noticed that his time was improving. It was good for us to get to know each other musically on these old jazz tunes.

Tackling the new song again, I counted it off and hit a loud crack just before Ray's intro. Jim hummed the first verse almost under his breath:

You know that it would be untrue
You know that I would be a liar
If I was to say to you
Girl, we couldn't get much higher

Robby found a nice rhythm on guitar, I was in the pocket with the tempo, and Jim opened up his throat:

The time to hesitate is through . . .

Suddenly he looked up from the paper he was singing from. "Hey, Robby, where's the rest of it?"

"I got stuck on the second verse."

Jim rolled his eyes, mulled it over for a second while Ray and I kept playing the groove:

No time to wallow in the mire . . . ?

Jim looked over at Robby, who nodded "Yeah, that's okay," as Jim carried on with the rest of the lyrics Robby had written.

Try now we could only lose . . .
And our love become a funeral pyre . . .

64

And then it all came together in the chorus:

C'mon, baby, light my fire
C'mon, baby, light my fire
Try to set the night on—
FIRE!

6

WHISKEY BAR

By the beginning of 1966, the marquee of the London Fog read "The Doors." We had made it to the Sunset Strip. After hitting the clubs along the Strip, we talked the owner of the Fog into booking us for a month, after we packed the house with friends. Our first real gig. Underneath our name we had them add "The Band from Venice." The place was a dump and a hangout for misfits, but it was on the same block as the Whiskey a Go-Go, so we were game.

We were hired to perform Thursday through Sunday, from 9 P.M. till 2 A.M., five hours of hardcore lounge music, for ten dollars apiece—way below union scale. I was used to at least fifteen dollars a night, standard scab wages on my wedding gigs (plus free food), but I knew the Doors had potential and felt that honing down the arrangements of our songs in front of an audience would be invaluable. There was extra pressure to get it together that couldn't be duplicated without people listening, even if it was only a few stragglers or derelicts, or our friends from UCLA.

But there was also the fear factor. How were we going to fill up five sets with music? We had about twenty-five originals—including "Light My Fire," "The End," "Break On Through"—and about five cover songs—including "Gloria," "Back Door Man," "Little Red Rooster"—which meant repeating a couple. If we played them early in the evening around 9 and then again at 1

66

A.M., the audience would have either turned over or gotten too drunk to remember that they'd already heard the songs. The management didn't seem to notice—at first.

Night after night of drunken sailors, perverts in raincoats, and lounge lizards. Hour after cramped hour in a funky club with nautical decor, stuck on a crow's-nest-size stage. Ray close enough to my drums that he nearly had to duck when I hit a cymbal crash. Robby squeezed in so tight nearby he could hit the opposite cymbal with his guitar neck. Jim perched precariously on the edge of the ten-foot-high stage. Directly across the room, suspended in a dancing cage hanging from the ceiling, was a bleached blonde named "Ronnda Lane: Go-Go Dancer," as she was advertised in the bar menu. A Rockette she wasn't. Skid City was more like it.

Since we had a kind of bizarre carte blanche to play what we wanted, we began experimenting. The long, jazzy instrumental solos in "Light My Fire" and the stream of consciousness poetry of "The End" were born at the Fog.

Jim's stage presence had a ways to go; he rarely faced the audience. We had a discussion one night after a lame set and confronted Jim with his shyness. We suggested to him that he try to turn around and face the people more often, which he accepted with no comment. We were used to facing each other in rehearsals, and Jim wasn't secure enough yet to break that circle of energy. He also didn't take nonmusical suggestions well.

Ray tells a story about when Jim was still living at his and Dorothy's apartment and he suggested that Jim might look better if he got a haircut. Jim's reaction was to scream at Ray never ever again to tell him what to do.

"I just told him to get a simple haircut," Ray relayed to me later. "I'm never going to try that again." Usually Ray came on as Mr. Confidence, flamboyant and articulate, but something in that confrontation took the wind out of his sails. It was a shock for Ray to be rebuked after bringing Jim so far. On the other hand, Jim wasn't going to take any advice from "Dad," and Ray was six or seven years older than the rest of us and hung out with Dorothy all the time. With a navy admiral for a father, Jim was sensitive to receiving criticism and interpreted any suggestions as orders from an archetypal father figure.

A few weeks after the haircut comment, Jim moved into an apartment in Venice with his UCLA film school buddy Phil Oleno and struck up with a new group of friends, including Felix Venable, the local speed freak. Felix was in film school but seemed to be majoring in drugs.

Meanwhile, Ray rented the bottom half of a crumbling mansion on a secluded beach south of Washington Boulevard. It rented for two hundred dollars a month, which was outrageously expensive at the time. He told us the band would rehearse there, implying that he and Dorothy would live there but we all would share the rent!

Two hundred dollars a month for one giant rehearsal room and one bedroom was not cool. Ray had an infectiously positive outlook on life, but he would get his mind set on an idea and wouldn't budge. Where the fuck were we going to get next month's rent? None of us said anything about it; silence was beginning to be the credo in the Doors Club. And so in July we began rehearsing at the Manczarek mansion.

Ray had managed to get himself a beach house at the band's expense. Meanwhile Robby, Jim, and I walked the streets, looking for more gigs to pay for the rent. Ray refused to join us, saying it was a waste of time. He was right. It was a waste of time inquiring at sleazy bars on Hollywood Boulevard that had never ever had live music, but the three of us were frustrated, and by going out it felt like we were doing *something*. Inevitably the resentment surfaced. Jim began grumbling about the "old fucker, all warm and cozy with his 'wife' at the beach." We began cruising over to use the beach house at odd hours, like six in the morning. After all, Ray had said we should treat it as our own, so. . . .

One morning after our gig at the Fog, Jim and Robby paid Ray and Dorothy a visit at dawn—on acid. They brought a couple of hookers we knew from the club. (None of us had partaken.) As the story goes, when they walked in they heard the familiar sound of Ray and Dorothy getting it on. (I say familiar because Jim, having lived with them, would often imitate the sound of Ray groaning and Dorothy saying "Oh, Ray, oh, God, oh, Ray, oh, God.")

Peaking on a double dose of pure sunshine acid, Jim began laughing and poking at Robby while gesturing to the noisy bedroom. He stumbled over to Ray's prized record collection and started taking records out of their jackets and throwing them across the massive room. Ray came out as Jim was walking on the records and said—carefully—"Okay, you guys, the party's over."

Robby giggled nervously in the background. The hookers slunk out of the room and headed for the water. Jim stood there with a glazed look on his face. Around his feet lay broken records with his sandy footprints on them. Ray's jaw tightened.

It was another standoff. Living side by side with Ray and Dorothy in two rooms for the previous year had had its effects. Jim had turned them into surrogate parents, and now he was breaking away.

Ray returned to the bedroom and closed the paper-thin Japanese curtains. The "boys" left. For revenge, Ray told Dorothy to get dressed because they were going over to Robby's parents' house in the Palisades for a nice warm shower. (The beach house had a very inadequate shower.) Stu and Marilyn Krieger were a bit surprised when they heard water running in the guest bathroom at 7 A.M. and their son was nowhere to be found.

After the shock of the rent money wore off, I started enjoying the beach house, sitting in our beach chairs during a rehearsal break, watching the planes taking off from LAX, and hearing Ray comment, "Someday we'll be on one of those." Ray talked as if we, or at least he, was destined for fame.

Morrison's prankish nature continued to surface at the Fog. Felix turned Jim on to amyl nitrites, or "poppers," little yellow capsules that you break (or pop) and stick under your nose, inhaling an ammonialike smell. They were designed for heart patients and would give you a quick twenty-second lift. During the second weekend of our performances at the club, my nose picked up a whiff of the stuff. There's no mistaking the smell.

One night in the middle of the solos in "Light My Fire," Jim whirled around from the microphone and stuck an amy under my nose. I tried to squirm away without getting up or stopping the song. I doubled over with laughter. My sides hurt. I could barely hold on to the drumsticks. Jim turned to Robby. But Robby, being mobile with his guitar cord, got away. Ray was next. Like me, he couldn't leave his instrument. He was laughing hysterically as Jim staggered toward him, leaned over the keyboard, and stuck the amy under Ray's nostrils. As Ray swayed back and forth, trying to avoid the popper, his hands flailed wildly at the organ and the tempo of "Light My Fire" sped up deliriously.

The audience didn't know anything unusual was happening. They were used to aberrant characters and were lost in their own stupor anyway. Actually there was hardly any audience at the Fog. Our friends had seen us several times now, and they stopped coming. The place was dead.

*

To our surprise, Billy James from Columbia Records came into the club. Dylan's label! He liked our demo and was head of A & R, (for artists and repertoire, the department in charge of acquiring new talent).

"My wife Judy will manage you because I can't while working for the record company. Conflict of interests. But I'll oversee everything," Billy said. They talked big, but after a month things seemed the same. A restlessness was setting in from a lack of new gigs.

One Monday afternoon we were rehearsing at the club because all of our equipment was there for the weekends. I walked into the smell of stale beer, peanuts, and shag carpet. Somehow, this ambience seemed okay at night, but in the afternoon—bluughh!

"I think we should all take acid and go over to Columbia and tell them we're going to make it so they better take notice right now!" Jim shouted.

"That's a refreshing approach to business," I quipped.

"That's a good idea, Jim," Ray said, trying to appease him. "But let's rehearse for now."

"If we're going to keep rehearsing we need some new songs," Robby said.

"What for?" I complained. "Billy James isn't doing shit. I'm sick of working up new songs."

"The Fog has offered us twenty bucks a night to play Tuesday and Wednesday," Ray interjected. "We could work on new material then."

"Wow, five dollars each," I retorted sarcastically. "I guess we could treat it as a paid rehearsal, 'cause nobody will be here."

"Well, I've got a new one, so let's work up a loose arrangement and we'll hone it down tomorrow night onstage," Robby suggested.

"What else is there to do?" Ray offered.

"I'm not going back to school for my master's, I'll tell you that," Jim said.

Once we got into the music I was okay, but my impatience over the snail's pace of our career was getting to me. After all, I was used to at least fifteen dollars for dragging my drums to a gig. The next night we performed to an audience of only four people—and one of them was a friend of Jim's, Phil Oleno.

Angry and disappointed, I rushed down to the Whiskey a Go-Go between sets and stuck my head in the door to watch Love perform "My Little Red Book" and "Hey Joe." I wished I was in their band. I was sure I could play better than their new drummer. The London Fog was depressing me, the prospects for the Doors were dismal, and I thought I was ready for a change.

On the way back to the Fog, Phil stopped me on the sidewalk.

"DRUMS, John . . . DRUMS!" Phil slobbered into my ear.

"Yeah, great, Phil. I gotta go play."

Fortunately, Robby's new song, "Love Me Two Times," was inspiring, so the next set back at the Fog wasn't too painful.

A few days later I decided to take things into my own hands. I dropped into Billy James's office at Columbia Records to see what was happening. Billy had gotten the company to sign us up to a record contract—no money but a chance to record—for which Ray dropped the "c" out of his last name. (Ray said it was hard enough to pronounce Manzarek without the "c.") But Columbia hadn't done anything for months, not even booking studio time to make a record. It seemed as if they were stalling. Billy didn't have much to say; I knew he liked us but he couldn't get the company excited. He excused himself for a moment, and in my boredom I scanned the room. Feeling paranoid, I got up and snooped through some papers on his desk. I saw one with "The Doors" on it! We were listed with about seventeen other artists under the heading "Drop List." There was another column with twelve acts, entitled "Pick-up List." My heart sank. Columbia was going to drop us. The pounding in my chest subsided as I sat back down and Billy returned.

I said I had to go.

That night at the Fog I told the guys what I had seen. "Columbia is just like General Motors. Capitol Records is probably like Chrysler. They're huge corporations who don't know what they like, except profit. They just sign a bunch of groups and drop a bunch. They don't care." My bandmates were bummed out, but we weren't going to give up. The first set was uninspired, but later we consoled ourselves, telling each other that people just didn't understand us yet.

The weeknights at the Fog had been a bust. The owner had to make over twenty dollars before going into a profit. Wow. After four months of small audiences, we were finally fired. Joey, the tough little streetwise bouncer, released some of his pent-up aggression in 86-ing some drunks, and a fight erupted. Somehow the fiasco was used to get rid of us. Imagine such a friendly group as us inciting a riot!

Fortunately, an extremely sexy, pixie-voiced blonde named Ronnie Harran, who booked acts at the Whiskey, saw us the very night we were fired from the Fog. She had an ear for talent and an eye for a lover. To her, the backup band was adequate but the lead singer was everything a rock star should be. Raw talent. An Adonis with a microphone. She had to have him. Ronnie convinced the owners of the Whiskey to hire us sight unseen.

And Jim moved in with Ronnie shortly after.

Ronnie had given us our first important break. Six months before our arrival, the Whiskey had been the home of go-go girls dancing in cages for acts like Johnny Rivers. But eventually it had started to book the new folk-rock acts. Elmer Valentine, part owner of the club, was hip to all the new trends, then as now. (After being closed during the dry period of the mid-seventies, Elmer sensed a new burst of creativity and reopened the Whiskey in 1973 to the new wave–punk movement.)

Between May and July of 1966 we were the opening act for groups like the Rascals, the Paul Butterfield Band, the Turtles, the Seeds, Frank Zappa and the Mothers of Invention, Them, the Animals, the Beau Brummels, Buffalo Springfield, and Captain Beefheart. We had to start the first set at 9 P.M., when there was hardly anyone in the club, but it was a major step in our career. Filling the first fifteen minutes with "Latin BS #2," we riffed on one chord with a salsa feel and Jim played his maracas. The song was an instrumental, which tightened up our ensemble. The Whiskey was finally a gig we could be proud of—and we were being paid like professionals: $495.50 per week for the four of us.

Before long the word was out: The Doors were the hottest house band on the Strip. "Artaud Rock," Bill Kirby from the UCLA *Daily Bruin* called us. Kirby called Jim "a gaunt, hollow Ariel from hell," singing "screaming terraced flights of poetry and music."

Ironically, the review that thrilled us the most was a somewhat negative one from Pete Johnson of the *Los Angeles Times:* "The Doors are a hungry-looking quartet with an interesting original sound but with what is possibly the worst stage appearance of any rock-'n'-roll group in captivity. Their lead singer emotes with his eyes closed, the electric pianist hunches over his instrument as if reading mysteries from the keyboard, the guitarist drifts about the stage randomly, and the drummer seems lost in a separate world."

That night in the dressing room before the first set, I bragged about our first *Times* review. "He was trying to dump on us," I said to Ray, waving the newspaper. "But I think the description of our stage presence was right on. If I was reading it, man, I would want to see that band! Ray, look at this, you're *'reading mysteries from the keys!'* Can you believe it? And I'm—'lost in a separate world'? Man, this guy must REALLY be straight." Ray smiled with that great smile of his, and Robby said it was time for another set. Jim closed his eyes in preparation for his stage emoting, and we led him downstairs as if he were blind. We were laughing so hard we could hardly play the first song. I got a side ache from the hysterics.

(Years later I met Johnson at Warner Bros. Records, where he was head of A & R, and the first thing out of his mouth was "I'm really sorry about that review."

"No, no, Pete," I assured him. "Your description of us was inspirational.")

※

By June we were enthusiastically awaiting the booking of the group Them and their lead singer-songwriter, Van Morrison. He had written some great songs, like "Gloria" and "Mystic Eyes," which were standard club fare.

Opening night the Whiskey was buzzing with anticipation. The VIP booths in the back were full. We opened tentatively with "Break On Through." I sped up the tempo and the song never settled into its proper groove.

"You're rushing, John!" Robby shouted over during Ray's solo. He started "Love Me Two Times," nodding his head up and down in tempo to make sure I stayed there.

Love me two times, I'm goin' away
bop-bop-bop-bop-bop-bop-bop-bop-bop-bop-bop
Love me two times, I'm goin' away
BOP-BOP-BOP-BOP-BOP-BOP! SCREEECH

The feedback from Robby's guitar spoiled the tight ending. Shit. Were we nervous.

During intermission it was every man for himself to find a seat. Mario, the bouncer, recognized me and let me stand on the "off-limits" stairway leading to the balcony.

Them brashly took the stage. They slammed through several songs one right after another, making them indistinguishable. Van was drunk and very uptight and violent with the mike stand, crashing it down on the stage. When he dropped his lower jaw and tongue and let out one of those yells of rage, something Irish in me made my skin crawl with goose bumps. Ancient angst.

I didn't understand why a guy with so much talent had to drink to get up onstage, or why he was so self-conscious up there. They were different, at least, I thought. It sure wasn't their performance; it was more their drunken, brawling foreign charisma. Jim thought they were great.

At 2 A.M., after the gig, I sat next to Van in the backseat of Ronnie Harran's Chevy Nova on the way to a small party at her apartment. Everyone was talking and drinking but Van. When we got there he sat on the couch, moody and glowering, and didn't say a word. All of a sudden he grabbed Ronnie's guitar and started singing songs about reincarnation, being in "another time and place with another face."

If I ventured into the slip-stream
Between the vine-dex of your dream
Where the mobil-steel runs crack
And the ditch in the back roads stop
Could you find me, would you a kiss a my eyes
And lay me down in silence easy

75

To be born again
(in another world, in another time, got a home on high,
ain't nothin but a stranger in this world, in another
time, in another place, and another face)

This was sheer poetry merging with rock 'n' roll. I wished Jim had been there. The apartment fell silent and all eyes were riveted on Van. Hearing him sing about "walking in gardens all wet with rain," I found my eyes welling up. It was as if he couldn't communicate on a small-talk party level, so he just burst into his songs. We were mesmerized. It didn't seem appropriate to shower Van with compliments, because his music came from such a deep place. So when he finished there was silence for a minute or so. A sacred silence. Then everyone went back to talking and partying. It was a special night and I was lucky to have been there. (The songs he sang that night, "Slim Slow Slider," and "Madame George," later became part of one of my favorite albums, *Astral Weeks.*)

We got to know the "boys from Belfast" well enough during their stint at the Whiskey to put their song "Gloria" back in our set. The last night before Them went home to the Old Sod, we all played "Gloria" together. Two keyboards, two guitars, two drummers, Alan—the lovable but always into the "drrrink" bass player —and two Morrisons. The song went on for about twenty minutes. What a night!

A few months later I was walking along Santa Monica Boulevard in West Hollywood when Van Morrison drove by. We recognized each other and Van motioned for the driver to pull over. He rolled down the window, said he was back in town, and asked how Jim was doing. I know Jim admired and cared for Van. It was touching that two rock-'n'-rollers with the same last name were looking out for each other.

As the months passed at the Whiskey, we began hanging out with the other bands. Don Van Vliet, alias Captain Beefheart, was eccentric but instantly likable. He had a unique sense of humor. Don did a monologue in the dressing room before their show about his toothbrush. Very bizarre. The man could rap about anything and make it fascinating. Once onstage, his Howlin' Wolf voice had us in awe. I had a gut response to his blues-based music, more so than the folk-rock groups like the Byrds. I dug the Byrds' lyrics, but their arrangements conjured up images of bodies with nothing below the waist. No balls. Their original, "Eight Miles High," had a nice melody and a hypnotic, electric twelve-string sound, but the rhythm didn't cut it for me. On the other hand, the Buffalo Springfield, with their multitude of singer-songwriters (Steve Stills, Neil Young, Richie Furay), was overflowing with talent.

We were starting to develop a following.

Including groupies.

I must say it bothered me a bit at first when one particular blonde and her girlfriends stood at the front of the Whiskey stage and stared at Jim and not me. They could almost reach out and touch him. They seemed to be completely hypnotized. Jim was now wearing tight velvet pants and no underwear. The blonde stared right at his crotch without embarrassment and kept giggling excitedly to her friends. For a twenty-two-year-old with a perpetual hard-on like me, her brazenness was tantalizing to the point of pain.

Ronnie Harran was now Jim's wardrobe mistress, encouraging him to discard his undergarments as she went braless. I couldn't believe seeing the outline of her nipples, as the groupies couldn't believe seeing the outline of Jim's crotch. I decided to grow muttonchop sideburns in hopes of attracting some of the attention.

I could tell we were mesmerizing the audience with our songs too. "Back Door Man" was deeply sexual and got everybody moving. "Break On Through" was a gas to play because the arrangement was so tight, and I got to show off my jazz drumming.

The audience thought we were stranger than usual whenever we played the Weill-Brecht tune "Alabama Song." I liked that reaction. When Ray first played us the song off the original cast album of *Mahagonny*, I thought it was a bit odd. But as we began arranging it, I realized what a great idea it was. I bet not one person in the entire club knew that we hadn't written the song, not to mention that it came from a twentieth-century German opera.

Paul Rothchild, who was later to become our record producer, remembered that Ray was an admirer of Brecht and Weill, "for obvious reasons. I suppose they were saying in the twenties what Jim was trying to get across in the sixties . . . in different ways they were trying to declare a reality to their generation. The inclusion of 'Alabama Song' was a sort of a Doors tribute to other brave men in another brave time even though the lyric is remarkably contemporary."

In those days the Whiskey always let in a strange cult of hippie freaks—Vito, Carl, and the gang. The management let them in free because they added a festive atmosphere. Vito was a fortyish bearded sculptor who had a beautiful but flirtatious wife, Sue. Carl, Vito's sidekick, who was also a little too old for the scene, wore skintight red and green leotards and a velvet cape. Hollywood Cheap. No one seemed to know what Carl did in the daytime. They came on like vampires who only lived at night.

Another notorious member of this clique was Errol's daughter, Rory Flynn, six feet tall, thin, and gorgeous. She was always wearing white, sheer, negligee-type clothes. I thought something was going on between her and Robby, but when asked, Robby would just give an impish grin. Vito had about twenty people in his crowd, and they danced to every song in a theatrical, free-form fashion.

They followed only what were considered the best groups on the scene—Love, the Byrds, and one or two more. So when they started to come to see us, it seemed like a good omen. It was great to have dancers who were "inside" the music, and it shocked the straighter suit-and-tie patrons. It felt like our very own scene. Sometimes their dancing inspired my drumming. When we played our heavier numbers, like "The End," they would just stop and stare at Jim. They didn't seem to notice that I was playing off their reactions, but it was those nights when I developed my technique of "vamping" Jim's wild singing with a kind of shamanistic drumming. That newfound power became a source of tremendous pride for me, so I looked forward to the receptive audiences who were coming to be aroused and excited by our blatantly primitive music.

Gonna make it, baby, in our prime
Get together one more time

The crowds were getting bigger and more stoned each night, but we still lacked a record contract. Columbia had officially dropped us, and Billy James said he was sorry he couldn't do anything about it. So much for management. A few record companies had sent representatives to see us play, but nothing had come of it. Ronnie Harran tried to get us to sign a management contract with her, as Love had, but even Jim thought that she was too regional to launch a group nationally.

Charlie Greene and Brian Stone, Sonny and Cher's old managers, wanted to sign us but they were taking 75 percent of the writing and publishing of the Buffalo Springfield. We felt that a publisher taking more than 50 percent was immoral, and the old way of bleeding musicians to death. Neil Young lived next door to me a year later when he was quitting the Springfield, and he told me that he was buying a house in Topanga Canyon for forty grand, his entire earnings from the group. He should have made more.

"Frank Zappa wanted to produce us," Robby remembers. "Terry Melcher [Byrds] wanted to produce us, but we didn't want a producer. We wanted a record label."

Finally we got some genuine interest from Elektra Records, because Arthur Lee of Love told them to check us out. The owner was Jac Holzman, a tall, lanky, bespectacled man who came down to see us several times and talked about signing us. Jac was self-assured and acted professional enough. He had started his career on his motorbike, with a little Nagra portable tape recorder, recording ethnic folk groups like Dave Van Ronk, Geoff Muldaur, and Koerner, Ray, and Glover. We dug him for that.

When he approached us, Elektra still seemed small compared to the big distributors, like Capitol and Columbia Records. Elektra had signed some folk talent—Judy Collins—and had recently broken into rock with Paul Butterfield and Love. Besides their good taste in music as a folk label, they were small enough that we wouldn't get lost in the shuffle. That was a definite plus. Our only worry was whether they had enough power to break a group across the country.

We held out for a little while longer, continuing as the house band at the Whiskey, but no offers came in. Finally we agreed to sign with Elektra: a one-year, one-album contract with two one-year options, and an advance of five thousand dollars.

Now we could buy some decent equipment!

Elektra Records flew us to New York for the official signing of our contract, plus they got us a club gig.

⅄

. . . *Jim, do you remember how nervous we were on our first visit to Gotham City? On the plane Ray sang the old Jimmy Reed song, "Go'n to New Yark, get on a New Yark quiz show." The Henry Hudson Hotel sure was a dump. A semi-fleabag on 57th and Eighth. You liked Max Fink, our brand-new lawyer who recommended we stay there, didn't you? One of your peers from the South. He knew the owner of the hotel, so we naively thought that with his connection the rooms would be free, or we'd at least get a discount. Getting back to L.A. we learned differently, didn't we? After being shown our rooms at the Henry Hudson, I remember Ray, Dorothy, and me going for our first walk. Robby went to sleep, and where were you? The rest of us felt the energy of the city coming up the sides of the walls of the hotel, so we went on the prowl. I have to admit that I was a little frightened. I now understood the Beach Boys' lyric, "New York's a lonely town, when you're the only surfer boy around." It seemed to be a tough place to survive if you were down and out. We learned to love New*

York, though, didn't we? And they loved us. Our best audiences were in Manhattan. Ray, Dorothy, and I walked over toward Times Square that night, and steam and voices were coming up from the subway grills in the potholed streets. Where did you go? You missed some great jazz. The Metropole, where Charlie Parker and Miles Davis played in the fifties, was our destination. As we approached the club, the street traffic and hustle vibe got thicker—then the marquee read "Dizzy Gillespie"! We looked through the blue-tinted front window and there was a go-go girl in a bikini dancing just on the other side. Way in the back we could make out Dizzy puffing up his cheeks like a grotesque frog as he stretched and bloated and blew mightily on that strange horn of his . . .

Our new Elektra Records producer, Paul Rothchild, had invited us to dinner at his home in New Jersey for the ceremonial signing, so the next night Paul drove us over the Hudson to his place. Jim responded in character by getting stone drunk and coming on to Paul's wife, talking soft and sexy, and running his hands through her hair after dinner. Paul tried to laugh it off, as if he didn't mind, but the feeling in the room was that something was drastically wrong. A week later Paul said it was okay because he and his wife had an "open marriage."

Things only got worse that night when he took us back to the hotel. While Rothchild drove, Jim began pulling on Paul's hair. Paul tried to brush Jim away and the car began to swerve.

"Cool it, Jim!" Paul finally shouted. But Jim just laughed as if it were a fraternity joke. Jim was jeopardizing our safety and I was pissed. It was another moment when our lead singer was proving to be unstable, taking his stage persona too far offstage. Was he acting? Or had we just signed a record deal with a madman in the group?

Before I could get too philosophical about it all, Morrison started in on Ray. He was pulling hard enough on Ray's hair to rip out the roots, but Ray just humored him until we got back to the hotel.

We hooked Jim's arms around our shoulders and carried him to the elevator and down the hall to his room. No sooner did we get him there than he immediately stripped naked and stepped out the window onto the ledge. Ten stories above Manhattan he began shrieking like a banshee.

Ray, Robby, and I pleaded, begged, and joked for him to come back in. Eventually he did, but then Jim grabbed Robby and began wrestling on the bed. Ray and I pulled them apart and the three of us left in a huff. We listened outside his door to hear if he had calmed down. It was too quiet, so Ray said he would go in and see what was happening. He slipped back into the room while Robby and I hovered nearby, listening at the door. We could hear Jim on the phone, putting the make on the hotel operator. Ray asked him to hang up, then there were some crashing noises and the sound of running water.

"Oh, no, Jim, please don't, please . . ."

As we all walked back to our rooms, Ray told us Jim had fallen over a lamp and when he stood up, he was wearing it. Then he began pissing on the rug.

"What are we going to do!" I said.

"Well, at least Rothchild now knows what he's dealing with," Robby said.

⁊

It felt good to be headed across town to our club gig the next night. I was getting the Big Apple down, and it gave me confidence. I stepped out into 57th Street and boldly raised my arm up into the air to hail a cab, unlike the first few times where my fear got to me and nobody would stop. Of course cabbies didn't like longhairs, either. Now I had my "don't fuck with me" New York street persona, which worked. The Upper East Side was crowded, as usual, as we made a right turn on 59th and stopped under the bridge.

It wasn't the narrow, closetlike dressing room where you could sit down against one wall and put your feet up on the opposite wall that made Ondine so great. Or the even smaller stage. Or the corny nautical motif. Or the last set on weekends at 2:15 A.M. It was the people. Brad Pierce, the manager, drew in the hippest crowd in Manhattan. Warren Beatty. Andy Warhol. The night Andy came down, he and his entourage sat in the large, round booth directly across from the stage. He was checking Jim out to be one of his "superstars." (He coined the phrase.) Andy's entourage was looking at us with awe, just like the audience at the Whiskey in L.A. We had started to hypnotize the East Coast. After our set, Jim headed for the Warhol booth. I was thinking of going over to the table, but Andy looked like a walking corpse, so I passed. Thank God Jim didn't get involved with Andy's underground movie crowd, Edie Sedgwick and all the rest, or he might have died even sooner.

Two nights later, after the last set at Ondine's, a group of us walked from the club to a bizarre Halloween party. New Yorkers *get down* on All Hallow's Eve. Not much on trick or treating, but the whole town dresses up. (When Peggy—the hat check girl at the club—and I stopped at a coffee shop on the way to the party, the waitress was dressed up as a nun.) After climbing the couple of steps to the ground-floor apartment where the party was, we entered this giant black room filled with characters dressed to the hilt. One guy was standing on a pedestal in a corner, frozen in a weird position like a statue. Ildiko, a girl from the club who claimed to be from Transylvania, came up to me and said that the statue-guy hadn't moved for hours. A beautiful black girl named Devon whispered in my ear that she wanted to talk to me. I turned around, looked at people behind me, then turned back to Devon, who was dressed in a Playboy bunny costume, and pointed to my chest.

"Me?"

She laughed.

"Why don't we go to your hotel room and bring my friend?" she said, motioning to another angelic dark-skinned beauty. I'd never been with two black girls before, let alone one, and I was afraid I couldn't satisfy them both. I told her to leave her friend behind and meet me at the Henry Hudson in an hour.

She showed, and boy, was I nervous. She sensed my reluctance and asked me which room Jim was in. After about an hour, it was apparent that she wasn't coming back. My confidence shrank back to adolescent size as I realized I'd been used.

٪.

Ray, Dorothy, and I decided to drive back home to L.A., to see the country before it was gone or changed. Since the Stones were our heroes, I wanted to take the advice on their cover record and

> Get your kicks . . . on Route 66
> If you ever plan to motor west
> Take my way, that's the highway, that's the best
> Get your kicks . . . on Route 66

We also didn't mind saving some money.

Ray pulled up to the front of the Henry Hudson with a 1960 Chevy in need of delivery to Los Angeles. The rental was free except for the gas.

"White is a good color . . . it looks like a low-rider car, though," I joked. "Big trunk space, that's good." We threw our stuff in the trunk, and Ray elected to drive first. Crossing the Hudson into New Jersey, we headed west.

> Well, it winds . . . from Chicago . . . to L.A.
> More than 2,000 miles, all the way
> Get your kicks . . . on Route 66

Pennsylvania was green, beautiful, and had a river running through it. We talked mostly about the potential of the band.

"That editor of *Crawdaddy*, Paul Williams, is a good writer," Ray offered. "He really understands what we're doing."

"I like Richard Goldstein from *The Village Voice*," I said. "He seems smart. I loved that parody he wrote, 'The Doors are mean, and their skin is green.' Funny stuff."

"I guess we conquered New York," Dorothy added softly.

"Yeah. We got the intellectual and literary circles as well as the teenybopper set," Ray concluded.

I wondered how far it was going to go. Ray wanted Jim to take it all the way. To the White House. He imagined himself secretary of state. Sounded like fantasy time to me, but I think a part of Ray hoped it would really happen. I thought Jim was too crazy to be as popular as he was already! I was scared by the idea of more power in his hands.

"Now this is what I call a white Christmas!" I exclaimed. Dorothy was driving through a beautiful snowstorm, which was intoxicating to us Californians.

"The road is disappearing. Maybe we better stop," Dorothy suggested as the visibility was getting worse and worse. You could feel the car weave a little.

"A little farther," Ray prodded.

"It's so quiet!" I said.

All of a sudden the back wheels skidded out and the '60 Chevy slid across the center divider line; we were going against the traffic on the other side of the road. Dorothy quickly pulled back across to the right side of the road and Ray spoke up, trying to humor our nervousness.

"On second thought, why don't we stop at the next motel!"

"We'll have to go back a few hundred yards and pick up my heart," I joked nervously. We pulled into a Howard Johnson's for the night. I called my mother, amazed at the ability to talk to warm, sunny California from the middle of a silent, white world.

Get hip . . . to this kind of tip
Go make . . . that California trip
Get your kicks . . . on Route 66

In Oklahoma, we spotted a real diner: a silver train with wheels intact. Our stomachs were having their own conversation, so we stopped. Besides, the place looked great.

Big mistake. Bad vibes. There weren't many long-hairs out between New York and Los Angeles yet, let alone with a Japanese girl. Two white hippie guys with a Jap. Bad combo for the Midwest. Lots of men with red paint on the backs of their necks sitting at the counter. Big men, with trucker caps on. They kept turning around, upsetting our digestion. One of them mumbled loudly to the waitress, "Hey, honey, you got any scissors around this joint?" They probably thought Ray and I were homosexuals. It pissed me off. Made me paranoid too. I hated anyone over thirty. At that moment I made a pact with myself to still have long hair when I was fifty—hair down to my feet.

The diner incident inspired us to drive straight through to the West Coast, which we made in two days. Ray and Dorothy had been great traveling companions.

Get your kicks . . . on Route 66

Back in L.A., we started our first album. It took only six days to record because we had worked on these songs for nearly a year. Paul Rothchild had recently gotten out of jail on a dope bust and Jac Holzman was giving him a break. Rothchild had produced Paul Butterfield, which impressed us. Doing time also appealed to our rebel nature.

The first few days were frustrating because recording wasn't the same as playing live. Rothchild held our hands as we learned the process. I didn't know you couldn't have the same "sound" as onstage. "Too live and echoey," Rothchild said. Paul wanted to damp my drum skins, and it hindered my technique but after a while I fell in love with the big snare drum sound it made. A fatter, dead drum sound recorded better than a live hollow one.

On the second day we laid down the track to "Break On Through." Robby said his guitar melody line was inspired by Butterfield's "Shake Your Money Maker." Jim did a "work" vocal, one that we could hear live in our headphones, but which could be replaced if he wanted. Listening through the 'phones bothered me so I put one on my right ear and the other on the side of my head so I could hear my drums naturally.

"You should try another vocal, Jim," Paul prodded. "We'll put the new one on another track and you can choose between the two."

Jim nodded and headed back out to the vocal booth.

"Just point your thumb up or down if you want more track in your 'phones."

After stumbling on a second take, Jim did a third, erasing the second because we were out of free tracks. (We were recording on four-track equipment, nothing like today's twenty-four-track recording.)

"I like the first half of the original vocal and the second half of my second performance."

"No problem. Bruce [Bruce Botnik, the engineer] and I will glue them together in the mix."

I found the recording process fascinating—getting a basic rhythm track (drums, bass, and other rhythm instruments), then overdubbing voices and instruments as needed. The danger of so much control was the possibility of losing the feeling, the soul of a song; the advantage was that each of us had the chance to be satisfied with his performance.

I always had strong opinions about which takes had the best feel and which songs needed more instrumentation. My years of music lessons, marching bands, orchestras, and dance halls were finally paying off.

We took a dinner break at seven-thirty and got take-out from Dukes, the coffee shop at Sandy Koufax's Tropicana Motel. Sitting in a restaurant would eat up precious hours of recording time, but the continuous diet of take-out pizza, Chinese food, and hamburgers got old fast. I got "Sandy's favorite," a mound of scrambled eggs with onions and stuff. After dinner, we worked till 1:30 A.M., when Paul called it a night.

The next day, when we arrived at Sunset Sound Studios at 2 P.M., Jim scared the shit out of me. We were scheduled to record "The End," and Jim dropped acid. I guess he thought it would help put him in a surreal mood, but it just gave him a foul mouth and he couldn't stick to the arrangement. I thought we'd never get the song down on vinyl.

After several trying hours Rothchild suggested a break.

We walked out into the blinding light of the neon lobby and bought some junk food out of the machines. Jim began chanting "FUCK the mother, kill the father. Fuck the mother, KILL the father." He looked deranged. He caught me staring at him, catching his eyes for a split-second glance, and he responded, "It's my mantra, man. Fuck the mother, kill the father." At that moment I thought that anything was possible with this guy. He could murder somebody.

In an interview with *Crawdaddy* done after the release of the first album, Paul explained Jim's position: "At one point Jim said to me during the recording session, and he was tearful, and he shouted in the studio, 'Does *anybody* understand me?' And I said yes, I do, and right then and there we got into a long discussion and Jim just kept saying over and over kill the father, fuck the mother, and essentially it boils down to this, kill all those things in yourself which are instilled in you and are not of yourself, they are alien concepts which are not yours, they must die. The psychedelic revolution. Fuck the mother is very basic, and it means get back to the essence, what is reality, what is, fuck the mother is very basically mother, mother-birth, real, you can touch it, it's nature, it can't lie to you. So what Jim says at the end of the Oedipus section, which is essentially the same thing that the classic says, kill the alien concepts, get back to reality, the end of alien concepts, the beginning of personal concepts." I wasn't so sure, but Paul indulged Jim the rest of the afternoon, and the next day we finally got the take.

As Jim was becoming more and more unpredictable, Ray and Robby and I were forced to take on more responsibility, almost in reaction to his pranks. We were worried about our fledgling career going down the tubes. Jim's pranks could be clever but there was an undertone of ugly aggressiveness, usually vented at the wrong time and place.

A week later he broke back into the recording studio after everyone had left and sprayed the whole place down with a fire extinguisher—instruments and all. The next day over breakfast at Aw Fongs Chinese Resturant on Sunset he pretended not to remember doing it at all.

"I did that? Come on, really?" Jim smiled. He plunged into his $3.95 egg fried rice, avoiding my eyes. In the morning, when he was straight, I had no problem looking him in the face.

"Well, I don't remember, but I've been thinking maybe we should get a place together up in Laurel Canyon." Changing the subject, huh, Jim! I was sure he was putting us on, but that straight pretty-boy face almost had me believing he was innocent. Or at least amnesiac. Later that day Rothchild confirmed that he thought he saw Jim climbing over the fence at the studio when Paul was coming home from a late dinner. Maybe Jim thought the take we did of "Light My Fire" the night before was so hot, he had to break back into the studio and put out the fire. He was obviously in another state of consciousness.

My life was changing. Robby and I had found a woodsy house for rent on Lookout Mountain Drive in Laurel Canyon. It wasn't big enough for Jim, too, and I didn't know whether I could live with Jim anyway. Living with Robby worked because we had the same outlook on life. Robby was my idol then; he seemed so serene. Nothing upset him. I was pretty sure we were best friends, although Robby never said much, so no one ever knew what he was thinking. Now we were in the canyon, where it felt like the country, even though we were ten minutes from the city. The Santa Monica Mountains were like the lungs of L.A. The housing developments in the hills worried me.

Now that I wasn't living at home, my parents could no longer ask, "When are you going to cut your hair, go back to school, and straighten up?" I always felt that Mom put Dad up to those remarks, he being so shy and she being pushy. Now that the band was paying my rent, my parents were beginning to see that my eccentricities might pay off. I appreciated their pride in my blossoming career, but the wounds they once gave me over what I was doing took a long time to heal.

I had been fairly close to my younger brother, Jim, when we were growing up, but now I was living on my own, going on the road a lot, and I didn't see as much of him. I hoped he was still painting; I loved his paintings. They were full of childlike fantasy in a sort of stark, surrealistic style with pastel colors. He played the flute well too. I envied his ability to write words and melodies; I could only create rhythm.

We finished recording the album in six days, but the mixing down to the final two tracks for stereo took another couple weeks. Mixing was tedious, but I liked the exactness that was necessary. The entire feel of a song could be changed by a slight drop or increase in volume on an obscure background instrument. The album cover was designed by Bill Harvey, Elektra's art director, from a series of photo sessions we posed for. I thought the cover looked beautiful, except that I was rather small and Jim was huge. Jim later reflected on these sessions: "I must have been out of my mind, I thought I knew what I was doing. The horrible thing about a photograph is once it's done, you can't destroy it. Can you imagine when I'm eighty years old and I have to look at myself posing for these pictures?"

❋

I was finally meeting some of the opposite sex on the road. One-night stands mostly. Then, while playing a week back at the Whiskey as headliners, I met Donna Port. She was standing at the side of the stage by the front door listening to us play a set. Her long dark hair was swaying back and forth as she moved her head in time to the music. Her eyes caught mine and she gave me a beautiful smile.

I went up to her after the show, and I found out she was a regular at the club. She seemed open and friendly. I went to the Whiskey on Monday and Tuesday, our off nights, hoping to run into her again. She came in late Tuesday and I bought her a drink.

"I know about a party. It's at a tacky motel, but it could be fun."

"Okay, great," I responded.

She held my hand as I drove east down Sunset toward Crescent Heights. I now had a Morgan, which I traded the Singer Gazelle for. It was like a stretch M.G. I changed the paint from pea green to chocolate brown with black fenders. Attention is what I wanted and now I could buy it. Jim was getting it his way, with black leather pants, so I was going to get mine.

The party was small but the booze was flowing due to the encouragement of the host who seemed to be trying to get us—or Donna, anyway—smashed. After a couple of hours I said I wanted to leave, and Donna told me that she would get a ride home. To my surprise, we kissed heavily in the doorway. As I drove up Laurel, I figured that she had another boyfriend. Or two.

I wasn't giving up. I couldn't give up. She had a great personality and she moved me below the belt.

John Judnick, the lighting man at the Whiskey, told Robby and me that he was moving in with his friend Lenny Bruce, the comedian, and that his house would be up for rent. It was a plastic cliffhanger in the canyon, which was not nearly as charming as our house on Lookout, but there was an apartment for rent right next door, both owned by the same landlord. We drove Jim up there and he liked the apartment, although the landlord lived downstairs. We got them both. Now, I thought, we won't have to track Jim down in crash pads from Hollywood to Venice. As Jim didn't have a phone, he was very difficult to get hold of.

It was in our new digs that Donna and I finally consummated

our relationship after seeing each other again at the club. As in the previous house, I had the living room, and Robby took the bedroom downstairs.

"Where's Robby today?" asked Donna.

"He's down there with his *older* girlfriend. Pretty quiet with two floors, huh?" Donna's eyes widened. I continued. "Yeah, occasionally this cute, *married* woman drops in during the day. I hope her old man doesn't find out. So, why'd you hold out so long on me, Donna?"

"I don't know. If I'd known it would be this good, I wouldn't have!"

We were inseparable for months. Then all of a sudden I started losing interest.

We were at the beach and she knew I was falling out of love from the melancholy in the air between us. Sitting on the sand looking at her down by the water, with her white skin bursting out of her bikini, I knew she knew it was over. What the fuck was wrong with me? She was intelligent and sexy. I guess it was the band. I knew there was some heavy career time up ahead and I didn't want to feel tied down to one person. I could feel subtle pressure from her about the next step in our relationship, whatever that was. But instead of clarifying my feelings and saying something to Donna, I just started to be mean to her. We weren't making love anymore, we were making sex, at least from my point of view. Going through the motions. Instead of talking about it, I just became cold.

It was starting. I was being drawn and quartered. I was making a choice between a beautiful, intuitive girl and our music, which had rescued me from my middle-class suburban background. Did I have to choose? I don't know. You see, we never talked. In any event, the choice was made. The thrill was gone.

٪

. . . Jim, I remember lying nude in a Denver hotel bathtub, putting my mind on the spot between my navel and my groin as the water drained out, reciting the word prana over and over in my brain—this was a

relaxation technique I picked up from Leon, our red-haired, Dutch-looking publicist.

I know, more Eastern bullshit! Well, Jim, if you'd found a positive crutch or two rather than alcohol . . . anyway, Leon (you couldn't forget Leon, the guy with incredible energy who talked us into hiring him as a European publicist because we would eventually get there and he would pave the way) was studying hypnotism and this was one of the things he'd learned.

Ray and I were amused because the hypnotist wasn't giving Leon a mantra, he was giving him the Sanskrit word for "breath." My laughter turned to respect as I used the technique to turn off my brain from thinking about why it wasn't working out with Donna Port.

Remember, I brought her to Denver on New Year's Eve weekend for that gig? The one where they tried to make a small Mason's lodge into a Fillmore-type hall by painting everything with Day-Glo paint? Donna and I both knew it was over, but we didn't want to be alone.

I didn't get to know your girlfriend Pam very well 'cause you rarely brought her along to any Doors events. Did you have a problem committing? She clearly was the "one" for you, but what a roller-coaster ride of a relationship! Did your military upbringing make it hard for you to put down roots?

We were sure committed to the band, weren't we? It was kind of like being married, only it's polygamy. Without the sex. Unless you're bent that way. I figure we had a yearlong honeymoon of rehearsing, then two good years of marriage peaking on success, and finally four years of diminishing tolerance of each other . . . which is sad. There didn't seem to be any other way. Back then at least. Hindsight is easy. My new thing is verbal communication. . . .

7

CRYSTAL SHIP

San Francisco, 1978

Before you slip into unconsciousness
I'd like to have another kiss,
Another flashing chance at bliss,
Another kiss, another kiss.

The cherry blossom trees are vibrating. The sculptured bonsai plants and trees look like statues, in 3-D. Water burbles loudly in the lotus pond as I throw a coin. I wish that this timeless feeling would last forever.

Deb and I climb to the top of the traditional Japanese hump-backed bridge and sit down, dangling our legs over the edge. The voices of Japanese tourists on the winding stone path below seem surreal. My ear picks up the last strains of Grieg's "Peer Gynt" coming from the Golden Gate Park bandshell we passed on our way from the aquarium.

The peyote buttons we brought up from L.A. have obviously kicked in!

"Are you getting a buzz yet?" I giggle while trying to focus on Debbie's face: high, round, reddish cheekbones surrounded by shaggy blond hair. A face I had fallen in love with.

"Yes, I feel a little light-headed," she admits with a smile. A

94

warm, infectious smile. Debbie is finally coming out of years of shyness living in the San Fernando Valley.

I turn my head as if in slow motion: There's the big Buddha where we took a publicity photo years ago. The very first publicity photos. Jim and Ray had climbed over the fence and sat right in his lap! Robby and I then crept next to them for the shot, feeling slightly sacrilegious. It was awkward being photographed over and over. We didn't know how to look. Casual? Angry? Pouting? Pompous? I think we mostly copied the attitude in old Stones' photographs that we had pored over.

I smile at the sudden memory flash. Staring down into the gently flowing stream, I try to refocus on the water but it appears to be pulsing wildly as the peyote intensifies.

"What are you thinking about, John?"

My mouth doesn't seem to be connected to my double-tracking brain. Nothing comes out. My mind continues to wander. It's hard to believe it's been over ten years since the Doors finally broke on through. When I see the pictures now I can't help thinking of how—

My thoughts move back to Morrison like a moth to the flame . . .

/.

. . . Jim, do you remember our first photo session? No one talked about it, but when the photos came back, it looked like we'd studied posing as rock-'n'-roll rebels. Personally, I admired the Beatles, but you were going for a bad boy look. . . . I loved the part of your bio where you described your life as being like a bow string, Jim, pulled back for twenty-two years and suddenly being let go, but the stuff about your attraction to ideas of revolt, disorder, and chaos was ridiculous to me. I thought they'd never play our records with comments like that!

A slender hand clasps mine on the elaborately carved bridge railing. I hold it tightly, caressing it, thinking that her hands look like an artist's hands.

95

. . . Robby talked about how his flamenco lessons influenced his guitar-picking style; Ray, his Chicago blues upbringing; and you had to say you were especially interested in activity that seemed to have no meaning. Frankly, I thought your brain was full of "disorder and chaos!" after we signed the contract. It was the beginning of the erosion of my sanity. My ticket to manhood, to the world, was being shredded as I tried to cash it in. You—or what you stood for—fucked with my head. I wanted to believe that "All You Need Is Love." You forced me to confront the dark side of the world. I wanted to remain a child, I suppose. You wanted me— all of us—to see the things that haunted you. . . .

Morrison's "brass and leather" voice comes on slowly in my inner ear. Eerily crawling up the back of my mind, haunting me as I look into Debbie's big, sad green eyes.

The days are bright and filled with pain
Enclose me in your gentle rain,
The time you ran was too insane,
We'll meet again, we'll meet again . . .

. . . I remember how you had written "Crystal Ship" before we had our first gig, when you were in the middle of breaking up with an early girlfriend. Was that your way of leaving her behind before the band really took off?

God, psychedelics expand time. Seconds go by like hours. People come and go, come and go. I look around for Debbie and see her below, sticking her finger in the *koi* pond and allowing the bright orange carp to nibble on it.

How did she get down there?

She seems hypnotized. Each time they nip at her she laughs shyly. I've fallen in love with that shyness. For the first time in years I feel in sync with a woman.

"John! John! Down here!" she shouts up at me.

I smile strangely at her. Trying to stand, my legs almost go out

96

from under me. Slowly—very slowly—I make my way down the steeply arched wooden bridge to where she's waiting for me with a curious look on her face.

"What was going on up there?"

" 'The Doors are mean and their skin is green,' " I say slyly.

"What?"

"Thinking about the old days, of course."

She laughs lightly again, smiles coyly. "C'mon, John, let's go to the teahouse, okay? Maybe we can get something to drink to help us come down a little."

"Good idea," I say as I take her hand.

"That was a line from a guy named Richard Goldstein, who reviewed our first gig in New York." "Joycean Rock," he had called Jim's lyrics. I shake my head with amusement as we sit down with cups of hot tea among hordes of tourists.

"Ya know, since I've been up here," I resume, "I've been obsessed with the fuckin' band! I can't get it out of my head. Everything—this beautiful park, Haight-Ashbury, North Beach, Golden Gate Bridge—it all reminds me of what happened after we had recorded our first album and then flew up here to try to convert San Francisco to our brand of—"

"Yes . . . your brand of . . . ?"

"Uhhh . . . our music," I say tentatively. "I was gonna say our brand of insanity. You know: The game called insane!"

She looks at me quizzically.

"Oh, I don't know. I was always scared about being too heavy. I want to please everybody. Sometimes it was like a horror movie."

"What was like a horror movie?"

"Our concerts. 'Come and see the Doors and they'll scare the shit out of you!' " I answer her sarcastically. I can feel the old anger again, the anger against fate for putting me in the band in the first place.

"John, you're confusing me. I thought you loved having your audiences on the edge of their seats."

"Well, I'm proud of what we did. But back then . . . oh, God, it's so hard to put into words. I just wanted to be liked. I had no idea how deeply the music was affecting them. *And me!* I still don't understand. I still don't understand why we're so important. Okay, so nobody explored the dark like the Doors. Even Jerry Garcia admits it. He says that, 'Everybody says the Dead are so dark. Well, what about the Doors? They were the dark band of the sixties.'

"In the early days we didn't fit up here. Actually, we didn't fit anywhere. Except for the Dead and the Airplane, San Francisco groups had a mellow sound: 'Wear some flowers in your hair' and all that shit. God, we were dark compared to all that flower power stuff. But why have we lasted? The scream of the butterfly?"

I feel the rage rising again. "Is that it, is that why we lasted? Darkness? Because we represented the dark side of the psyche? Well, look what happened to Jim. He's dead. That's where darkness gets ya! Holy shit, what am I talking about?"

"Why didn't you quit, then?"

" 'Cause this was my only chance! The only card I had to play. I dropped out of college. Plus . . . I love music. It's like a positive addiction for me. I'll tolerate any musician's obnoxious personality for a chance to play. I'm sure I'm obnoxious at times as well, but one of the great things in my life is the brief moments when I'm in sync with other musicians. Jammin'." By now I am gesturing wildly with my hands as if I'm drumming. I look up at her.

"IT'S LIKE SEX!"

She blushes immediately, her eyes flashing, and she nods in agreement.

I reach for an almond cookie in hopes of leveling off a little from the peyote. "Do you feel up to riding some more?"

"Definitely," she answers softly.

"Let's take a ride to the Hall of Flowers. It's another place where we took some photos. It'll knock your eyes out."

We unlock the bikes we had rented earlier that Sunday morning from a shop on Stanyan Street and pedal slowly to the Conservatory of Flowers.

"It's great to ride, isn't it? Instead of driving," Deb confirms.

"The trees seem to be screaming how green they are," I exclaim.

"You're so funny! What exactly was a love-in?" she asks curiously.

"Haight Street was where George Harrison led thousands of hippies into this park for a 'love-in.' It was just a large gathering of folk decked out in their paisley shirts and beads. A prerequisite to protest marches. We realized that with this many people we not only could enjoy the sheer numbers of each other, we could do something. Say something. There were a lot of common feelings: freedom of speech, boycott the draft, stop the Vietnam war. It felt like we were taking over when I joined a huge peace rally through these streets."

"Sounds like a riot to me."

"When you're with people you love, your peers, you feel safe."

A few minutes later we ride up in front of the conservatory, a magnificent glass Hall of Flowers, a replica of the Crystal Palace in London. Sunlight glints off the panes. We park our bikes outside and walk in.

A tropical paradise. I sit down on a bench in front of the giant palm tree from the South Seas. Debbie wanders off on her own.

Oh tell me where your freedom lies,
The streets are fields that never die,
Deliver me from reasons why,
You'd rather cry, I'd rather fly.

Being there with Debbie in the tropical garden I think I finally understand the true meaning of the verse. Morrison's cryptic lyrics were like that; sometimes it took years to fathom what he was trying to say. Now it seemed like one of Morrison's few rays of hope. After going through one marriage already and finding myself back on the street again, the words taunt me to leave the wanderlust years behind me. Living off the streets had killed him; I can't let it happen to me. Meeting Debbie is like being reborn.

The crystal ship is being filled,
A thousand girls, a thousand thrills,
A million ways to spend your time,
When we get back, I'll drop a line.

Jim had asked me before the recording session for the song whether I thought "a thousand girls, a thousand thrills" was better than "a thousand girls, a thousand pills." Was he trying to be careful about advocating drugs? I think so. But was he fooling around with Methedrine like his buddy Felix?

The Crystal Ship, the Crystal Ship . . . the phrase turns over in my mind. It was a pseudonym for the Doors, the four of us together in the band. Maybe the "we" in "when we get back, I'll drop a line" was simply the four of us. We really were together then, or at least that's how we felt when we got on the plane to fly to our first S.F. gig.

٪

San Francisco, January 1967

It was only my second plane ride. I had a window seat next to Robby and stared nervously out the porthole as the plane shimmied up the runway. When we lifted off the ground, I leaned over the seat in front and smiled at Ray and Dorothy; Ray grinned back as if to say *we're on our way.*

Jim was across the aisle next to Robby's brother, Ronnie (our roadie for the tour), poring over his journal, taking a few notes. When he raised his head for a moment, a little grin crept across his face. I could tell how much he was looking forward to this first road trip.

Our first album, simply called *The Doors*, had just been released. "An existential album," as Ray said in an interview, by "four incredibly hungry men, striving and dying to make it, desperately

100

wanting to get a record, a good record, out to the American public and wanting the public to like it."

We had no idea it was to become a classic and our biggest seller ever. Something in my bones did tell me that "Light My Fire" was special. The transition from the verse into the chorus made something inside of me weep. On each song we had tried every possible arrangement, so we felt the whole album was tight. No excess. And Jim was happy with "The End," his dark poetic stream-of-consciousness vision accompanied by Robby's sitarlike guitar.

When the album was released, each of the band members got ten copies. I held off for a few days and then finally played the album for my parents. I was very proud of it but worried about their reaction to "The End."

"Did you drive up Sunset Boulevard and see the billboard?"

"Yes, it's so huge!" Mom exclaimed.

"I think Jac Holzman is very smart. He's the record company president. It was his idea. Up till now, of course, billboards have been used exclusively to sell junk." Radio newscaster Bill Erwin had interviewed us at the new billboard a few days earlier, and was teasing us about the ad. "This is kind of a strange way of using a billboard, guys. I mean, you really can't *hear* a billboard. And nobody has heard of the Doors yet." Holzman retorted that the billboard was Elektra's notice to the music industry that the record company was committed to the group. Jac, who was normally tight, must've had his finger on the pulse of what was happening next in music to spring for the fifteen hundred bucks for the advertisement.

"Well . . . the first cut is called 'Break On Through,' " I continued. "It's fast and loud . . . this next one is 'Soul Kitchen.' It has a nice groove . . . uh . . . a nice feeling. I like the rhythm. Check out the lyrics: 'The cars crawl past all stuffed with eyes, street lights shed their hollow glow, your brain seems bruised with numb surprise, still one place to go' . . . Jim's words are incredible. . . . 'Crystal Ship' is a beautiful ballad. You'll like this one . . . 'Twentieth-Century Fox' is a little cutie . . . 'Alabama

Song' is different . . . kind of European . . . and the last cut on side one is 'Light My Fire,' which I think could be a hit."

"It sounds very nice," my dad offered as I turned the record over.

Wait till you hear "The End," Dad, then see if you still think it's "nice." What was I going to do? . . . I could play it real soft . . . or just skip it.

"This is an old blues, 'Back Door Man.' We didn't write this one . . . 'I Looked at You' is another cutie. . . . 'End of the Night' is kind of eerie. It's fun to create a mood around Jim's lyrics. . . . Jim got the title 'Take It As It Comes' from one of Maharishi's teachers . . .'"

Well, here it goes . . .

"This is called 'The End' . . . it's kind of weird. . . . It's long . . . about ten minutes . . . Jim wrote some stuff about Greek tragedy . . . uh . . . Oedipus or something. . . . Do you know the story?"

Silence.

"I didn't either . . . it's about a son killing his father and then . . . uh . . . messing with his mother. It's all symbolic . . . I mean, Jim doesn't mean it literally."

My mother shifted her sitting position, and then shifted again; she couldn't get comfortable. I quickly put the needle on the record to dispel the awkwardness.

I listened with them, reliving every drum beat.

"Yoga explains perhaps how a man built as slightly as Densmore can cut into a drum with the stunning power he displays in the quiet passages of 'The End,'" said a reviewer from *Vogue*. When the listening party was over at my parents', we all sat silently for a few minutes. Drained. My mother looked teary; my dad, stoic. They complimented me cordially and I left. Whew. That was over.

✗

"Break On Through" was chosen as the single, even though I was worried that the beat was too eccentric for the mass market. It was

102

a fast bossa nova, a beat from Brazilian music I had incorporated into my drumming for the song. Brazilian musicians had by that time penetrated the American record charts with a bossa nova in a jazz idiom, "The Girl from Ipanema" by Antonio Carlos Jobin, but "Break On Through" had a stiffer rock feel to it. We had considered "Twentieth-Century Fox" as a single, but the chorus sounded too commercial, too cute, and we didn't want it to be representative of our sound, which we considered more hard-edged.

When the single of "Break On Through" came out, we convinced friends and relatives to start calling the stations to request it. Getting the band off the ground was a twenty-four-hour obsession with each of us. If we weren't practicing, we were sleeping. If we were eating, we were talking about the group.

One day I called the KRLA request line for what was probably the fortieth time. I said I was Fred Schwartz from West Covina and they said, "We know who you are, and if you don't stop calling we'll pull the record!"

I hoped I hadn't ruined our career before it began.

"Break On Through" slowly rose to number eleven in Los Angeles. It even made it to the bottom of the national charts, but just for a few weeks.

Dave Diamond, a local disc jockey who spun his records from the psychedelic depths of the Diamond Mine (the name of his radio show), invited Robby and me over to his house to show us piles of letters from listeners requesting "Light My Fire"—the seven-minute version he was daring enough to play in an era of the strict three-minute format. He said we should consider cutting the song down to the standard three minutes and put it out as a single. We didn't like the idea of shortening our jazz solos, but Robby and I agreed with him that "LMF" could be a hit. Rothchild, however, was less than excited when we took the idea to him. Grudgingly he agreed to edit the song, saying he still didn't think the record had a chance. Fortunately, our album was selling ten thousand copies every week, so Jac Holzman was willing to try one more single while we hit the psychedelic ballroom scene in San Francisco.

※

The City by the Bay. Only an hour after leaving L.A. we were driving through the Broadway tunnel to the Swiss American Hotel in North Beach, a fleabag joint across the street from the Jazz Workshop and Mike's Pool Hall, where writers and poets like Jack Kerouac and Lawrence Ferlinghetti hung out in the fifties. City Lights bookstore was just down the street from the porn palaces that were beginning to creep into the Italian café part of town.

It felt bohemian to be playing San Francisco, the city of poets and acid rock bands. The groups up here had a semicamaraderie among them that I admired. I say semi because the hardcore music freaks looked down on the Jefferson Airplane as they took off commercially. The Grateful Dead, who sometimes spiked ballroom punch with acid, were considered the real thing. Country Joe and the Fish sounded like acid itself. With heavy echo and repeat, they sang: "YOUR your SILVER silver STREET street FLASH flash ACROSS across THE the TINY tiny DOOR door OF of MY my EYES eyes eyes eyes eyes." The locals said we sounded like Country Joe, but that was only because we had similar instrumentation—we both used an organ. Jim's lyrics were certainly different from "I hunger for your porpoise mouth and stand erect for love."

San Francisco was symbolic of the counterculture movement. Bill Graham, the local rock entrepreneur, put it succinctly in the *Chronicle:* "The combination of the influx of people from all over the country, and the fact that the law and the powers that be made no attempt to stifle that desire for expression by all these young people through their music, poetry, and theatre was the reason San Francisco became Mecca."

All the hallucinogen-induced paintings on the sides of walls and buildings throughout the city gave a kaleidoscopic feel to S.F. The Dead's house in the Haight-Ashbury, with its rainbow colors, came to represent the hippie movement. And across the bay, the

U.C. Berkeley campus was a hotbed of liberal activism. Lyndon Baines Johnson had been inaugurated as the thirty-sixth president of the United States two years before, and he was continuing the escalation of the *undeclared* war in Vietnam. So much for the "Great Society" and the "War on Poverty." Rebellion was in the air.

Later that afternoon we took a cab across town to the Fillmore Auditorium.

The Fillmore. A rather nondescript brown brick music hall on the edge of a rough, black neighborhood. Bill Graham, the transplanted New Yorker with a New Yorker's energy, booked groups like the Airplane, the Dead, Country Joe, and Big Brother and the Holding Company. The truly inventive thing about Graham was the way he booked these groups on the same bill with blues and jazz acts like B.B. King and Woody Herman. It was quite a coup for Jac Holzman to pressure him into booking us, but "Break On Through" was out and that earned us third billing to the Young Rascals and Sopwith Camel, two considerably more clean-cut groups. Our cab pulled up outside the auditorium to a street scene of a few hippies trying to get tickets for the night's performance. Just around the corner to the left, it looked like Watts, with local brothers drinking out of paper bags.

We walked into the empty hall and were a little intimidated by its size. All of a sudden this mean-ass guy with an unmistakable New York accent started shouting and grabbed a kid and said, "Try and get in free, eh? Get the fuck outta here!" Then he threw him down the stairs. It was a shocking introduction to Bill Graham.

That night we were shown to the dressing room on the side of the balcony. As the audience came in before our set, I said to Ray, "I'm going downstairs to check out the vibes."

"Don't drink the punch," he warned jokingly.

Robby looked up from tuning his guitar, lost in his pre-gig haze. He wasn't as interested in audience response; he was too obsessed with his music. I wanted to get a feel for where the audience was at. I figured it could help me gauge our performance, make changes if necessary.

I couldn't believe the hordes of freaks pouring into the seatless auditorium. Graham greeted them at the door by handing out apples from an enormous barrel. He had totally changed personalities and now seemed eager to please. Some of the people were dancing free form to Otis Redding on Graham's spectacular sound system. He certainly did things right. Others were lying on the floor in their beads and dashikis. Street pageantry.

The crowd was hyped up from the "Human Be-In" in Golden Gate Park, we had attended earlier that day. It had felt like a huge outdoor picnic, with marijuana as the food. Twenty thousand hippies had celebrated a new spirit of consciousness, initiated by beat poet Gary Snyder blowing on a conch shell. Other Dharma Bums in attendance at the park that day were poets Allen Ginsberg, Lawrence Ferlinghetti, and Michael McClure, who later was to become Jim's close friend. Also present, representing the drug/ guru culture, was Richard Alpert (a.k.a. Ram Dass) and Timothy Leary, the acid king. They had been promenading for peace in the first love-in in the country.

That night the crowd was kind of quiet, possibly because we were the opening act for the Young Rascals, or maybe they just didn't know what to make of us. We didn't have a bass player, like most rock bands they were used to hearing, and we put out an ominous vibe. It was partly a coverup for stage fright, but after the first couple of numbers, Jim realized it worked, and he stayed with it.

Still, it felt as if we were being scrutinized because we were from L.A.

That night we didn't blow anybody off the stage, but the faces in the first few rows stared at us like we were from another planet. Mouths open and eyes pinned. In Robby's solo in "Spanish Caravan," Jim got down on his knees to get a closer look at Robby's fingers. In rehearsal I always asked Robby to play flamenco so I, too, could watch his picking. His right hand looked like a crab with many legs crawling over the strings.

The reviews said we were a band to watch, probably because of Jim's leather pants. We'd gotten a little bread over and above food and rent money, so the next thing in line was wardrobe. We didn't discuss group outfits anymore, although Ray did continue with the suit or sport coat look. Jim got into leather and Robby and I went into full flower power. Tie-dyed shirts and Nehru jackets. Rainbow City. In weaker moments, I worried that one might have to wear dark glasses to look at me in some of my outfits.

The biggest roar that night at the Fillmore came when Ray said that we'd been in the park for the love-in.

After we finished our set, I found a space for myself in the middle of the auditorium to hear the Rascals. My attention centered mostly on their drummer, Dino Danelli, who was quite good, twirling his sticks and not missing a beat. I had to admit that the group was slick. The guitar player and singer had all the standard rock concert moves down. Listening to their pop sound, though, convinced me how serious we were in comparison. We wanted to be more than just entertainment. As Ray said at the time, "We want our music to short-circuit the conscious mind and allow the unconscious to flow free." In other words, we wanted to be the band you were forced to think about when you got home.

Three weeks later, the Doors were back at the Fillmore playing third bill again, this time to the Grateful Dead and Junior Wells and his All-Stars.

Owsley Stanley III, the underground chemist and sound man for the Dead, came backstage for a chat. He had long, stringy hair and wore wire-rimmed Ben Franklin glasses.

One pill makes you larger and one pill makes you small
The ones that Mother gives you don't do anything at all

I thought the "white rabbit" was going to give us samples of his famous pure LSD, but he wanted to discuss music.

"You guys need a bass player. There's a hole in your sound and a bass would make it fuller." Ray and I nodded as if we agreed, and the doctor left.

"If we're making *him* nervous, we're on the right track," I stated.

"Yeah, let's definitely *not* get a bass player now!" Ray confirmed.

⁒

We played the club scene in L.A. —the Hullabaloo and Gazarri's, among others—for the next couple of months before being booked into San Francisco again in March. Because our album was climbing the charts, this time we were the headliners.

The Avalon was the other "psychedelic ballroom" in San Francisco. It was run by mellow Chet Helms, a local promoter with shoulder-length blond hair and a full beard. Between Helms and Bill Graham at the Fillmore, there was serious competition for musical groups. Early on, the supposedly more hardcore, underground types preferred the Avalon, knocking Bill Graham for his aggressive entrepreneurship.

Like the Fillmore, the Avalon was a large, empty auditorium. Another echo chamber. You had to fill these places with bodies for more than economic reasons; they absorbed the sound and made the acoustics tolerable. There were white sheets all over the walls and ceiling for the light shows, which consisted of colored water on plastic or glass wiggled in time to the music and projected on the walls and ceiling. Just walking into one of these places would put you into another time zone. The music was hypnotic and the walls were moving and pulsating with light moving through colored liquid. A trip.

The Avalon was one stoned gig. We followed a band called the Sparrow and a hallucinogenic set by Country Joe. The crowd was more out of it than usual, more receptive to our surreal imagery.

The psychedelized crowd wanted *head* music—they wanted to be transported. Their vibes encouraged experimentation.

With most of the packed-in audience lazing on the floor rather than dancing—it looked like a huge dope den with the marijuana smoke swirling in the air—the stage was set.

We took a break between "Light My Fire" and "The End." During this pause, before our crowd-hypnotizing encore, I got up from my drum stool and walked over to Ray seated at his organ.

"Looks like someone is ejaculating with a zoom lens up there on the light show crew," I joked, pointing to the balcony where the light booth was.

"Eisenstein montage, man," Ray quipped.

The Avalon was the first place where "The End" got real attention. People seemed entranced by the Oriental tuning, as if they were hearing something new. They were meeting us halfway. They were willing to let us lead them a little farther down and then out —of where? Rock's heart of darkness? The rabbit hole? The back door? With Jim as the "Back Door Man"?

The light show, which was projected directly on the stage as well as the walls, oozed in perfect time with my rhythms. From the drum riser at the middle of the stage, it felt like I was playing in the center of a giant, pulsating womb.

Jim was really coming into his own that night. We all were. Ray locked into a groove and started hanging his head down, swaying to the music. It was trance time.

There's danger on the edge of town
Ride the king's highway, baby
Weird scenes inside the gold mine
Ride the high-way west, bay-by
Ride the snake, ride the snake,
To the lake, the ancient lake
The snake he's long, seven miles
Ride the snake, he's old
And his skin is cold

The west is the best
Get here, and we'll do the rest
Da blue bus is callin us
Driver, where you takin' us?
The killer awoke before dawn
He put his boots on
He took a face from the ancient gallery
And he walked on down the hall
And he went into the room where his sister lived
And then, paid a visit to his brother, and then he,
HE WALKED ON DOWN THE HALL
And he came to a door . . .
And he looked inside . . .
Father—yes, son—I want to kill you
MOTHER . . . I want TO . . .
UHHAAHGGHHFUCKYOUMAMAALLNIGHTLONGYEA

We knocked them out.

After the concert, I was helping one of the roadies pack up when I sensed someone staring up at the stage. I turned around and looked out into the empty auditorium where I saw, standing among all the leftover plastic cups, a beaming face and a soft, round female body.

Pam was the epitome of Earth Mother. Just my type. I said hi and noticed her pupils totally pinned back in acid-induced dilation.

She took me to the archetypal crash pad that she frequented. There were so many hippies living in San Francisco at the time that one could survive almost rent free, rotating from one old Victorian house to another every couple days.

"You don't live here?" I asked.

"No. This guy Chris pays the rent, but it's okay. Everybody crashes here," Pam assured me.

Hmm. What if this guy Chris shows up? Maybe he's her boy-friend!

Before I knew what was happening, Pam took off all of her clothes, which was pretty stimulating for a young Catholic boy like me. She let me run my hands all over her body as she stretched her arms to the ceiling. She was totally free, blissed out. She was also ripped.

I was lucky to get it inside before making a mess. I tried thinking of numbers, counting. My sexual immaturity kept me from knowing that women too can have orgasms or that they want affection as much as performance.

The next morning Chris showed up, and he looked displeased. Not too angry, but displeased. Pam said hi and sort of cooled him out . . . I guess free love wasn't that free after all.

I took a cable car down to Fisherman's Wharf. I remember looking out across to Alcatraz shimmering in the bay and thinking I had found The One.

So, like most modern adolescents, I learned my sexuality on the street. I continued to see Pam on our next trips to San Francisco, tracking her down to crash pads or knocking on her boyfriend's apartment door. No one seemed to mind.

The fact that we were actually making a living off our music was satisfying, and it gave us a sense of confidence and power. Robby, having grown up with money, wasn't as affected by the two hundred fifty bucks a month, but he did get off on having his songs out in public. "Manzarek is grateful to success for the first chance he's ever had to live a thoroughly comfortable life," a writer from *Vogue* commented about Ray. Jim and I thought that we must be special with all the money and attention. I used yoga to help ground me, thinking every once in a while that all this excitement was actually *maya* (the Indian word for illusion). I'd been an outcast in high school, why was I so great now? There was a bitter taste in my mouth. I was getting my revenge, wasn't I?

After our hypnotic debut as headliners at the Avalon, we played a weekend at the Winterland Ballroom. I was surprised that San Franciscans liked the Doors. Our lyrics weren't about love and peace; they were about sex and death. Morrison dressed

111

all in black, a stark contrast to the rainbow-colored San Francisco dress code—and he didn't wear flowers in his hair. (It was at this time, in 1967, that we started running into Morrison clones. Jan was a guy in the Haight who dressed in black leather and kept inviting us over to parties to which we all went at first. They were like a scene out of Fellini's *Satyricon,* just a bunch of people lazing around on the floor stoned out of their minds.)

At our Winterland concert, Jim kept sticking the flowers his fans were giving him under my drumsticks as I was trying to play. He laughed hysterically because he knew I couldn't stop unless I wanted to ruin the performance; so my sticks smashed the daisy petals. Maybe it was his way of fucking with my image as a flower child.

That night, in between sets, Paul Kantner of the Airplane suggested that we drive over to the Avalon, about two miles across town, to hear Big Brother and the Holding Company. The female lead singer was so good, we were told, it would be worth the hassle of getting back for our last set. I remember thinking that a girl who called herself "Big Brother" must be kind of butch. I was setting myself up to be disappointed. Still, Robby and I rushed over in our rental car and arrived in the middle of a torching rendition of "Down on Me"—"Looks like everybody, in this whole round world, is . . . Down on me, down on me." I couldn't *believe* the sound! No way did it jive with the white girl onstage. If I hadn't been looking up at her, I could've sworn she was an old black blues singer like Bessie Smith. She sang with lust and pain in her voice, wrestling with the mike as if she were being electrocuted. Later they would call her the female Jim Morrison.

After the set I went back to the dressing room to tell her how great she was. She thanked me kindly and offered me a slug of her gallon of rotgut wine. Seeing Janis Joplin up close wasn't as appealing as from a distance, but she was warm and friendly, and that deep, husky voice kept reminding me how powerfully she could belt the blues.

The next morning the unshaven manager of our sleazy hotel

burst into our rooms at 8 A.M. and yelled, "CHECK OUT, HIP-
PIES!" We found out that he was mad because Jim had scored a
chick from the Winterland and she'd spent the night, and bringing women back to the room was not allowed. I bet if the manager
had gotten more rent, he would have totally approved.

The next day we were in Enrico's Café down the street for
cappuccino and the morning papers. There was nothing in the
San Francisco Chronicle, but Ray found a review in *The New York
Times.*

"When The Doors came on to do their thing," wrote Robert
Windeeler, describing the Winterland performance, "there was
sudden silence and the crowd sat as if it were about to hear a
chamber music concert."

"Chamber music!" roared Jim above the traffic on Broadway.

"Dig it," I said as I ordered an Italian pastry.

"Far out," Robby murmured.

Ray nodded, as if everything were on schedule.

The Crystal Ship had left the safe confines of California and
was headed out into the high seas. We didn't know that we were
never to return to the pleasures of the harbor.

TWENTIETH-CENTURY FOX

Well, she's fashionably lean
And she's fashionably late . . .

She's the queen of cool
She's the lady who waits
Since her mind left school
It never hesitates . . .

She won't waste time on elementary talk
She's a Twentieth-Century Fox

⚹

The summer of 1967 was one of traveling the country from coast to coast, from gig to gig, studio session to studio session. We were trying to crack New York again, appearing at the Scene in June while the Monterey Pop Festival, the first of its kind, was going on in California. I was depressed that we were in this dumpy club across the country while all of the important groups of the sixties were in Monterey. Of course, we weren't even invited! Later Derek Taylor, one of the organizers, was to say that we'd been overlooked. Bullshit. They knew about us. They were afraid of us. We didn't represent the attitude of the festival: peace and love and flower power. We represented the shadow side. My flower-

114

child half strongly wanted to be tripping and dancing at the festival, but I was in the demon Doors.

The days and weeks blurred as we performed continually. I began dreading the drive down to the airport to get on yet another plane. Especially with Jim. Sometimes it felt like I was trapped on an airplane with a lunatic. I thought that if these other passengers knew what was going on in Jim's mind ("Confusion, all my life's a torn curtain, all my mind comes tumblin' down"), they would head for the exit, find a parachute, and jump out, 'cause he's gonna open the exit door anyway. He'll wait till we're good and up in the air. On one flight during this tour, Jim got so loud and drunk that the stewardess summoned the captain. Jim snapped to attention, said "Yes, sir," and quickly sat down at the captain's mere presence. Interesting.

My feelings about live performances were bittersweet. Was the magical hour onstage worth all the craziness and rootless feeling of the road?

Jac Holzman, who was, after all, president of a folk label, had Paul Simon over for dinner and played him some of our demos for our second album. He told Paul the Doors were going to be the biggest group in America, and Simon agreed. Simon also agreed to have us play second bill with Simon and Garfunkel at Forest Hills. Ten thousand people!

You could feel our nervousness backstage when Paul came in to wish us luck. He was very friendly. I don't know whether it was nervousness, or just that Jim hated folk music, but he gave Simon the worst vibes, in short of saying "Get the fuck out of our dressing room." To the guy who hired us! Then we went out onstage and Jim didn't give an inch. He didn't try to connect to the audience in any way. At the end of our set, during the "Father, I want to kill you" section, Jim put all the bottled-up hatred and rage and whatever was bothering him into slamming the mike down and screaming. It lasted about one minute. The audience woke up a bit and started thinking about what they were seeing.

After intermission, Paul and Artie walked out onstage to thunderous applause.

٪.

In July "Light My Fire" hit number one on the charts and stayed at number one for a month. It remained on the charts for an unheard-of twenty-six weeks. A rumor spread like brushfire that the song was the anthem for race riots in Detroit that summer.

That July we headed for New York for a club gig at the Scene and a series of interviews. It was all set up by the record company. When "Light My Fire" started racing up the charts, we began crisscrossing the country on airplanes. This was to be our way of life for the next few years. Airports, baggage claim checks, and limos became our steady environment.

This time around in New York we were minor celebrities because *Newsweek*, *Vogue*, and *The New York Times* all gave our album favorable reviews. It seemed as if they were trying to outdo each other with wild descriptions. *Time* magazine ran Jim's old quote from our Elektra biography: "I'm interested in anything about revolt, disorder, and chaos."

I'd hated the quote from the beginning. In spite of the attention it got, I had a feeling that it would lead to Jim's demise.

Howard Smith gave us a terrific review in the *Village Voice*, calling Jim the first real male sex symbol since James Dean. "If my antennae are right," he wrote, "he could be the biggest thing to grab the mass libido in a long time."

Steve Harris, head of promotion for Elektra Records-New York, set up interviews with 16 magazine. At first I couldn't figure out why a teenybopper rag would be interested in us, since we were becoming notorious as a radical group. I was soon to find out.

Tell you about my baby, she come around
She come around here, just about midnight
Make me feel so good, make me feel alright
She come around my street, she come to my house . . .
Knock upon my door, climbin' up my stairs

One, two, three, ca pup, daca, ch ch come on baby
Umm, here she is in my room . . . OH BOY

I thought I was a renegade Catholic until I met Gloria Stavers. A thirty-year-old ex-model and head of *16*, she was the first woman I had met who could trade on her power for sex, and it shocked me and shattered my illusions about how liberated I was. The scene at her magazine office was another nail in the coffin of my innocence. Gloria personally selected the teen idols who graced her covers, and Steve said if she liked us—that is, if she liked Jim—it would be great for our career. She liked. When Gloria invited the band over to her apartment, she instructed Steve to tell us to leave early so she and Jim could take some photos. Hmmm. . . . This felt like a new form of payola. But Jim seemed more than comfortable with the setup. Gloria wasn't a knockout, but she was the publisher.

Hey, what's your name? How old are you?
Where'd you go to school? Uh huh, yea,
Uh huh, yea, oh, oh, yea, oh, huh.
Well, now that we know each other a little bit better
Why don't you come over here . . . and
MAKE ME FEEL ALRIGHT!
GLOOORIA, G-L-O-R-I-A GLOOORIA

A not-unattractive, slightly older woman. I had heard that if you took a look at the old covers of *16* you could see her conquests.

I've always wondered what happened later that night. The pictures that resulted from the photo session were strange. Jim looked androgynous. It surprised me that he consented to being photographed in Gloria's fur coat. Having his shirt off wasn't new, but draping his concho belt around his neck? At the time I thought it looked like a soft-porn shoot. She got him into poses

117

that turned her on, and then after the session, I imagine that he got her into poses that turned *him* on.

I am . . . a BACK DOOR MAN
THE MEN DON'T KNOW
But the little girls UNDERSTAND!

Obviously Jim knew something *I* didn't understand.

His guttural grunts in the intro of "Back Door Man" were those of an old black man in the bayou who had been through the wars with women.

You men eat your dinner, eat your pork and beans,
I eat more chicken than any man ever seen . . .
Cuz I'm a Back Door Man!
Da men don't know, but da little girls understand . . .

It took me a while to realize that the verse was about other men only sleeping with their wives while the singer was sleeping with *all* of them, but having to steal away in the middle of the night. That's the sort of thing *men* are famous for, but Jim found his match in Gloria. Robby had warned Gloria about Jim, but had anyone warned him about her?

You were my queen and I was your fool
Riding home after school
You took me home, to your house
Your father's at work,
Your mother's out shopping . . . around
You took me into your room
You showed me your thing
Why'd you do it?
Gettin' softer, slow it down . . .

118

Recording *Strange Days*.

Recording, 1967.
(PHOTO CREDIT:
FRANK LISCIANDRO)

Waiting for the Sun
sessions.
(PHOTO CREDIT:
JERRY HOPKINS)

Jim and Pam, 1968.

Ray and Dorothy.
(PHOTO CREDIT:
BRENDEE GREEN)

(PHOTO CREDIT: EDMUND TESKE)

Robby and Lynn.
(PHOTO CREDIT:
BRENDEE GREEN)

Julia and me, at my surprise birthday party.

Adding percussive comments to Jim's singing.

Jim (well on his way),
wishing me a happy
birthday.
(PHOTO CREDIT:
BRENDEE GREEN)

(PHOTO CREDIT: PAUL FARRARA)

(PHOTO CREDIT: PAUL FARRARA)

I was surprised that Gloria would take the risk of publicizing Jim so much in light of his antics. And you could feel his potential for antics by just meeting him. *16* magazine was for young girls, and I thought it might be a problem if one of its cover subjects ever got into trouble. And Jim did.

> *. . . Wrap your legs around my neck*
> *Wrap your arms around my feet*
> *Wrap your hair around my skin . . .*

I guess Jim was just too charming to pass up. Gloria could have put me on the cover, but I'm sure Jim's face sold more magazines. My face would probably be good selling shotguns on the cover of *Soldier of Fortune.*

> *It's gettin' harder, it's gettin' too darn fast*
> *Too late, too late, can't stop*
> *MAKE ME FEEL ALRIGHT!*
> *GLOOORIA, G-L-O-R-I-A GLOOORIA*

%

We were staying at the dumpy Great Northern Hotel on 57th Street. Convenient location, but the place smelled of old people. I was rooming right next to Jim, which turned out to be better than TV. Not that I was the drinking-glass-to-the-wall type, but the racket that was coming from next door one night was hard to miss. Jim brought Nico, the Velvet Underground's famous German vamp, back to his hotel room, and I'd never heard such crashing around. It sounded as if they were beating the shit out of each other. I was worried but never dared to ask what happened. Nico looked okay the next day, so I let it slide. Later Nico was to say in the press, "Ja, Jim ist crazzy!"

%

A dark-haired girl at the press party for our first album kept batting her eyes at me. While I was looking at the incredible exhibit of huge Salvador Dali paintings, she came up to me.

"The security guard said the boys in the band like girls who don't wear bras, so I took mine off." Such ingenuity, on both their parts. I looked down at her breasts and sure enough, they were peeking through a fairly transparent blouse.

"I have to go to the bathroom," I said mischievously.

"Can I watch?" she replied.

Quite a line.

"Sure, sure."

Watch she did, and then she took off her blouse. I noticed a cigarette burn very close to her nipple.

"How'd you get that?"

"My boyfriend did it in an argument."

"Pretty heavy boyfriend," I said. "Is he here?"

"No, no, he's out of town."

I received badly needed, detailed instruction in fellatio, and then she left. Didn't even leave her phone number.

In the morning our publicist, Leon, told me that the same girl knocked on his door around 2 A.M. that night, came in, and gave him an oil and lube job. Such service!

The Doors weren't the typical macho rock-'n'-rollers who bragged to each other about their conquests. Jim, Robby, and I were having casual affairs drawn from the music scene. We were still looking for The One, but is there ever *one* for a rock-'n'-roller? The problem with notoriety is that you're not sure whether someone is interested because of your image or your soul. Ray still had Dorothy, but he had had her before our climb to the peak. They were inseparable. In fact, Dorothy was now a permanent fixture, present at everything from record negotiations to dinners and rehearsals. Silently.

Robby was subtler than I was about picking up girls. But he had them all the same.

Whenever we were in New York, Jim would see a girl with short, pixyish blond hair and a gregarious personality. Her name was Lynn Veres, and she was raised in New Jersey. She came to Manhattan and started out as a dancer at the Peppermint Lounge.

Lynn was full of hilarious stories about her life in the fast lane in NYC, like the time one of the dancers at the club had her falsies pop out of her bra while onstage.

⁒

Jim looked a little pale on the limo ride to our first reserved-seating concert gig at the Village Theater on the Lower East Side. The paleness wasn't from the limo, which we all loved, with its velvet upholstery and silent, smooth ride. Nor was it from Jac Holzman's black limo driver, George, who had a great smile and a big knife scar across the back of his neck. ("We's just joy-ridin'," he said when we couldn't find the stage door and circled the block a couple of times.) No, Jim was pale because it was radio station WOR's anniversary show, and this was our first "concert" concert. With all the gigs I'd played, I still found my heart pounding while standing in the wings waiting to go on. This was the big time. A huge proscenium stage with long red curtains at the wings. And the sea of faces out there.

Vince Treanor, our new "electronic genius" roadie from New England, was running behind setting up the equipment. Vince was thin and nervous, a workaholic. The theater management told me not to play longer than thirty minutes. But before I could relay the message to "the boys," the curtain started rising. Vince was still onstage, so Jim grabbed the curtain as it went up. It kept rising, and Jim wouldn't let go! I was worried that he'd reach the point of no return and get hurt, but he knew what he was doing. At the halfway point Jim let go, dropped to the stage, landed on his feet, grabbed the mike, and started singing "Break On Through." What a show, what a show. The audience thought it was all part of the act and ate it up. I didn't know Jim was into acrobatics.

After a few numbers, Janis Ian's manager started yelling at us from the side of the stage. We were running overtime and his client, who was on next, was only seventeen and had to go to school in the morning.

Ray, Robby, and Jim didn't hear the complaint because they

were downstage, and they started "The End," which usually lasted fifteen to twenty minutes. I do know they heard Murray the K, the deejay, screaming "We're dying, we're dying!" during the first few soft minutes of the piece.

This is the end, beautiful friend
This is the end, my only friend
The end, it hurts to set you free,
But you'll never follow me,
The end, of laughter and soft lies,
The end, of nights we tried to die

Can you picture what will be, so limitless and free,
desperately in need, of some stranger's hand,
In a desperate land

Jim pretended to be oblivious to the sideline distraction. The song was loosely based on classical Indian ragas, so the first two-thirds were very subdued. Then it built from the double time to the turbulent finale, with the tempo increasing to a musical orgasm. If you can be patient enough to let the hypnotic droning sound of the first half take you, then your imagination gets wildly fulfilled at the climax, but at this performance I felt pressure to wrap it up. I was upstage, and out of the corner of my eye, I could see Murray's beet-red face and his finger pointing to his watch. He wasn't about to surrender to the trance.

We cut the song by five minutes, but there were still bad vibes backstage from the agents and managers after we finished.

٪

It was when we got back to L.A. that Jim met Pam Courson at the Whiskey. It was a relationship that would last through the rest of his life. She was a redhead, short and shy and straight from Orange County, complete with a high school principal for a father. With brown-ricelike freckles and emerald-green eyes, Pam had the innocent face of a snow princess, and a soft, lilting voice to boot.

122

She also had the fire to be Jim's match. Jim liked to dominate women or treat them with great respect. At nineteen years of age Pam came up to Hollywood to find herself; instead she found Jim. Jim chatted her up at the bar, just as I had done with Donna Port. They quickly moved in together, taking an apartment behind the Canyon Market in Laurel. My hopes were high that Jim might stabilize a bit.

Lynn Veres came out to the coast with her friend Peggy, and Robby started dating Lynn! Hmmm. There was no dialogue between Robby and Jim about Jim's former lover.

As I said, Robby had grown up with money, but I was still surprised when he bought a Porsche with his first royalty check. I was more surprised when he also bought an antique Oriental rug, which he cut up and used as upholstery for the car! Why not? The single of "Light My Fire" had taken giant leaps up the charts, and Elektra predicted that the group would hit the top soon.

Ray bought a house with a pool.

Me? I was still tooling around in my Morgan and playing the field.

9

Strange Days

Los Angeles, August 1967

When Robby and I were still roommates on Lookout Mountain Drive in Laurel Canyon, Jim came by one afternoon when I was out. Apparently he was deeply depressed, pacing the floor and saying that everything was fucked up. Robby was taken by surprise, since Jim rarely confided in us about his problems, only his music. After rapping for a little while, Robby suggested that they take a walk up the hill to Appian Way for the spectacular panoramic view of L.A., saying it could be just the thing for a little perspective.

Half an hour later Robby returned, and Jim followed shortly thereafter. He was euphoric.

"What happened?" Robby asked him.

"Look at these lyrics," Jim said excitedly.

People are strange, when you're a stranger,
Faces look ugly, when you're alone,
Women seem wicked, when you're unwanted,
Streets are uneven—when you're down.

"These are great, Jim. Have you got a melody to go with it?" Robby asked.

124

Jim smiled strangely and hummed a few bars. Robby's ears immediately perked up. He knew a hit when he heard one.

"That melody has a nice hook."

"Yeah, I really feel good about this one. It just came to me all of a sudden . . . in a flash—as I was sitting up there on the ridge looking out over the city." His eyes were wild with excitement. "I scribbled it down as fast as I could. It felt great to be writing again." He looked down at the crumpled paper in his hand and sang the chorus in his haunting blues voice.

When you're strange,
Faces come out in the rain,
When you're strange,
No one remembers your name . . .

"My dad says we should get a manager," Robby said, going up the elevator to Max Fink's office.

"I guess it's time," I confirmed. "All the big groups have managers."

"Yeah," Ray and Jim chimed in, nodding their heads.

"My dad said Max can help us find one."

"Very good," Ray replied.

We met several people, finally settling on Salvator Bonafetti, who used to manage Dion of Dion and the Belmonts, and his partner Asher Dann, a Beverly Hills real estate broker. To this day, I have some regrets about the choice. Our career was escalating rapidly and they seemed like the best at the time. The trouble was, they didn't really have any feeling for the music, let alone for us as individuals. They were first and foremost businessmen. They certainly weren't our peers.

Sal and Ash did convince us to hire a press agent. We were sitting in their Vegas-like office on Sunset when Derek Taylor, the Beatles' press agent and our new one, came in. He was a handsome, terribly British gentleman who wore ascots and had an upper-crust accent. He had a warm personality, though. Following

Derek's dialogue—and he did like to talk—wasn't that easy because he seemed to wander a bit from his train of thought. He had a great rep, though.

It was clear that Derek understood the music scene. I was a little embarrassed that he might have thought our new managers were out of touch.

"You know the boys [Beatles] got the news of the death of their manager, Brian Epstein, a couple of days ago. They're in India meditating with this guru. He's the one who gave them the news. Who better to? Here's a newspaper article about it."

Holy shit! It's Maharishi!

"Robby, look at this!" I exclaimed.

Our secret little ritual was going to be exposed to the masses.

Robby looked up from the article in amazement.

Oh, well. Many people, especially our younger fans who are vulnerable to peer pressure and emulating rock stars, could use the calming technique.

٪

We started our second album back at Sunset Sound Studios that August. Elektra announced a record-breaking advance order of 500,000 copies, so we were excited about delivering the goods to a receptive audience. As we were feeling that Max Fink was an old-school lawyer, and we could use some new blood, my old girl-friend Donna Port urged us to see a friend of hers, Abe Somer. The contract had options for two more albums, at the same royalty rates, but Abe felt with the huge success of "Light My Fire" and the album having already sold a half million copies, he could vastly improve our deal.

"First of all, you should own your own songs. That's your gold, and it belongs to you. It's nothing to have your own publishing company. It costs two hundred dollars and we'll take care of the paperwork. Jac owning it is slightly immoral. Second, I think I can get a better overall deal. I'll call Jac in New York right now, and you'll see the guilt coming through the phone. Elektra may *seem* like a family, but wait until we audit them."

"Hi, Jac." Abe had his finger to his lips, indicating that we should be quiet. "It's Abe Somer."

"How's the weather out in L.A.?" Jac said. "It's a 150 degrees here!"

"A perfect 78 degrees, Jac," Abe said, winking at us. "About the publishing, Jac . . . you *know* the boys should own their own songs and not Nipper Music. Nipper is the nickname you have for your son. These songs are the Doors' babies."

"Well . . . you're right, but then no percentage increase."

"I think up a couple points is fair, in light of 'Light My Fire' holding number one for weeks and weeks and weeks."

"You drive a hard bargain, Abe." Jac sighed.

"These boys deserve it," Abe said, smiling at us.

"Okay . . . but seven and a half is it!"

"I'll have it in writing by the weekend. Thank you, Jac. I know the boys will appreciate it. And come out and enjoy this weather sometime."

⁂

The recording of the new album began very well. We polished up "My Eyes Have Seen You," which was written in Ray's parents' garage before Robby even arrived, and rehearsed "People Are Strange" for a couple of weeks. It turned into a catchy song with single potential. Jim's latest song was especially poignant to me because the lyrics not only had his patented strange and dark trademark, but now they were raw and lonely, even personal. I thought his vulnerability was finally showing through the bravado and that he was finally admitting he was afraid.

Paul Rothchild, our producer, was very open about listening to everyone's input in the recording studio. If he had been an old-line producer, we probably wouldn't have been invited to the mix, where the final sound is put together. But Paul was wise enough to know that the new groups who wrote their own material were very concerned about every stage of recording. He arranged for Paul Beaver, the expert programmer of the new Moog sound synthesizers, to come down and distort some of our instru-

127

mental and vocal sounds for interesting effects. We certainly made Jim's voice sound "strange" on the title cut, "Strange Days." For "Unhappy Girl," Rothchild actually had Ray overdub the chord changes backward on piano while listening to the song backward, and then played it back forward. The backward piano track sounded like some melodic percussion instrument—a rattle or shaker—playing the correct chords.

Late that summer our engineer Bruce Botnick got a mono (one-track) reference disk of the yet-to-be-released Beatles' album, *Sergeant Pepper*, from the Turtles. He had just recorded the song "Happy Together" with them, and he played the new Beatles album for us. Rumor had it that the Beatles had bought ten copies of our first album, but their new one was both inspirational and intimidating. We had thought we were on the cutting edge of experimental pop music, but the Beatles seemed to have done it all with *Sergeant Pepper*. As Robert Hilburn of the *L.A. Times* said, "All previous albums seemed like black and white as opposed to Pepper's technicolor."

Ray remembers those days vividly. *"Strange Days* is when we began to experiment with the studio itself, as an instrument to be played. It was now eight-track, and we thought, 'My goodness, how amazing! We can do all kinds of things—we can do overdubs, we can do this, we can do that—we've got eight tracks to play with!' It seems like nothing today, in these times of thirty-two-, even forty-eight-track recording, but those eight tracks to us were really liberating. So, at that point, we began to play . . . it became five people: keyboard, guitar, drums, vocalist, and the studio."

We were all smoking a lot of grass during those sessions. Through the haze of Mary Jane, the music kept sounding greater and greater—louder and louder. One writer described our music as "people trying desperately to reach each other through the choking haze of drugs and artificial masks."

Meanwhile, we were refining our so-called California sound, with "spooking organ tones, the traces of raga and sitar . . ." as another rock writer described it at the time. And Jim's lyrics kept astounding me:

My eyes have seen you
let them photograph your soul,
memorize your alleys
on an endless roll.

His stuff was great—erotic, but not pornographic; mystical, but not pretentious. His poetry was a source of his power as much as his sexually charged "David" looks or his "brass and leather voice."

One night we got a call from the Jefferson Airplane. They were in town and wanted to drop by the studio. Both of our groups were working on our second albums, and we were curious about what the other was doing. I was pleased that the Airplane walked in right when Jim was screaming the lines for the poem "Horse Latitudes":

When the still sea conspires an armor, And her sullen and aborted currents breed tiny monsters, true sailing is dead.
Awkward instant, and the first animal is jettisoned, legs furiously pumping
their stiff green gallop, And heads bob up, Poise, Delicate, Pause, Consent,
In mute nostril agony, carefully refined, And sealed over.

The studio was dark except for the red exit sign, and we scared the shit out of our San Francisco rivals.

During the recording of the *Strange Days* album, Morrison's attitude was more confident. For all of us, the studio was becoming a familiar place; we were more relaxed there. It was almost like a second home. Botnick was using more and more microphones on my drums, which my ego liked. Getting a "sound" on the drums took forever. I had to play each drum and cymbal over and over individually in simple, monotonous patterns until Rothchild was satisfied with what he heard. I, too, wanted a fat drum sound, but I felt it didn't warrant half a day's work.

Because of glitches like these, Jim started avoiding the sessions until he absolutely had to be there. When he did arrive, there was incredible tension in the room for a while, but no one expressed his anger over Jim's rudeness or tardiness.

One day a mousy little writer was standing in the corner of the control room being very quiet. How did she get in here? I wondered. I didn't like people coming down and seeing our dirty laundry being exposed. I never even invited my family down, Jim was so unpredictable. I would certainly have been embarrassed if Jim were in his Mr. Hyde phase and pulled one of his stunts when my parents visited.

Of course, being over twenty-five, they were taboo anyway. Ray was actually taboo too. When *Time* magazine had proclaimed the 1966 Man of the Year for their cover, it was anyone under twenty-five, and Ray had just turned twenty-seven. Psychologist Dr. Timothy Leary coined the phrase "Turn on, tune in, and drop out." Of society, that is. Fuck the old people. At the time, I was quoted as saying the idea of having a family made me sick. I had my own life and I didn't want my parents involved. Especially if they caught Jim on a binge. As Paul Rothchild would say years later, "You never knew whether Jim would show up as the erudite, poetic scholar or the kamikaze drunk."

But now the public was about to get its first exposure to the side of the Doors that Ray Manzarek is still trying to cover up. In 1973 in Germany, Ray tried to distort Jim's vision into his own, saying that "I want to talk about love, Jim wanted everybody to love everything." But what about the secret, unspoken pact to cover up the fact that something was wrong in the band? Jim was turning down the darkest road available, short of suicide, and the tension was in the air. Jim's decay was the dark side of an already very dark vision. The writer picked up on that. She must have had some angst of her own. Her name was Joan Didion.

"The Doors are different," she wrote in her book *The White Album*:

> They have nothing in common with the gentle Beatles. They lack the contemporary conviction that love is brotherhood and the *Kama Sutra*. Their music insists that love is sex and sex is death and therein lies salvation. The Doors are the Norman Mailers of the Top 40, missionaries of apocalyptic sex.
>
> Right now they are gathered together in uneasy symbiosis to make their album, and the studio is cold and the lights are too bright and there are masses of wires and banks of the ominous blinking electronic circuitry with which the new musicians live so casually. There are three of the four Doors . . . there is everything and everybody except one thing, the fourth Door, the lead singer, Jim Morrison, a twenty-four-year-old graduate of UCLA who wears black vinyl pants and no underwear and tends to suggest some range of the possible just beyond a sui-cide pact. . . . It is Ray Manzarek and Robby Krieger and John Densmore who make the Doors sound the way they do . . . but it is Morrison who gets up there in his black vinyl pants with no underwear and projects the idea, and it is Morri-son they are waiting for now. . . .
>
> It is a long while later. Morrison arrives. He has on his black vinyl pants, and he sits down on a leather couch in front of the four blank speakers and he closes his eyes. The curious aspect of Morrison's arrival is this: No one acknowledges it by so much as a flicker of an eye. Robby Krieger continues working out a guitar passage. John Densmore tunes his drums. Manzarek sits at the control console and twirls a corkscrew and lets a girl rub his shoulders. . . .
>
> Morrison sits down on the leather couch . . . and leans back. He lights a match. He studies the flame awhile and then very slowly, very deliberately, lowers it to the fly of his black vinyl pants. Manzarek watches him. The girl who is rubbing Manzarek's shoulders does not look at anyone. There is a sense

that no one is going to leave the room, ever. It will be some weeks before the Doors finish recording this album. I do not see it through.

٪.

A few nights after the Didion visit, we were smoking a bunch of hashish and mixing "You're Lost Little Girl" down to the final two tracks for stereo. Ray came back into the control room from the hallway, where he occasionally listened to the playback with the door ajar. He was trying to "distance" himself from the sound, which we had heard over and over, to gain some objectivity. Plus, Rothchild usually *blasted* the playbacks.

"I think your song, Robby, is perfect for Frank Sinatra," Ray suggested with his tongue thoroughly inserted in his cheek.

"Frank should dedicate it to his wife, Mia Farrow."

We all chuckled. The vocal had a serene quality, which may have been due to Rothchild's idea of having Jim's girlfriend Pam come down and give head to Jim while he sang. On one particular vocal take, Jim stopped singing in the middle of the song and we heard some rustling noises. Rothchild appropriately dimmed the lights in the vocal booth, and who knows what was going on in there? We went with a later take, but Paul's idea may have affected the vocal we went with. It had a tranquil mood, like the aftermath of a large explosion.

When we finished mixing "You're Lost Little Girl," we listened to it twice again, at extremely high volume. It sounded great.

We took forever to get from the studio to our cars, and I sat for half an hour in my Morgan trying to figure out how to start it up. When I finally got home, I was still so high that I staggered out of the car and didn't go into the house immediately. I started rubbing my hand over the felt-covered belt across the car hood. Maybe it was a way to remind myself that my dream was real. All the hassles seemed worth it at that moment because deep inside me I knew, we were waxing some heavy cuts. What a night!

With a few days off from recording, I dropped into my old watering hole, the Whiskey a Go-Go. I passed Mario, the legendary doorman, and asked how it was going, getting the same joke he'd told every night for years. "SOS—same old shit."

A new friend, a professional magician named Jordan, came up and said a couple girls invited him to their apartment, where he was going to do some sleight-of-hand. Ha ha. Would I like to come along? Sounded like fun. Especially since one of the girls had long, long brown hair and a great smile.

We all drove together to Beachwood Canyon, and I sat in the back with the great smile. She was conversational and friendly to me. This girl had LRP: Long Range Potential, as I was later to call it. Her name was Julia Brose, and her father was Bill Ballinger, a writer of mystery stories; he'd won the Book Award for Mystery in the thirties. He was remarried to a bubbly blonde who supposedly looked like Julia's real mother, but wasn't as crazy. Apparently the real mother drank quite a bit. She died rather young.

Julia and I consummated our brand-new relationship that night. There were no male blue balls in the sixties!

⁊.

The Strange Days kept getting stranger. By September Jim was beginning a secret life of his own, so secret that years later I learned that he had participated in a witch wedding. Jim would have several hours to kill while we were overdubbing on the instrumental tracks before we needed him to replace any work vocals, so he would run out to a bar or pick up someone and they'd get wrecked on downers and alcohol. Sometimes Jim asked me to go out drinking with him after our sessions. But I couldn't do it. I felt it would be hard to resist the peer pressure to drink, so I declined the invitations. When you meet someone and he becomes your brother, and you create stuff together that is possibly greater than your individual parts, you'll go down the road a little farther with that person than you should because you love him. But accepting would have meant compromising something inside me. Jim was becoming so unpredictable and so unreliable, I even began begging Vince, our roadie, to pour out any liquor he found lying around backstage or in the rehearsal room.

Coming home late after one of the *Strange Days* sessions, Robby and I walked into our place and it was a wreck. We wondered for about thirty seconds who'd done it, and then thought of Jim. It turned out that he'd taken one final acid trip before truly committing to booze. Pam had joined him in the excursion, and they'd ventured next door to our apartment . . . and freaked out. Jim got the idea to piss on my bed. I was livid. Robby thought it was funny. Sigmund Freud would have had a field day. At times like those, I wondered what Ray was doing—hiding with Dorothy while we baby-sat?

Cancel *my* subscription, Jack. Morrison wasn't only "writing as if Edgar Allan Poe had blown back as a hippie," as Kurt Von Meir wrote in *Vogue,* he was living like him—headed straight for a sad death in a gutter.

The psychedelic Jim I knew just a year earlier, the one who was constantly coming up with colorful answers to universal questions, was being slowly tortured by something we didn't understand. But you don't question the universe before breakfast for years and not pay a price. What was worse, his response to his demons was becoming glamorized.

In an interview with *Time* magazine, Jim labeled us "erotic politicians," a tag I loved; in turn, they called the Doors "black priests of the Great Society" and Jim the "Dionysus of Rock and Roll."

And the more secretive Morrison's personal life became, the larger the legend grew.

Jim didn't show the night we were supposed to record "When the Music's Over"—our first epic song since "The End." The Stones had done "Goin' Home," an eleven-minute cut that was attributed to our influence. We recorded the track without Jim. The problem was that since the song was about ten minutes long, there was a lot of improvisation in the middle section. Jim would read different poems he felt like doing at the moment, and we would respond spontaneously with melodic and rhythmic comments.

Fortunately, we'd done this song many times in person, so we could pretty much estimate where the poems would be.

Finally, the next day, Jim showed and recorded his part for "When the Music's Over." It worked perfectly, thank God. I couldn't imagine Jim not showing for a vocal, especially a song of his own and one I knew was important to him.

My violent jabs on the cymbal were a little late, but they answered the "what have they done to the earth" section, as I had intended. It was as if Jim and I were having a dialogue.

What have they done to our fair sister?
blop-che-blop-che-blop-che-blop-che-blop-che
Ravaged and plundered and ripped her
and bit her, brap-um-um-che
Stuck her with knives in the side of the dawn
and tied her with fences, che-che-che-che
and dragged her down. BBRAP-CHECHE-BBRAPP-CHECHE
BRAPP-BOUMPBOUM-BODIDIDOOOM!

Ray, Robby, and I sensed that Jim would do his new little vignette, "The Scream of the Butterfly," so we left space.

Before I sink, into the big sleep,
I want to hear, I want to hear,
The scream of the butterfly.

The obscure reference to the butterfly came from our most recent New York gig. On a drive past Eighth Avenue and 40th Street, a sleazy part of town, a porno theater had *The Scream of the Butterfly!* blazing across the marquee. If Jim could borrow from William Blake—as in "End of the Night"—he could also borrow from skin flicks.

When we finished *Strange Days*, we felt it was better than our first album. The worry was that there was no hit single. I had learned that it was difficult to choose which song would be released as a single; the tendency was to select a catchy number, but would it hold up to repeated listening? Jim didn't concern himself that much with singles, but the rest of us did. If we could get a hit, it would expose the album material to a much greater audience. I wanted as many young people as possible to hear the line "We want the world and we want it now" from "The Music's Over."

The record was released in October 1967, and "People Are Strange" was finally chosen as the single for its unique sound and hook-filled melody. I wondered if people would notice how vulnerable Jim's lyrics were. The song went top 10 nationally but at the time I was disappointed that we didn't reach number one. I was twenty-two, and the feelings of immortality I had were coupled with the relentless desire for *more*.

We all loved the photograph on the cover, with the posters of the first album in the background all ripped and torn. Elektra art director Bill Harvey had put it together on his own. Did anyone realize that the photographs on the front and back were actually one wraparound shot?

"The themes, symbols, and imagery of the Doors are stronger in their second album," wrote John Stinckney of the *Williams College News*, "which manages to transcend the fever-pitch intensity and macabre beauty of their first. The Doors have grown, a good sign.

"Significantly titled *Strange Days*, the new album's music is just as erotic, just as hard-driving, just as compelling but twice as terrifying as their first effort."

The album was a critical success as well as a financial one. In overall album sales it hasn't fared as well as the others, but it will always remain one of my favorites—like our last studio album, *L.A. Woman*, it has that inherent sense of swing. The groove.

✷

On October 30, 1967, Elektra announced that both *The Doors* album and the single of "Light My Fire" had sold five hundred thousand and one million copies respectively, apparently within hours of each other. We had our first gold records.

I was on top of the world until I drove home later that night. As I turned left at the corner of Laurel and Lookout, I saw my brother, Jim, walking up the hill. He was six feet tall now, had a long, scruffy beard, and looked greasy. I hadn't seen him in months and barely recognized him.

"What have you been up to?" I asked as he got in the car.

Not only did he look awful, he had terrible body odor. He was also very nervous, constantly bouncing his leg against the car door. It seemed as if he'd completely stopped taking care of himself. My breath became shallow and I quickly opened the car window.

"Well . . . I just got out of Camarillo. I just thought I'd pay you a visit."

"What?"

"Yeah, the state looney bin. I was hitchhiking, I got bored, and I borrowed a car. I drove it into a lake."

After an uneasy dinner, I invited him to play a game on my pool table, hoping to defuse some tension. My mind was racing. What the fuck was happening to my younger brother? I watched him closely after I broke. He could barely control the cue stick. He fidgeted for a moment, then shot clumsily. I felt bad for him, but I was also preoccupied with having to leave for a short tour of the Midwest in a few days.

I didn't see him again until I visited him during his second stay in the state hospital.

10

ROADHOUSE BLUES

Keep your eyes on the road, your hands upon the wheel
Yeah, we're goin to the roadhouse, gonna have a real
Good time

I woke up this morning, I got myself a beer
The future is uncertain, and the end is always near.

⁒

We never discussed it, but our stage presence, especially Jim's, evolved to meet the size of the growing audience. First we played clubs, then second bill at small two-thousand-seat auditoriums like the Cheetah.

"Wow . . . what a mind blower!"

"Whew, man."

I couldn't believe my eyes. Someone had turned Lawrence Welk's Aragon Ballroom on the Santa Monica Pier into a mock spaceship called the Cheetah. Ray's jaw dropped in amazement. He adjusted his rimless glasses in the reflection of the silver-mirrored walls.

"Whoever decorated this place must have taken a lot of drugs!" I said.

"Ha ha ha." Ray laughed.

Across the gleaming hardwood floor Jim ambled slowly onto

the ten-foot-high islandlike stage. A cocky smile flashed across his face. He knew he belonged up there.

Returning that night, I passed the Jefferson Airplane–Doors poster in the lobby and was pleased to see the place fairly full.

"It's still pretty echoey out there," Robby said to me as I walked into the dressing room, "but with the audience it won't be as bad as today's sound check."

"I heard 'Break On Through' driving over here! It was on KRLA," I said loudly so everyone could hear me. What a high: hearing one of your own songs come on the radio while driving in your car! I rolled down the car window when I was stopped at a traffic light to see if the car next to me was listening to the same station. They weren't, so I turned up the song real loud.

"THAT'S ME!!!" I wanted to shout out to the world. I was bursting with pride. The Doors *were* road music. On-the-road music. Freedom on the freeway.

I couldn't believe how our sound cut through the airwaves. We had found our sound. An original sound. No bass player, no backup singers: raw energy.

"I hope this works," Ray commented. His reference was to tonight's concert being sponsored by radio station KHJ, one of twenty or so large AM stations across the country programmed by Bill Drake. Mr. Drake had a tight grip on the playlists. If he didn't like your song, it wouldn't get added to the lists, and if you couldn't pick up the Drake chain, you couldn't have a hit. So here we were playing for peanuts—a couple of hundred dollars— in hopes that they would add "People Are Strange" before it died as a single, even though the rumor was that Bill didn't like the song. If "Boss" deejay Humble Harv, who was the announcer for tonight's show, liked the song, maybe he could influence the strict playlists. No deejay was allowed to vary from the list and spin a personal favorite. But Humble Harv, whose voice was the antithesis of "humble," was the most powerful deejay in Los Angeles. Maybe he could help. It was the first of many necessary compromises. I felt weird to know that *someone* was making a small fortune (2,000 people at $3.50 each) on the Cheetah concert, but I would have done anything to break our second single. It was a twenty-four-hour obsession. For a year and a half already we had been at it, and something was driving me hard, propelling me fast to get there. I didn't think too much about where "there" was.

✗

The lights dimmed. We climbed up the steep ladder at the back of the stage and took our places. I tightened the top skin of my snare drum nearest where my left-hand stick came down. The impact always loosened the lug. Looking over, I saw Robby stooped down to untangle his cords. Jim double-checked us with furtive glances over his shoulder, then coiled around the microphone. Ray hovered over his keyboards, glanced up at me and—"LADIES AND GENTLEMAN, THIS IS HUMBLE HARV FROM KHJ—BOSS RADIO. HERE THEY ARE . . . THE DOORS."

Ray's hands crashed down on the keys of his Vox organ and the first chords of "When the Music's Over" sliced through me and seemed to take the breath away from the crowd. Into the suspended silence I began to jab at my bass drum, snare, hi-hat: boom, snap-ba rap bap—hssst boom . . . brap! I was tightening the tension in the room with every beat.

Then I came to an abrupt halt. And I waited. And waited. This was one of my moments. I remained silent until the tension built to the breaking point and then finally released the sorcerer:

RAT-TAT-TAT-TAT-TAT-TAT-TAT-TAT-TAT-TAT-TAT-TAT-TAT

CRASH!

And like an animal in excruciating pain, Jim was jolted into his scream just as Robby hit a wailing, anguishing bass note. Jim cried out,

Eeeeeee-aaaahhhhhhhh,
When the music's over
When the music's over
Yeaahhh

When the music's over
Turn out the lights

Then came the dark silence. I twirled my drumsticks, held them over my head, and smashed the cymbals as Robby roared into his guitar solo that sounded like a snake being choked.

"EEEEAAAAAHHHHH!" came another gut-wrenching scream, then the angry scatting, the mumbled obscenities.

Jim's rebel yell ignited the band. Riffs exploded off Robby's guitar; Ray went into his hypnotic head-bobbing trance, and I drove the soloist, pushing him to the edge. Always the edge.

The acoustics weren't much better with a full house, but the crowd seemed to worship us. Did they get off on our sense of danger? Or was it the absurdly high stage?

Whatever it was, as I watched Jim teasing the crowd I realized that it was all happening! We were making the transition from dives to concerts. I wanted it all.

We finished the first song to a fair round of applause, but the audience was staring at us, especially Jim, and I knew we had made a lasting impression. It was in their faces.

Robby started "Back Door Man" with that low, mean guitar lick, and I came in with fat-back drums.

You could tell that Jim loved to sing the blues, those rural blues. It was the most dramatic way he could deal with his pain and the most effective release valve for pentup rage.

JESUS CHRIST!!! Jim just fell off the stage!

The audience has broken his fall and they're trying to push him back up! The stage is so high they can't quite get him back up there. We continue vamping and Jim finally scrambles over the edge and grabs the mike. The audience lets out a cheer and I'm laughing so hard the tempo is dragging.

We finished our five-song set (ten to fifteen minutes per song) and I mimicked Ed Sullivan on the way back to the dressing rooms.

"*What* a shew! . . . what a shoe! It was an echo chamber, but the audience got *off!*"

"Pretty neat, pretty good," Jim agreed.

⁊

Our performances were becoming rock theater. As Jim told a *Time* magazine reporter, they had "the structure of poetic drama . . . a sort of electric wedding."

The Doors' popularity would eventually grow enough to fill ten- and twenty-thousand-seat arenas, which were built for sports events, not music. We never sat down and planned how we were going to communicate to larger audiences, but as we faced bigger crowds, our intuition—especially Jim's and mine—told us to exaggerate a bit to reach the back row.

Ray played with his head hanging down over the keyboard, so his style didn't change much. If Robby wanted to get a little showy, he never let on. Rothchild illuminates: "If you watch Robby play, even when he's playing very quickly, he looks like he's playing slowly." Robby still wandered a lot onstage, looking as if he didn't know where he was, but that glazed look in those hazel eyes was easy to misread. Rothchild again: "If you watch Robby's face, it looks like someone's just asked him a question and he's thinking very seriously about what the answer might be." Robby didn't know how to milk the audience, but he was not unaware of where he was going with his improvs. I once asked him what he was thinking about when he played a solo because he looked so distant. He said lately he was thinking of "the fish in my fish tank" while playing. Wherever his mind was, his solos soared with liquid magic. Robby started playing the melody from "Eleanor Rigby" in the middle of his solo in "Light My Fire." A short exchange evolved between the guitar and drums in this section, which Robby and I had fun with. We'd give a little nod to each other after it was finished. Like athletes on the playing field; we were bros.

As for me, on some songs I got rather dramatic with my drumsticks. My arms became extensions of my sticks, and I began waving them threateningly over my head between beats in "The Music's Over" and "Light My Fire." I don't know why these two songs brought out my showmanship except that they seemed passionate to me. What I was doing seemed natural, and I could feel that I was reaching the back row in larger auditoriums with emotions as well as my volume. I taped my fingers for more grip power, and on the last chord of our set I began standing up, still playing a roll on the cymbals, and then on a cue I gave for Ray and Robby, we would hit the last note, me with both my sticks on the snare, making a loud crack. The sticks usually broke and I'd throw the remains into the audience. I refused to use thicker sticks because it would slow my technique down. Sometimes fans came backstage with the broken sticks and asked me to autograph them. Occasionally I noticed blood on the wood. When I looked at my taped fingers, red would be seeping through the white bandages.

"I've got blisters on my fingers!"

I guess I was somewhere *else* during those shows.

By the end of 1967, Jim had certainly come into his own as a performer. He began to move more onstage, going from side to side, talking to people in the balcony or jumping off the stage and going right up the middle aisle. "Sometimes he would fall on the ground and writhe around like a snake," Robby remembers. "I knew Jim didn't really mean all that stuff, but I knew he was into it, too, and I knew he had to push himself to do more and more as the crowds got bigger. I felt sorry for him."

He started pointing the microphone in front of the mouths of various members of the audience, encouraging them to sing, shout, or do what they wanted. Some were mic shy; most just let out a yell. Jim loved to get the audience to respond, not only on a mass level, but he was interested in individual opinions. We would be doing an instrumental vamp, waiting for Jim to come in singing; the audience would know from listening to the records that Jim's voice was the next cue, and Jim would purposely wait until everyone, especially me, got very restless.

It was the maximum in foreplay. There was a similarity to Ravi Shankar's ragas. One has to wait a long time for a *good* climax. I didn't like our new label, though: "Kings of Orgasmic Rock." Similarly, Ravi Shankar didn't like his music becoming popular enough to be used as soundtracks for porn flicks. He sued! What Shankar describes as "the sound of God" became the soundtrack of sex.

At our concerts, several people in the audience would start kibbitzing with Jim. Jim would give a quick retort, trying for more response.

"All right, all right, what do you wanna hear next?"

"Crystal Ship!" "Love Me Two Times!" "People Are Strange!"

They were shouting different song titles all at once.

"No, no, one at a time!" Jim kidded.

"Break On Through!" "Light My Fire!" "Back Door Man!"

Finally releasing us all from the built-up tension, Jim would continue the song.

"It was like Jim was an electric shaman," Ray has said of our concerts, "and we were the electric shaman's band, pounding away behind him. Sometimes he wouldn't feel like getting into the state, but the band would keep on pounding and pounding, and little by little it would take him over. God, I could send an electric shock through him with the organ. John could do it with his drumbeats. You could see every once in a while—twitch!—I could hit a chord and make him twitch. And he'd be off again. Sometimes he was just incredible. Just amazing. And the audience felt it too!"

✌

With stardom, someone else dealt with the tedious parts of traveling. It was easy to become spoiled and act like a child, because all the responsibilities were taken care of. From this point on we would be boarded on the airplanes first—special groups go first. The Optimists Club and the Doors Club. All these straights would be standing in line to go from Pittsburgh to New York, and here were these long-haired freaks being boarded before everyone else, and into first class! I could read the other passengers' minds: "What the fuck is this country coming to?"

The constant touring did blur the mind. Sometimes I didn't know which city we were in. Cleveland? No. Pittsburgh? No. Connecticut? Yeah. New Haven, Connecticut. Where did I live? Los Angeles. Right.

⁊⁄⁊

New Haven, Connecticut
December 5, 1967

Just before we went onstage that night, I had Vince move my drums back so that my ears were behind the amp line. I wasn't about to lose my hearing, even for "these creeps," as I jokingly called Jim, Ray, and Robby in the first bio for Elektra Records.

After Vince moved my drums, he told me that Jim had been Maced in one of the dressing rooms by a policeman. Apparently Jim was "chatting up a fan" in a side room and a cop came in and thought they were supposed to be in the audience. In his subtle Mr. Hyde manner Jim had told the cop to fuck off. The policeman reacted by spraying Jim in the eyes.

When Morrison came onstage, I could sense that something confrontational was going to happen. His eyes were red and he looked mad. In the middle of "Back Door Man," Jim told the story of the backstage incident and started taunting the police who were standing directly in front of the stage, supposedly protecting us from the audience. The cops started turning around, frowning at Jim. Jim continued baiting the crowd like I never heard before—daring anyone to do something.

Two or three policemen came onstage from the sides and behind the back curtain. My heart started double-timing. Jim stuck the microphone under the nose of one of the officers and said, "Say your thing, man!" They started to drag Jim off, and I left the stage via the back curtain. The mood in the auditorium was getting hysterical, ugly, even violent. Standing in the wings, I

145

thought that this is what war must feel like. I felt real panic in the air.

Suddenly Vince grabbed my arm, scaring me half to death.

"What are they going to do with Jim?" he asked.

I could hear the crowd starting to chant "To the police station! To the police station! To the police station!"

Ray came around the back and encouraged a few fans to go to the station. I gave Ray a worried look and he responded with "It's okay, a reporter from *Life* magazine is here tonight." I thought to myself—what about Jim? Are they going to beat the shit out of him? I was frightened. The group was too out of hand. Jim was crazy. And I wanted to escape from the growing fear that this was just the beginning.

Ray later said that at the time, he, too, was worried that New Haven was the beginning of the erosion of everything we'd worked for.

⁊.

To my surprise, the Lizard King seemed in pretty good spirits after having spent the night in jail, and we were off to Philadelphia, despite some post–New Haven paranoia. As usual, everyone tried to sweep it under the rug, as if it were now a part of the act. We went to a big AM radio station in Philly, kissed their asses by shaking deejays' hands, and on the way out one announcer said, "Love that single you have out, 'Light My Fire.'" He hadn't heard of "People Are Strange," which had been out for three months. I rubbed the brown off my nose and got in the limo.

That night when we got in our limo to go to the gig it was raining. I could have sworn our driver looked like a narc. His head was shaved and he gave off the coldest vibes. At the gig, we found out that the vice squad was there. They planned to tape and film us to see if we violated any laws.

Just before we went on, Bill Siddons, another roadie, begged Jim not to say fuck or shit onstage. Of course, Jim began cursing as soon as he reached the mike. Miraculously, it didn't register with the officers amid all of the noise.

This was not the greatest atmosphere for creating music. Our performance that night was tentative, to say the least. I was worried about what Jim might say during the whole set, and Jim was upset over being censored.

Going to a party afterward at a fan's apartment, we told our driver to wait and climbed the wet half flight of stairs into the red brick building. It was your usual sixties' gathering, with people sitting around in a circle on the floor passing a joint around, listening to music, and not relating to each other verbally except for a few "far outs" and "wow, mans."

After an hour or so, remembering our uptight driver, we returned to the limo, acting very cool and together. He drove us back to the hotel with no complications. It was a relief to see him go.

I took off my clothes, which had been drenched in sweat a couple hours ago but by now had dried. Then I felt an itch behind my knees. I drew a bath. I knew that water, especially warm water, irritated the rash, but I had dried sweat on me and sitting in the tub would relax my mind. My skin would pay later.

I sat back and went through the entire set we'd played that night, savoring the good moments—although they were few that night—and trying to figure out how to avoid the weak ones. I loved going over everything that happened onstage, but tonight wasn't very fulfilling. This isn't the way it's supposed to be, I told myself. It's *supposed* to be relaxed and fun being in a famous rock-n'-roll band.

٪

"I'm sick . . . so I can't perform this weekend in the Northwest," I lied to Sal.

"You *have* to, it's all booked!"

"How come you guys never come to any of the gigs except the fun cities like New York? You still get your fifteen percent, though, don't you?"

"We'll get another drummer!"

"Fine!"

147

I hate doing this, but I just can't get on another plane. I hope Ray, Robby, and Jim aren't too pissed.

"You're not going?" Robby says over the phone.

"I'm sick," I mutter.

"You're not sick, you're just tired of baby-sitting Jim!"

I didn't respond. We didn't actually baby-sit Jim. We worried about him all the time. Me the most. It was clear that Robby was tired, too, but he wasn't ready to do anything about it.

In retrospect, Robby says that it was at this point—around the end of '67 and beginning of '68—that he began to dislike Jim intensely, thinking that the band's future was a day-to-day thing.

%

"I shall not seek, and will not accept, the nomination of my party for another term as your president." The radio news bulletin blares out President Johnson's shocking statement. The protesters have driven LBJ out of office, and I feel partly responsible. Proudly responsible. A surrogate witness for the defense of the Chicago Seven.

You can see the guy aging before your eyes on TV. Nothing personal, I just hate his policies. The nominees are promising to end the war. There is hope.

%

Ray was right. New Haven *was* the beginning of the erosion of everything we had worked for. Our second single off the second album, "Love Me Two Times," was racing up the charts when it got banned because of New Haven. We were too controversial. Shit.

Word came down that John Kilor, the drummer for the Daily Flash who substituted for me in Seattle and Portland, didn't work out very well. That made me feel good. Wanted. I didn't expect that. John's a very competent drummer, but I guess my fills are unique and hard to duplicate.

Julia Brose and I were dating and it felt pretty natural, except that an old flame of hers came into town from Georgia and my intuition told me they were rekindling. So one night I drove up

Laurel, made a left on Stanley Hills Drive off of Lookout, and slowly cruised her cozy apartment, two houses up on the right. Her lights were on, so I turned around and parked across the street, banking my wheels into the curb. I quietly walked across the steep road and up her steps. I could see from the front window that Julia was with someone in the back bedroom. Instead of leaving, I knocked on the door.

There's just one way out of here, and I just can't go out the door.
There's a man down there, might be your man, I don't know.

My jealousy surprised me. I guess I really liked this girl. They got themselves together and let me in. I tried to pretend that I hadn't seen anything, but I found myself being rather cold and hostile as Julia introduced the guy to me. He looked like a surfer and his name was Gregg Allman. I made some excuse and left rather quickly. Maharishi says not to stir up the mud of the past. It's not worth it. I agreed. I was off to Europe soon, so maybe I'd meet somebody over there.

✗

Before we went to Europe, Robby and I took a month-long meditation course. Maharishi was leading it at Squaw Valley Conference Grounds near Lake Tahoe in northern California, and I wanted to experience more of that love vibe, as described by Buckminster Fuller: "There is coming to the western world through Maharishi manifest love. You could not meet with Maharishi without recognizing instantly his integrity. You look in his eyes and there it is."

The Doors' business locomotive hadn't gotten to the runaway stage yet, so the agents and managers didn't pressure us into not going. Nor did Ray or Jim. Too bad Jim didn't look into alternative ways to relax and forget the rat race.

You got the dog race,
You got the horse race,

You got the human race,
But dis here is a rat race.

—Bob Marley

Robby and I rented a large cabin on the north shore of the lake along with Paul Horn, the jazz flute player, Emil Richards, Paul's vibraphone player and a much sought-after studio percussionist, and Jordan, my magician friend. It was called Moon Dune, and Maharishi had stayed in the place a year before. Paul insisted on the rishi's old room.

We were meditating most of the day between lectures by Maharishi, and in the evening there was time to read or socialize. Late one afternoon, as Maharishi passed me on the way out of the auditorium after a lecture, I got his attention by bowing my head. "In a few years you will blossom," he said.

Later that night some musician-meditators set up their equipment and we had a great jam session. On a couple of numbers I played with Emil, Paul, and Robby. I was playing with guys I used to idolize at Shelley's Manne Hole! I had seen the Paul Horn Quintet several times there, so I started a fast jazz waltz in their style. Robby had to hustle to keep up 'cause he wasn't used to the idiom, but Emil kept turning around and giving me the thumbs-up, which encouraged me to burn a hole in the drums even more. On the drive back to the cabin, Paul and Emil were complimentary about my playing. It was a great thrill.

Another afternoon, halfway through the course, I volunteered to take Jordan's girlfriend to the airport in Reno. Robby let me use his Porsche and Jordan came along for the ride.

After leaving the airport, we cruised back through Reno. It was a shock. Any city would have seemed intense after hanging around Maharishi's love vibes and meditating for two weeks. I had experienced some strong heat coming from my third eye, encouraged by a little Tiger Balm, and an overall feeling of well-being was paramount. Mellow yellow.

Except that I kept seeing hamburger stands on the side of the

150

road, and a craving for meat surfaced in my stomach. Maharishi had said nothing about diets, but most of us meditators were vegetarians or semivegetarians.

"Dare we get a burger, Jordan?" I asked with raised eyebrows.

"I'd love one."

"But what about our diets? I hardly even eat chicken, let alone red meat."

"Yeah, but with all this purity, we need a little grease!"

I laughed and then almost started drooling.

"Let's do it!" I exclaimed, and pulled into Froster's Freeze. We pigged out on cheeseburgers with everything. Chili included. Satisfied, but with a growing knot in my stomach, I hopped back in the car. Jordan followed. As we made a right turn to get back on the highway, a cop put on his siren and pulled us over.

"GET OUT OF THE CAR!"

What the fuck did we do? Maybe I still had a little chili dripping from my mouth. I braved a question.

"What did we do?"

"YOU FORGOT TO TAKE A BATH THIS MORNING . . . OR MAYBE IT'S BEEN MONTHS SINCE YOU TWO BATHED!"

Uh-oh. Harassment.

"PUT YOUR HANDS ABOVE YOUR HEADS, TURN AROUND, AND LEAN AGAINST THE PATROL CAR."

This was straight out of *Easy Rider!* What were they going to do, butt-fuck us with their nightsticks?

They frisked us, slamming their hands with extra pressure as they passed over our crotches.

"Guess we're gonna have to take you girls in on a vagrancy charge."

"Vagrancy! What about Robby's car? How can we be vagrants with an eight thousand dollar Porsche?"

"PUT YOUR HANDS BEHIND YOUR BACKS!"

They wrenched our arms down and handcuffed us as tightly as possible. My wrists started getting numb and I was thinking about my drumming career being shortened. All my power came from my wrists. I could play as strong as Buddy Miles, a two hundred and fifty–pound black drummer, because of the snap of my wrists.

I caught a glimpse of the more aggressive cop's name tag as he shoved me into the backseat of the patrol car. Glancing over at Jordan as he was being shoved into the opposite side, I gave him a scared look. He managed a weak smile.

They were leaving Robby's car right there on the street! At the police station they unlocked the cuffs, which had made a deep imprint in my skin. My wrists seemed okay except for the stiffness.

After dumping all of our possessions on the counter, they gave us each one thin dime and pointed to the phone on the wall.

Simultaneously on the verge of tears and rage, I called the band's old lawyer, Max Fink.

"Max, I will pay any amount of money it takes to get this cop reprimanded!"

After the ultimate in humiliation—they took mug shots, finger-prints, and looked up our assholes for dope—we landed in the drunk tank and started laughing. It was so pathetic that it became funny. I started doing yoga, standing on my head, which was easy because the floor was made of rubber to prevent any winos from hurting themselves. Periodically, one of our cellmates would go over and throw up in the toilet sticking out of the wall.

"Why don't you do some magic for the guard and maybe we'd get out of this gray rubber tank quicker?"

"Hey . . . *hey* . . . I'm a magician. . . . Got a coin?"

The guard came over and peered through the bars. "Huh? . . . really . . . uh . . . *yeah.*"

He handed Jordan a quarter. Jordan made it disappear and come back out of the guy's ear.

"How did you do that? That's great!"

I'd seen Jordan work for years and I knew how most of the tricks were done, but I had a lot of respect for his talent. Close-up magic is the real art; sawing people in half is an illusion anyone could buy at the magic shop.

"You guys are all right. It was a mistake booking you in here. I'll see what I can do."

It was the first friendly voice we'd heard all night. They let us out at 6 A.M. We got Robby's car back at the pound, to the tune of sixty fucking dollars, and drove back to Satoriville. Totally shattered.

11

TELL ALL THE PEOPLE

Los Angeles, 1978

I am pacing back and forth across the stage arrogantly, my short-cropped hair slicked back with grease. Peggy had gently suggested I cut it. She'd said musicians are "internal," and they hide behind their music. Actors are "out." Their bodies are their instruments, and if you really want to be an actor, she'd said, maybe you should get your hair out of your face.

I had. For Peggy Feury, yes; for my dad, years before, no. I knew I had stumbled onto the best acting teacher around and I trusted her instincts.

It's kind of fun wearing a three-piece suit, overcoat, and gloves, pretending to be somebody else. It was also scary enough for me to think my heart is going to bust the buttons off my vest.

At this moment, I definitely have more stage fright in front of these twelve people in class than when I had to face 21,000 people at Madison Square Garden with the Doors.

Thursday night class. Advanced class. First scene. I wouldn't ordinarily be so nervous, since I've been doing this for a year and a half now in day classes and I think I have a knack for it. But Annette O'Toole and Jeff Goldblum are sitting with the others, Sean Penn might show up, and I want desperately to impress them 'cause I admire their talent.

I make my entrance. My acting partner is doing his long monologue, and I'm listening with a condescending air while sitting on an ottoman.

I deliver my opening lines, get up and walk downstage left, and gaze at an easel. My partner responds meekly, which pushes a button in my character.

"You must have told her some real horror stories," I blurt out insolently.

The class roars! Their laughter is *with* me, not at me. I'm on the right track. Feels like improvising the right drum fill behind Jim's vocals. Strindberg's words are the chord changes you follow as your framework.

We finish the scene and I can tell that it went well. Peggy waves the two of us down to her corner, and she says I conducted myself wonderfully up there. My pride is swelling. This is only the third time I've felt I was really in character, that I knew him so well that through him I could do anything, I was totally free. It's a long haul across L.A. to these classes, but as with my drumming, studying craft for a few years is vital foundation-building. And what better teacher to have than the former director of the Lee Strasberg Theatre Institute in New York.

I lean back in the folding chair against the wall and watch the others rehearsing. I've always wanted to get up from my drums, and now I'm finally doing it. Peggy's critique is short, as it usually is when you're good. But when you're off, her critique goes on forever.

Reminds me of the time we did the *Jonathan Winters Show.* When was that, anyhow—'68? Boy, was Morrison off . . .

Jim, what was bugging you just before the taping of the Jonathan Winters Show? *You seemed down. Sal and Ash even tried to talk to you. I overheard them telling you that it was an important show and for you to try to be dramatic and give a good performance. We'd been careful about which television shows we would do because the sterile working conditions stifle performances into mediocrity. "Doing television wasn't real," Robby recently said.*

155

Strange days have found us
Strange days have tracked us down
They're going to destroy
Our casual joys
We shall go on playing
Or find a new town

But hadn't we agreed that we needed more exposure, just as long as it wasn't on a show we considered lousy? We'd done Ed Sullivan 'cause the Beatles, the Stones, and Elvis had been on. Remember when Ed walked in on our rehearsal and Robby was writhing around on the floor doing his Three Stooges imitation? We were all laughing and Ed said, "You boys look great when you smile. You should do that tonight. You're too serious." Hadn't we turned down lots of offers before agreeing to the Smothers Brothers' because their politics were cool and controversial, and Winters because we liked his bizarre sense of humor? But you showed us all by not moving an inch during "Light My Fire," didn't you? It was an uptight, stiff vocal performance, and I felt you were hurting the band as the end of the song approached and you were giving nothing as far as emotional singing goes. When your voice started to crack at the last chorus, I was worried. Then when you leaped into that weird prop rope fence, none of us could believe it. Did you even hear the stifled laughter when you knocked it down and got tangled up in the ropes? You must have noticed the big silence from everyone after we ended the song. I wondered if you were okay, Jim. Fuck the career, did you need help? It felt like we had just witnessed a short seizure from a schizophrenic. . . . How did it feel to you? Of course, no one asked you, did they? We all just sort of avoided you for a few minutes and then acted like nothing unusual had happened. Jim, no one dared confront you. It seemed as if you were out of control, possessed or something. Was it the pressure from everyone for you to be great all the time, or were you getting restless with it all, getting sick of singing the same songs over and over again? Maybe you sensed that now that we had business managers and press agents, we had started something that had a life of its own, a machine that didn't allow for valleys in a career, only peaks. Creativity vs. Business . . . We sensed rage and a *possible explosion too near the surface to mess with in dealing with you. It seemed to have a lid on it—Pandora's Box with all the demons that wanted to be released. We never opened the box—had a dialogue with you about deeper undercurrents in one's psyche—so we had to deal with your demons seeping out of the sides. A hopeless situation. I keep blaming myself for not having done anything to help you, to stop you, but I was only twenty-three. It's time I forgave myself. . . . But hey, I have to admit that I was very curious and excited to see what your "tantrum" looked like on national TV. Remember we happened to be playing the Winterland, Graham's new ballroom, in San Francisco the night the show was to air? Did you know it was I who insisted that we include a "rider" in our contract for a backstage television so we could see the show? You wouldn't believe how bands are sticking it to the promoters these days by demanding elaborate food and liquor supplies in their riders. If you recall we were watching Jonathan Winters in the dressing room, and right in the middle of his hour-long TV show we had to go onstage—just when our segment was due to come on any second. So we brought the television onstage with us! Positioning it on top of a large amplifier, I tuned it to the correct channel and turned the sound off. Remember it was Robby's job to keep an eye on the TV for our appearance, since he had the best angle to see the screen? We started the set with our usual, "Break On Through," and then in the middle of the second song of our set, "Back Door Man," we appeared on the TV screen on the Jonathan Winters Show! I got up immediately and walked around the drums, turned up the sound on the set, and sat down on the floor of the stage facing the TV. As the live song petered out, you and Ray and Robby joined me on the floor in front of the set with our backs to the audience of several thousand people. Our TV performance was rather subdued until the end, when you freaked out. It looked like you were in a trance. Very bizarre. Our growing image as a strange group was intensified on national TV. The reaction from the live audience at the theater was amusing. Some of them laughed; some of them must have thought we were so arrogant that we'd brought a tape of ourselves—it couldn't have been being broadcast then, that would have been too coincidental. Maybe some of the audience thought that possibly they had taken too much acid! We turned the TV*

off, went back to our instruments, and started playing "Back Door Man"
from the middle of the song where we'd left off! I'm sure most of the
Winterland audience thought we were out of our minds. It sure was fun,
sometimes. You weren't too stoned that night, we were on as a band, and
everything else was forgivable when we were tight.

Well, almost everything. . . .

⁊.

Ohm. Aum. Ohhhmmm. Auuummm.

By early '68, Robby's and my fascination with Indian culture
had prompted us to enroll in the recently opened Ravi Shankar
Kinara School of Indian Music in Los Angeles. Robby studied
sitar and I studied tabla, the most difficult percussion instrument
in the world. In the classical Indian tradition you have to learn to
sing the notes before you can play them—tita-gita-tita-nana, tita-
gita-tita-da. Drummers must master the singing part along with
their playing or they'll be discouraged from continuing their studies.

Ravi gave a lecture one night to the entire group of about forty
students. With his wife sitting right next to him, he stated that
sometimes, if one has the inner strength, the sexual drive can be
sublimated into a musical instrument. My God! Ravi was so dedicated that he practiced music when he got horny! I'd heard of the
yogis sending their sexual energy up their spines, around to their
foreheads, but I knew that it wasn't my path in life. I was too
aware of the all-encompassing throbbing in my pants.

When Robby and I went to the meditation retreat before Europe, I noticed that my sexual drive cooled down a bit, the proba-
ble reason being that I didn't have all the usual stimulation from
television, movies and magazines. I remember halfway through
the retreat having a nice feeling that it was possible to gain some
control over my carnal desires. I also knew, in the words of the
Indian teachers, that I was to follow the path of the "house-
holder" and not the "recluse." I processed Ravi's words through
my old Catholic filter and came up with guilt instead of the idea

158

of channeling or transmuting. It takes a long time to transcend old, ingrained modes of thinking—that sex is bad, for example.

And here I was playing the "devil's music," the very thing that aroused sex. In the fifties, a group of Southern zealots figured out that the rhythm of this new "nigger" music was sinful and would lead to fornicating, and riots, and orgies. "Rock and roll and other monstrosities . . . are muddying up the airwaves. It is the current climate on radio and television which makes Elvis Presley and his animal posturings possible. . . ." So said producer Bill Rose in 1956 to the House Judiciary Anti-Trust Subcommittee.

Then in the sixties they began breaking rock-'n'-roll records over the air, cracking them right across the microphones. And burning them in big bonfires. Later on in the seventies, sanctimonious Christian TV preachers accused the Beatles of corrupting the nation's youth with lyrics containing satanic undertones.

And I was the drummer with the one group that was delving into the dark, shadow side of human nature. Driving the listeners into possession!

Or as John Stinckney wrote, "The group does not cater to the nameless faces beyond the footlights. . . . The Doors are not pleasant, amusing hippies proffering a grin and a flower; they wield a knife with a cold and terrifying edge. The Doors are closely akin to the national taste for violence. . . ."

※

February 1968

Third album syndrome.

"Usually a group will have enough songs in their repertoire to record one, or maybe two albums," Robby explained at the time, "and then what'll happen is they go on tour and they don't have time to write any more stuff, so by the third album, you find yourself trying to write stuff in the studio, and it shows."

A couple months after the New Haven fiasco, we were supposed to start rehearsing. It was time for the recording sessions, and the pressure of the process had caught up with us. We were going into the studio to record and we didn't have enough songs worked out to fill an entire album. There just wasn't enough time to write the songs and digest them like we used to. The Doors had finally gotten a giant business machine going, lawyers and managers, and now it was picking up speed, gaining its own wild momentum. No time for writing songs like in the early days. Success began to feel like a runaway train—and we couldn't slow it down.

One night at TT & G studios in Hollywood, where we were recording at $100 an hour, Paul Rothchild took us all by the hands and dragged us from the control room into the studio for one of his little talks. He said that we needed a hit soon and that "Hello, I Love You," with a tight arrangement, could fit the bill. We'd written the song a year ago but hadn't fleshed out the arrangement.

It turned into an unusual song with tons of distortion on the guitar via the latest electronic toy, the fuzz box. Robby had also suggested a catchy way of turning the beat around à la Cream's "Sunshine of Your Love." Though I liked the lyrics very much, the new arrangement seemed contrived. When it climbed to number one, I was baffled.

⅄

Got a night off and went to see *2001: A Space Odyssey*. It was slow going but worth the wait—kind of like a raga. I got goose bumps at the end, and I'm not sure why. Something to do with having a sense that what I was watching I already knew about. Reincarnation or something. Déjà-vu.

⅄

Another time in the studio, after Robby and I finished our fifteen-minute meditation break—a practice we continued for several years—Jim started bugging me to play something very basic, very primitive, on my drums. I had resisted his suggestion in the past because I wanted to play more challenging rhythmic patterns. I hadn't played jazz for years for nothing. Finally I gave in and started playing the dumbest 4/4 beat I knew, and Jim started singing, "Five to one, one in five, no one here gets out alive."

160

Robby found a guitar lick and Ray moved in on the organ, and we got something really powerful.

"What does five to one mean, Jim?" I asked.

"That's for me to know and you to find out," Jim said with a mischievous smile. He went to the bathroom.

I turned to Rothchild. "Paul?"

"Well, I think it means that by 1975 there will be five younger people to one older person, the dividing line being over twenty-five."

"Great."

Our roadie Vince Treanor reflects: "The first album was knocked down in a matter of days; Paul did a beautiful job. Same with the second. Then Paul got into *Waiting for the Sun*, which took a goddamned century to make. He made them go over it and over it until it was wrung dry. A beautiful album technically, every line was clean, distinct, you could hear Robby, you could hear him breathe. But as far as an exciting performance was concerned, it wasn't."

"Let's try it one more time, guys . . . we're almost there," Paul would say carefully. We were with him the first twenty or thirty takes, but at number fifty-nine, "The Unknown Soldier" was running out of ammo. And it was only the first half of the song! (We were doing it in sections.) Paul pushed us nearly as hard on the last half of the song. To perform the execution action in the middle of the song, we marched around the studio and shot off a real rifle filled with blanks. It was fun, but I think we spent about two hours getting one gunshot. It seemed absurd. The spontaneity was lost.

It may have had something to do with the K.D. Paul had a little film jar that he kept his grass in labeled "K.D.*: Killer Dope!" At the bottom of his homemade label it read: *Don't drive under the influence of." I had an impulse to add "Don't record under the influence of!" Experimentation, yes. Rehearsal, great. But performing—no.

Recording became ridiculous. The crowd Jim began hanging

161

out with made me want to puke. At least Tom Baker, the star of one of Warhol's films, was talented once. He's dead now. At times I've fantasized that Jim and Tom are knocking back Courvoisier right now with the late Jimmy Reed. But those two other creeps, Freddie-the-male-groupie-leech and the blond guy with the Charles Manson vibes, were the worst. Freddie, who seemed high all the time, played half-assed piano. When Ray, Robby, and I rejected Jim's new song, "Orange County Suite," after having worked on it unsuccessfully several times, Jim turned to Freddie. Or Freddie got Jim loaded and. . . .

One night, after the Morrison entourage left, I asked Paul what we were going to do about Jim. He said he would think about it that night. The next day Rothchild asked for the band to assemble in the recording room.

"Jim . . . you don't seem interested in participating much in the recording of this album. What are you doing? You don't look like a rock star anymore."

Jim brushed back his greasy hair and stroked his stubble. He didn't respond verbally, and the usual quiet tension in the room intensified.

"Well, I'm going back to work," Paul said, heading for the control room. Jim got up and went into the lobby, and I threw up my hands in a gesture to Ray and Robby. Ray let out a big sigh and Robby just shook his head in frustration.

We actually got some work done that night, but the next day Jim came in and shocked us. He was clean shaven and had the stupidest haircut I had ever seen. He had apparently gathered his hair into a ponytail at the back of his head and taken a scissors and snipped it off in one fell swoop. When he let go, the little ends dropped down on each side of his face, dangling in his eyes. He looked like the boy in the Dutch Boy Paints commercial. This was the first time I noticed a little double chin coming in on that beautiful Grecian face. I thought, Oh, God, grow the beard back, he's starting to look like the Pillsbury Dough Boy.

Another afternoon, during the *Waiting for the Sun* sessions, we

162

all arrived at the studio an hour or two late, which was now the norm. I guess no one wanted to be there, except that we loved making records. Jim always came in an hour or two after the rest of us. Around 5 P.M., he straggled in with his new "family"— Freddie, the blond guy, and a female version of Charles Manson. It was amusing when Jim's buddies pulled up Mrs. Manson's skirt in the vocal booth and were playfully encouraging any comers to have themselves off in her ass, but it was also disgusting and pathetic. She was clearly in a drunken, downer stupor.

What the fuck happened? We had created such a great thing and it was going sour. I told Paul Rothchild I was quitting. He sat me down and told me I was in one of the most envied and re-spected groups in the world. I kept thinking of what Paul had said about Jim a few nights before, after one of his binges. He told Ray, Robby, and me that we were witnessing a special psychological experience, and we should get as much tape on Jim as fast as possible because he didn't think he was going to be around long.

"There's the Beatles, the Stones, and the Doors," Paul was now saying to me as we sat in the studio hallway. It wasn't enough. I would have rather been a martyr and sacrificed my future career than to go on in this direction. God, it was depressing. In an interview, when reflecting on our third album, Robby said, "There was a lot of Jim getting drunk and bringing drunken friends into the studio and Paul throwing them out. Scenes, heavy pill-taking and stuff. That was rock 'n' roll to its fullest." But I felt something more. The Grim Reaper.

I couldn't see how Ray and Robby could turn the other cheek. I knew Robby could feel Jim's pain, but he was too shy to do any-thing. I knew he liked the success and didn't like confrontations. I wished Ray would, or could, have stopped the madness. He was the one who put this group together. At least that's what the press has been saying the last several years.

So I wasn't waiting for the others to stop Jim. I walked back into the studio, took one look at Jim and his friends, and said, "I quit!" Then I threw my drumsticks down on the floor and stormed out the door. It was my statement against this insanity.

I didn't know what I'd do with myself the next morning. When I awoke, I made some herb tea, did my yoga, and cut my fingernails. Keeping them short helped me resist scratching my rash, which had resurfaced. At noon I decided to go back to the studio. I was drawn back because I didn't know any other way to live. I didn't want to give up the one thing that had been consistent in my life for many years: music.

I felt real stupid driving down from my house in Laurel Canyon to TT & G recording studios at Sunset and Highland. I also felt the black Morrison cloud still hanging over the place as I walked in, but, thank God, I got the same treatment Jim always got when he fucked up: silence. I couldn't have stood being ridiculed about coming back.

I took a deep breath, walked into the control room, and said, "What song are we working on today?"

"Bruce and I are involved in a technical problem with the studio," Rothchild said. "Probably take several hours . . . but in the meantime you might be interested in making an appointment with those two girls in the lobby. They're the Plaster Casters!"

"What the hell is that?"

"Check it out, John."

With the encouragement of Frank Zappa, these two industrious groupies had a show in an art gallery. But was their work art? They took plaster molds of rock stars' cocks! One girl was the brains—she thought up the idea—the other was the "plater." The plater? What the hell was a plater? She aroused the client just as the other was finishing making the brew of plaster in a coffee can. Timing was essential. They didn't want the client's member to get stuck in cement that hardened too quickly. Nor did they want to get cement all over anyone's pubic hairs. I decided to pass. None of the other band members signed up, but our assistant engineer, Fritz Richmond from the old Jim Kweskin Jug Band, went for it.

I did see the exhibit of the Casters' work: a cast of a very large Jimi Hendrix, a keyboard player with a curved one, and another of the drummer from Canned Heat, Frank Cook.

✶

"Unknown Soldier" was released as our second single off the third album, *Waiting for the Sun*, following the huge success of "Hello, I Love You." The prospects weren't nearly as good because of the political nature of the lyrics. I was proud of Jim's first obviously political statement and proud of the record company for having the courage to push it.

> *Breakfast where the news is read,*
> *Television children fed,*
> *Bullets strike the helmet's head,*
> *And it's all over, for the Unknown Soldier.*

I didn't realize back then that with Jim's father an admiral in the navy, "Unknown Soldier" was a direct challenge to dad. The lyrics weren't talking specifically about the Vietnam war, but I thought it was more powerful with its universal imagery. That was Jim's gift.

> *Make a grave for the Unknown Soldier,*
> *Nestled in your hollow shoulder,*
> *It's all over . . . for The Unknown Soldier,*
> *The war is over . . .*

Our "anti-war philippic," as *Time* magazine called it, reached number twenty-four on the national charts. Music people said we were lucky to get it played at all on the radio during those Vietnam years.

Apparently we were one of the more popular groups in 'Nam.

> *We had no cameras, to shoot the landscape*
> *We passed the hash pipe, and played our Doors tapes*

165

*And it was dark, so dark at night, and we held on
to each other, like brother to brother,
We promised our mothers we'd write.*

*AND WE WILL ALL GO DOWN TOGETHER
WE SAID WE'D ALL GO DOWN TOGETHER
YES, WE WOULD ALL GO DOWN TOGETHER*
              —*"Goodnight Saigon," Billy Joel*

To some, our music meant a longing for back home, a momentary escape valve, and a way to feel connected with what was going on back in the States.

To others, we were the dark soundtrack raging in their minds when they were under fire. The more rebellious infantry soldiers who were in the Ah Shau Valley, where it looked like the Fourth of July every night, tied their growing hair in bandanas, took acid, cut off ears and heads of dead Viet Cong for warmup, building courage for taking lives, and machine-gunned the enemy to Jim's singing "This Is the End." The look in their faces scared the shit out of the "straights" back at the base.

In a radio talk show we did a few years ago, John Milius, cowriter of *Apocalypse Now*, talked about how he used active imagination when listening to our songs.

"When I hear 'Light My Fire' I imagine killing gooks from my 'copter in 'Nam . . . or driving a tank through a village." Milius was never in the service; he received a 4F classification due to asthma. I had heard personal "Light My Fire" stories for years—the first time people made love while listening to it; the first time they smoked pot; the first record they ever bought—but Milius's story upset me. When I talked to some vets, I found out that the army programmed the boys into depersonalizing the "enemy" to get them psyched up to kill. Hence terms like "gooks" were encouraged.

Milius said that he used our music as background on the set for actor motivation in his gladiator films. Drums have always been

166

the instrument to stir men to war, but I didn't play so that it would help Arnold Schwarzenegger decapitate the "enemy."

What disturbs me today is that rock 'n' roll is being exploited into "battle" music for patriotic war movies. Enlistments skyrocketed after *Top Gun* glamorized the air force. Vietnam was called a rock-'n'-roll war because the *soldiers* chose to listen to it to help them survive, which is quite different from some of today's film directors (modern-day generals) using rock to drum up patriotic reverie.

"When I want some good pagan carnage I put on the Doors," said Milius.

WAITING FOR THE SUN

At first flash of Eden we raced down to the sea,
Standing there on freedom's shore,
Waiting for the sun
Waiting for you to come along,
Waiting for you to hear my song,
Waiting for you to tell me what went wrong.
This is the strangest life I've ever known.
Waiting for the sun.

June 1968

Just before leaving for our series of concerts in large arenas—
the first would be the Hollywood Bowl—I got two important
phone calls, one good, one bad. The good one was from our old
lawyer, Max Fink, who told me that the "peace" officer who had
hassled me in Reno had been reprimanded. Max didn't know if
he was fired or demoted, but he definitely got his hand slapped.
The attorney's fees cost me several hundred bucks, but I felt vin-
dicated.

The other call was from my parents. They said my brother was
back in Camarillo. He had turned on the gas stove in his apartment without lighting the flame. I was shocked. On the way to the
sound check at the Bowl, I reflected back to when my parents had

taken Jim to Minnesota on a business trip years ago and he'd refused to attend school back there. Was that the beginning? It was too much to figure out, if it ever could be figured out. I buried my thoughts about my brother.

The Hollywood Bowl didn't look as famous in the daylight as it did at night, but unfortunately the night light didn't save our performance. We were worried about the acoustics at the outdoor amphitheater, where there were no walls to bounce the sound off. We had played outdoor concerts successfully before, but you couldn't hear the sound coming back to you and it could be difficult to judge how loudly to play. We didn't want to take any chances, so Vince, our dedicated and obsessed road manager, built additional amplifiers, fifty-two speakers in all, with seven thousand watts of power. For a four-piece band!

I used four mikes to amplify my drums and had eight speakers all for myself. Ray and Robby had about fifteen speakers each and Jim had a few less, but his voice was also fed through the house PA system.

We wanted to reach the back of the Bowl and we didn't want to get caught short. As it turned out, the people who lived in the homes behind the Bowl had complained about noise the previous month or so, and the Bowl had hired a sound man to walk around the theater during performances and check volume levels on a portable meter. The sound level was not to exceed eighty decibels, or he would pull the plug. Robby was very unhappy. Typical—a guitar player. Power! I was actually pleased, because as a drummer I always fought to be heard. Whenever Ray and Robby turned up a knob, I had to use more muscle.

Unfortunately, eighty decibels was not enough to fill eighteen thousand seats with the punch we relied on. Thinking the Bowl would be an important gig, we also had a movie crew of old UCLA film school friends of Ray and Jim's shooting 16 mm color and sync sound. A small crew had been following us around on tour for a documentary we were making. For the Bowl we had a couple additional cameramen. (Although I wasn't into guys, I noticed how strikingly handsome one of the new crewmen was. And he had a weird name: Harrison Ford.) We got a call from Jimmy Miller, the Stones' producer, and he said that he and Mick would like to come to the Bowl. Mick Jagger! We were impressed until they drove up in front of our office to go to dinner with us. Robby said, "John, look at the car they're driving." It was a Cadillac, and not even an old one. Was Mick selling out? I excused them because it was probably a rental, but still I thought, Couldn't they have had more taste? Our entourage went to Mu Ling's Chinese restaurant on Sunset Boulevard and unfortunately, since there were too many people in our group, we sat at two separate tables. Mick sat at the other table. Jimmy Miller talked up a storm, but I wanted to hear the interaction between the two lead singers, and maybe put my two cents in. As we drove to the back of the Bowl, it felt like attending a huge baseball game. I felt a twinge of nervousness looking at the crowd as we walked into the dressing room. I got a piece of paper and we agreed to the first three or four songs. Out of the corner of my eye, I could see Mick watching very attentively.

Jimmy Miller and Jagger snuck around to one of the reserved boxes, and we went out onstage to eighteen thousand roaring people. I wanted to show the Stones' lead singer how good we could be. Not tonight. Damn it! I wished we were better. Several close friends were right in the front seats and I couldn't even look at them. Jim wore a cross and smoked a lot of cigarettes, which seemed out of character for him. He wasn't born again and it was the first time I ever saw him smoke. I detected some self-conscious image-building.

The audience lit matches when we played "Light My Fire," a trend that continues at rock concerts today, but as beautiful as it looked from the Bowl stage, there was little spark coming from the music. It wasn't a bad show; it was just off.

I couldn't put my finger on what went wrong. The lights were very bright for the film crew, and I could tell they were affecting Jim's performance. The mood of the show wasn't there. We didn't have enough power and Jim's pauses were too long on some songs. Jim's gold crucifix didn't even help. I had noticed Roger Daltrey of the Who sporting a cross on TV, so I asked Jim why he had followed suit.

"I like the symbol visually, plus it will confuse people."

"What went wrong?" I asked Robby, walking back under the shell to the dressing rooms.

"Jim took acid right before going on."

"GOD DAMN IT!" I hurled my drumsticks to the floor. "It's one thing to take it on your own time, but the Hollywood Bowl? That's probably why he took it. Damn."

Later Jagger was very kind when *Melody Maker*, the English music magazine, asked him how he liked the Doors. He said, "They were nice chaps, but they played a bit too long."

%

I was driving the hour and a half north to Camarillo to see my brother. Visions of Terry and the Twilighters, the first band I was ever in, came to me. We used to play for free at the VA hospital at Christmastime. I visualized going into the locked wards full of World War II veterans and playing holiday songs. The guy who stuck in my mind was pathetically trying to keep the five pairs of pants that he had on from sliding down his legs. It was a constant job, but he worked at it cheerfully.

"Play 'Jingle Bell Rock,' would you?" he kept requesting over and over and over.

"Do you guys know 'Jingle Bell Rock'?"

"Hey, ha ha ha . . . how about 'Jingle Bell Rock'?"

So I had visions of further confrontations with crazy people as I approached the hospital. R. P. McMurphy I wasn't. Maybe the big fear was that if they got onto my trip they'd probably lock me up too.

It was yet another sunny southern California day and I was enjoying one of my favorite parts of the coast north of the Los Angeles County line before I turned the radio on and heard the news. It interrupted the dread already gnawing at me from the inside about my brother. I wanted to see him, as I was leaving for Europe soon. The yellow wildflowers hanging from the Point Mugu cliffs, which always reminded me of Big Sur, couldn't distract my mind from dwelling on mental hospitals. The radio news riveted me into pulling over to the side of the road. Robert Kennedy had just been shot after winning the Democratic primary for president. It was getting insane: Martin Luther King, Jr., assassinated a few months back . . . our singer was unstable . . . my brother was in trouble . . . anarchy in the U.S. I loved Robert more than his brother. He seemed even smarter. There was no hope.

I pulled into the institutional grounds and found the correct building. After getting out of the car, I went in, down the beige hallways with the beige vinyl couches, and spoke with the nurse. After about ten minutes of watching TV with a couple of "the guys," my brother, Jim, came out. He looked okay except for the crusty stuff in the corners of his eyes, the stuff you get from sleeping too much.

He suggested we go outside and sit on the grass, which I thought was a great idea. I had to get out of those depressing buildings. It crossed my mind that he could just walk right out of this place if he wanted to.

Not to touch the earth, not to see the sun,
Nothing left to do but run, run, run,
Let's run.

"They said it looks pretty good for me to get out of here in about two weeks, so could you pick me up?"

"Sure."

He seemed fairly coherent except for his drowsy disposition. It was clear they were giving him tranquilizers. State hospital policy: Keep everybody anesthetized so there's no trouble. Sort of like putting an invisible straitjacket on the patients.

172

So how was my brother supposed to sort out what was going on in his mind when he was sleeping fourteen hours a day?

We talked a little while longer and then I left, promising to pick him up when he called.

⅄.

Rumor had it that we were getting a reputation in England as a serious group with political overtones, a group to be reckoned with. At first our records were underground favorites, but by the third album "Hello, I Love You" was a hit across the Atlantic. So in August of '68, off we went for two weeks to conquer England and Europe. On the eleven-hour flight my mind wandered between looking at the polar icecaps and daydreaming. I decided to add to my muttonchop sideburns and grow a mustache. Something to do on the long plane ride. I looked over at Robby; he had plugged the movie headphones into his electric guitar and was playing up a storm. Silently. I got up to take another walk up and down the aisles. The plane wasn't full so our entourage was spread all over the place. Jim was sacked out across five seats in the center aisle, and Dorothy was sitting all alone in the business section watching *Goodbye, Mr. Chips.* She was crying. Must have been a tearjerker.

In London we played the Roundhouse, an old circular barn in a northwest suburb called Chalk Farm. It held a few thousand people, and we were there for two nights with the Jefferson Airplane. Someone told me that Paul McCartney was there, but I didn't see him. It was packed; the "West Coast" sound comes to England. The BBC was taping us for an hour-long TV special that would later be called *The Doors Are Open.* The Airplane played for two and a half hours. San Francisco groups were notorious for not being able to get offstage without playing forever. Maybe it had something to do with drugs! They must have thought they were playing in slow motion.

That night Jim was on and we played our asses off. Best performance on tape. I felt totally concentrated during both sets. Since we opened the first night, I insisted we go on last the second night. There was a hassle, but I was adamant. It was supposed to be equal billing. We went on second.

About this time I felt I was developing a sense of where the audience was at during a concert. It was like having an antenna out and being extra sensitive to the audience's feelings—as a whole—as if they were one giant being. If the audience was getting bored or wanted a change of pace, which was instant feedback on your performance, I not only sensed it early, I figured out what song would be good to play next instead of the one planned, to take them to a different level. In Copenhagen we started fighting in front of everybody over what to play next, but it was worth it to me.

"How 'bout 'Little Red Rooster'?" Jim said.

Ray and I immediately looked disappointed. The Stones had already covered that song, and our version wasn't as good. Jim *always* wanted to play it now. Robby was noncommittal, and all of a sudden, Ray started "Soul Kitchen." I was relieved.

No one seemed to have the initiative to get a piece of paper and figure out a set to play, so the job landed in my lap. I figured you needed a dramatic opening: "Break On Through" or "Back Door Man"; then take it down for a while: "Music's Over" or "Five to One"; and then slowly build to a strong climax: "Light My Fire." "The End" evolved into our encore, which shellshocked the audience into leaving.

At the press party in London, Jim dazzled reporters with his rhetoric. He controlled the conversation with long pauses between each sentence while he weighed his answers. You could *see* the wheels turning in his head as he took the maximum time tolerable in answering.

I liked to try to find some humor in my answers. A reporter asked me about the blending of rock and jazz. I said, "It could never happen, but if it could, we're it!" In the middle of the noisy London press party I shouted out, "LET ME SAY THIS ABOUT THAT," mocking the seriousness of the whole affair. Ray responded confidently to the interviews, sometimes in long roundabout ways. He would work himself into a place where he evaded the question entirely and said what he wanted. He gave a short answer to one question.

"Do the Doors advocate drugs?"

"Well . . ." Ray responded, smiling at Jim. Jim smiled back. I felt it was a glib, irresponsible half reply. I decided right then to give a donation to the TM movement in hopes that other young people would be exposed to meditation. TM helped me survive the drug scene; maybe others could benefit.

Robby hardly said anything. He just twisted a strand of his frizzy brown hair and evasively kept quiet. I knew he had thoughts about all these questions but he was too shy.

⁒

"You vill open ze bag, I vill look!" the customs officials barked in their German-accented English. When we arrived in Frankfurt on the next stop of our tour, I thought I was in an old World War II movie. Once we got out into the country, though, the people were very friendly and I was surprised at how green the landscape was. I thought it was going to be gray. I'd seen too many films stereotyping Germany.

The promoters were two young men who were very warm and catered to our every need. They had a vivacious blonde in tow who seemed to be available for the groups who came into town. We arrived at that conclusion after the promoters told us that José Feliciano had enjoyed reading Braille all over her chest. (We all loved his version of "Light My Fire," because he had found a way of interpreting it rather than just copying our arrangement.) Another beautiful German woman, Francesca, latched on to Jim. Pam Courson was nowhere in sight, and Jim had started occasionally staying in motels when we were back home. I guess he was available.

That night as the curtain rose, I was optimistic about our set. I could feel the audience's anticipation. We roared into "Break On Through" and finished it with a bang. Silence. As we quickly started our second number, "Back Door Man," I could still feel the silence. Maybe they were transfixed by Jim. The song ended and the response was still very quiet. Curious.

We thought "Whiskey Bar" would get a rise out of them, since it was written by one of their countrymen, Munich's own Bertoldt Brecht.

Nothing. Quieter still. Maybe the pre-Hitler song was in bad taste. We continued and Jim started berating the audience for a reaction. He stalked around the stage using the mike stand as if it were a javelin, pretending to throw it into the audience. He got a vicious look on his face and ran from the back of the stage, in front of my drums, to the edge of the stage, threatening to impale members of the audience on his mike stand. I thought he was going too far. The audience didn't flinch. Each time he did it, I gasped.

We finished the set to the same lukewarm response, and the curtain came down. Everyone backstage was very quiet. The once-friendly promoters avoided us.

"What happened out there, Ray?" I asked.

"Beats me!"

I was mad at Jim for being so hostile, but, in retrospect, I think he struck a nerve in all of us. Here was this rock singer, dressed in his "leathers," stomping around the stage threatening violence. He wasn't doing the goose step, but the young Germans got the message. Rage and anarchy. Just what they had been trying to forget since the war.

Afterward we were taken to an Israeli club called Das Kinky. It was full of life. My impression was that the young people were trying to make up for what their parents had given in to. The blonde came on to Robby after realizing that everyone else was taken—Jim with Francesca, Ray with Dorothy, and me with a German Jewess from the club—but it was to no avail.

Lynn was to catch up with Robby in a few days and he was committed to her, so he passed on the blonde. It was heart-warming that for a few years Lynn had lived the sixties' version of

McInerney's *Bright Lights, Big City* and was now settling down with Robby.

Unfortunately, the German girl I ended up with didn't speak a word of English. Excuse me, I didn't speak a word of Deutsch. German is close enough to English that occasionally a sentence would pop out of her conversation that I would understand perfectly. I was worried about making love with someone I couldn't talk with, but we had no problem communicating physically. She looked very exotic sitting on my hotel bed, with her coal-black hair practically covering her face. The problem was that I had to get on a plane the next morning and I had no way to tell her. When morning came and I began to pack, she got the idea. She looked very surprised and sad. I didn't feel too good either; the only thing I could say was "Auf wiedersehen."

A week later we were sitting in a pristine side room of the Amsterdam Concert Hall, surrounded by statuettes of Mozart, Chopin, and the rest of the classical lads. It was half an hour before we were supposed to perform, and Jim and Robby had wandered out somewhere in the auditorium. All of a sudden Jim was being carried past on a stretcher, out cold. He was put in an ambulance and he was gone.

"What the fuck happened, Leon?" I screamed to the publicist. "You were supposed to watch Jim this afternoon!"

"We were on the street and someone came up and gave Jim a little block of hash, and he popped the whole thing in his mouth right there," Leon replied with exasperation.

"Vince! Go out and make an announcement that Jim got sick and they can have their money back. Or the three of us will play, I guess." Ray didn't sound so sure.

"We can do it." I jumped in. Vince came running by in a fancy green sparkle jacket he'd put on just for the announcement.

I went up to the Airplane's dressing room. Grace Slick said Jim had been onstage in the middle of their set and acted kind of crazy, but everyone had thought it was part of the act. The Airplane *was* mellow. Marty Balin was quiet, but Grace and Paul Kantnor were very friendly.

When I got back downstairs, Vince ran up and said the audience wanted the Doors, with or without Jim.

A couple of members of the Airplane, including Spencer Dryden, their drummer, came down to the wings to see how we would do. Ray handled the vocals fairly well; I exaggerated my performance because there was no lead singer blocking my view of the audience, and therefore, for once, I was the focal point. I liked that. The Dutch seemed to like us. Our lyrics weren't in Dutch, anyway, so they had to go with the mood. That's the way I judged new records, anyhow. If the mood got me, I would listen again to pick up all the lyrics.

After the concert we called the hospital. Jim had recovered after taking a nice nap.

The next morning, walking out of the hotel, we noticed that I was on the front cover of the local newspaper! An interpreter translated and said they liked my playing and stage presence. I glanced at Jim; he was expressionless. I was feeling very proud of myself. Check it out, Jim!

⅃

Back from the successful three-week European tour, my sense of the world had expanded. I'd known there were many different cultures out there, but now I had experienced them directly. Europeans seemed to know how to relax. They took long lunches and weren't so obsessed with huge record sales. They had a practical policy: Record merchandisers had to sell what they ordered. No returns. No inflation.

⅃

Julia and I began dating again. She asked me over for a home-made dinner—her famous halibut with sour cream sauce—and it felt like the Song of the South (Gregg Allman, that is) was in the past. Our dating evolved into a warm relationship, and then she brought up the idea of living together. I hadn't given it much thought, but I started thinking about it now.

We spent the fall of '68 trying to sort out the documentary, *Feast of Friends.* We had dropped thirty thousand dollars into it, but completion was still eluding us. I knew we had the coverage, but the editing seemed poor. I complained so much that Jim offered to buy me out for six thousand dollars. I pondered the offer as we hit the road for another tour.

Now armed with six black bodyguards in pinstripe suits and natty pimp derbies, we opened in Minneapolis with a blues-heavy set. The bodyguards were our manager's idea. Actually, it was cheaper hiring six detectives out of the Sullivan Detective Agency from Philadelphia than employing a couple of security guards from L.A. (Besides, we could find out who was cheating on whom!) Mr. Sullivan would go right up to any cops at the venues and say, "Everything is taken care of, we're taken care of the boys, thank you very much, we'll see you later." It made me feel secure. Protected from the heat, as well as the fans! The Sullivans seemed to be having fun watching out for us, but they took their job seriously when we went onstage. At an average of 250 pounds each, several bodyguards went in front of us, and several following behind. Our entrance must have been impressive; it felt like we were boxers going down to the ring.

Jim seemed depressed as he sat down on my drum riser in the middle of the show, put his head in his hands, and wouldn't get up. After about five minutes, I came around and sat beside him, asking what he would like to play. The audience sat motionless. Another five minutes. Jim finally got up and began humming a slow blues, "Rock Me," and we followed suit. Local harp player Tony Glover sat in with us on "Little Red Rooster," which perked Jim up even more.

Columbus the next night was an average gig.

Then the tide turned. In Madison Jim destroyed the microphone. In Phoenix the powers that be pulled the plug on us after we had played an hour set. The kids clearly wanted more, so we said we'd pay any overtime for the union electricians or whoever ran the place. They said, "No go." Jim went back out onstage with all the lights on and yelled, "Do you want more?" The crowd roared, but the promoter still said, "No go." Ray, Robby and I started doing some hand-jive; slapping our thighs and finger-popping, and Jim started singing without any power. The fans dug it. The promoter still said, "No go." Someone started ripping the seats apart and several chairs started flying. We went backstage and the crowd dispersed.

The music reviewer from the local paper, *The Phoenix Gazette,* wrote up the concert as if he were covering a political riot:

At least seven persons were detained after last night's appearance at the Coliseum by the Doors, and Arizona Highway Patrol Captain Bill Foster said he feared the incident was going to develop into a full-scale riot.

Phoenix Gazette photographer Brian Lanker said the singer, identified as Jim Morrison, invited the youngsters to leave their seats and approach the stage. The youngsters milled in the aisles, threw things onstage, and pushed against a line of security police ringing the stage.

Witnesses said Morrison made obscene gestures with a scarf and then threw it into the crowd of screaming youngsters.

The singer reportedly commented on the presidential race by saying: "Four more years of mediocrity and h----s---. If he [President-elect Richard Nixon] does wrong, we will get him."

Dick Smith, vice-chairman of the State Fair Board, said the group "won't be back here. They certainly shouldn't be in our building."

Phoenix police said today they were holding four persons, including one girl, in connection with use of vulgar language, one person accused of assault, and also had detained two juveniles accused of disturbing the peace.

Twenty were arrested. There were arrests, injuries, and riots at our concerts in Chicago, Cleveland, and St. Louis.

180

In a later interview with the *Los Angeles Free Press*, Jim reflected on the crowd phenomena:

The Doors never really had any riots. I did try and create something a few times just because I'd always heard about riots at concerts and I mean I thought we ought to have a riot. Everyone else did. So I tried to stimulate a few little riots, you know, and after a few times I realized it's such a joke. It doesn't lead nowhere. You know what, soon it got to the point where people didn't think it was a successful concert unless everybody jumped up and ran around a bit. I think it would be better to do a concert and just keep all that feeling submerged so that when everyone left they'd take that energy out on the streets and back home with them. Rather than just spend it uselessly in a little crowd explosion.

No, we never had any real riots. I mean a riot's an out-of-control, violent thing. We never had too much of what I call a real riot.

⅞

In December, in the middle of rehearsing for our fourth album, we played the eighteen-thousand-seat Forum in L.A. We now had the power to dictate who the second act would be, and we wanted to give a nod to a fifties' rock-'n'-roller who helped get things started. We suggested Johnny Cash because of "I Walked the Line" but the promoter said no, since he was an ex-con. (Before his hit TV show, Johnny Cash couldn't get the time of day. Within the next few years, he would become a rebel hero.)

We were thrilled that Jerry Lee Lewis was "acceptable." They said he wouldn't draw, but we didn't care. They said he only played country music now, but we didn't care.

His band showed up at the gig without any instruments.

"Can my boys borrow your drums?"

"Sure, Jerry Lee." I smiled.

He turned to Robby. "Can we borrow a gittar?"

"What kind of guitar do you want? I have several."

"Any old rock 'a day Fender gittar!"

Ray tried to start "World Music" twenty years before its time by having a Chinese musician, Mr. Chin, open the concert.

"Now I want you all to try and be quiet and listen to some ancient Chinese music played on the pi-pa," Ray pleaded in his introduction of the concert.

Later Jerry Lee obliged the audience with "Whole Lotta Shakin' " and "Great Balls of Fire," which got a rise out of them, but throughout his set they persisted with obnoxious Doors' chants.

"Jim, Jim, Jim. Doors, Doors, Doors!"

I had snuck out into the audience with the bass player we had on this tour, Harvey Brooks. We were experimenting with our sound for our fourth album, so we had horns, strings, and a bass onstage. Harvey was a jovial guy who had played with Dylan and the Electric Flag. He and I were eager to hear the "killer."

"Jim, Jim, Doors, Doors." The audience was turning into a restless mob.

"I wish they'd shut up," I whispered.

"He doesn't seem to mind." Harvey laughed. "Don't worry about it."

I did anyway. We were the headliners, but now we were also the producers. I worried about everything.

After combing his hair, playing the piano with his feet, and jumping on top of the grand, Jerry Lee spoke up loudly into the microphone at the end of his performance. "FOR THOSE OF YOU WHO LIKED ME, GOD LOVE YA. FOR THE REST OF YOU, I HOPE YOU HAVE A HEART ATTACK!"

When we came out, the audience baited Jim by hurling lit matches at him and calling for "Light My Fire." The tables had turned. They weren't coming to hear our jazz solos or Jim's "dark-green lyrics" anymore.

"Hey, man," Jim said, his voice booming from speakers on the ceiling. "Cut out that shit." The crowd giggled.

Meditating.

Up on the roof.

East meets West.
(PHOTO CREDIT: PAUL FARRARA)

On the road.
(PHOTO CREDIT: PAUL FARRARA)

Rehearsing *The Soft Parade*
album.
(PHOTO CREDIT: JERRY HOPKINS)

Set discussion before going onstage.
(PHOTO CREDIT: JIM MARSHALL)

Seattle Pop Festival.
(PHOTO CREDIT: JIM MARSHALL)

Press conference at London Airport, 1968.
(PHOTO CREDIT: UPI)

Lipsynching a German
TV show.
(PHOTO CREDIT: MICHAEL
MONTFORT/DOORS PHOTO
LIBRARY)

The javelin thrower,
Germany.
(PHOTO CREDIT:
MICHAEL MONTFORT/
DOORS PHOTO LIBRARY)

New Haven bust ("Say your thing, man!").
(PHOTO CREDIT: TIM PAGE)

The Sullivan Detective Agency takes control of the situation.
(PHOTO CREDIT: PAUL FARRARA)

Backstage, the isolation has begun to set in.
(PHOTO CREDIT: MICHAEL MONTFORT/DOORS PHOTO LIBRARY)

next page
"I like the symbol visually, plus it will confuse people."
(PHOTO CREDIT: HENRY DILTZ)

"What are you all doing here?" Jim went on. No response.

"You want music?" A rousing yeah.

"Well, man, we can play music all night, but that's not what you *really* want, you want something more, something greater than you've ever seen, right?"

"We want Mick Jagger," someone shouted.

Jim ignored the comment.

Half an hour after the show I went back onstage and played some classical piano as the crew cleaned up the array of junk-food cartons and musical equipment. It occasionally used to center me back into a tranquil state after all the hoopla. It also broke the barrier between me and the audience, because there were always a few stragglers around to talk to.

There was a backstage party at the Forum Club. Jim was in the corner, with the Orange Julius stand decor in the background, being interviewed by Michael Lydon from *The New York Times*:

After the show, Morrison said it had been "great fun" but the backstage party had a funereal air. It was one of their biggest concerts, a prelude to the biggest ever in Madison Square Garden next Friday, and the kids dared laugh, even at Morrison. Not much, but they had begun.

The Doors' lead singer showed he knew their first rush of energy was running out. "Success," he said, looking beat in the orange chair, "had been nice. When we had to carry our own equipment everywhere, we had no time to be creative. Now we can focus our energies more intensely."

He squirmed a bit. "The trouble really is now that we don't see each other very much anymore. We're big time, so we go on tours, record, and in our free time, everybody splits off into their own scenes. When we record we have to get all our ideas then, we can't build them night after night like the days in the clubs. In the studio, creation is not so natural.

"I don't know what will happen. I guess we'll continue like

this for a while. Then to get our vitality back, maybe we'll all go to an island by ourselves and start creating again.''

The audience was coming for a freak show, and the "Shaman's Blues" had begun:

There will never be another one like you
There will never be another one
Who can do the things you do
Oh, will you give another chance
Will you try a little try
Please stop and you'll remember
We were together
Anyway . . .

How you must stop to think and wonder
How I must feel
Out on the meadows
While you're on the field
I'm alone
For you
And I cry

18

ABSOLUTELY LIVE

I've been around the world
Had my pick of any girl
You'd think I'd be happy
But I'm not
Ev'rybody knows my name
But it's just a crazy game
Oh, it's lonely at the top

People were starting to call us the American Rolling Stones; we received another gold record for our third album; the BBC-TV special aired in England, portraying us as on the forefront of the liberal political movement in the U.S. All four of us felt the producers were reading a little too much into our lyrics, with their heavy intercutting of U.S. political turmoil in the middle of our songs, but the performances were dynamic.

We were getting kudos from the masses, but the hardcore record critics said we were slipping. They thought our third album didn't live up to the promise of the first two.

Pressure.

The mansion is warm at the top of the hill
Rich are the rooms and the comforts there

185

Red are the arms of luxuriant chairs
And you won't know a thing till you get inside

. . . and you, Jim, were sowing new seeds of creativity with a book of poetry. I was so mad at you for your self-destruction that I didn't give a shit about it. You didn't even give me a copy when it got published. Looking at it now, though, sifting through the despair and disconnected images, I'm blown away by the sensitivity.

There are no longer "dancers," the possessed.
The cleavage of men into actor and spectators
is the central fact of our time. We are obsessed
with heros who live for us and whom we punish.
If all the radios and televisions were deprived
of their sources of power, all books and paintings
burned tomorrow, all shows and cinemas closed,
all the arts of vicarious existence . . .

We are content with the "given" in sensation's
quest. We have been metamorphosed from a mad
body dancing on hillsides to a pair of eyes
staring in the dark.

. . . so, as we were peaking in the outer world, you were still searching for transcendence, not letting up for a moment to enjoy the fruits, and it inflamed your wound. Your birth wound. I can just hear the angst under the lyrics you were writing at this time, before we went into the studio to record our fourth album.

Successful hills are here to stay
Everything must be this way
Gentle street where people play
Welcome to the soft parade

January 1969

During rehearsals for our fourth album, the tension within the group intensified. Jim had a problem with Robby's "Tell All the People." When Robby first brought it in to rehearsal he was very excited, saying he couldn't wait to show it to us, describing the song as the perfect vehicle for Jim.

Jim must have been squirming over not liking the lyrics for months, but he kept it to himself out of respect for the band. Finally he couldn't contain his disapproval.

"I don't want the audience to think I wrote these lyrics, Robby," Jim said. Then he abruptly went into the bathroom of our rehearsal space.

"Why? It's a good song," Robby yelled.

"Yeah, but I don't want the public to think they should 'get their guns and follow me!' " the voice echoed from the bathroom.

The mood darkened. Jim returned and continued to bicker with Robby until Paul Rothchild, who had been listening to the argument, lost his patience.

"I came here to check out your new batch of songs. This dialogue makes me sick." He paused, afraid to go any further. "Can't we go on to something else . . . another song?"

Jim and Robby cooled out, as if to say "We'll let it go for now." I was surprised to see Robby get so passionate about anything. He certainly cared about his songs, and he valued Jim as his mouthpiece.

The Soft Parade cost around two hundred thousand dollars to make, which was a lot at the time, and Ray and I fulfilled our dream of having more of a jazz influence on the record. We got Curtis Ami, a West Coast jazz saxophonist, and George Bohanan, former trombonist with the Chico Hamilton Quintet, and told them to play like John Coltrane and Archie Shepp on Robby's "Runnin' Blue." Rothchild contacted Paul Harris to arrange an orchestra of horns and strings for overdubs. Horns and *strings*? Well, Rothchild's intuition had paid off so far. . . .

George Harrison was in town and dropped by to see Elektra's

new studio, and we got to meet a Beatle. Alluding to all the extra musicians, he commented that our session looked like the one for *Sergeant Pepper*. I guess that's what we were trying to do. It was a thrill meeting him, although I found myself tongue-tied.

Jim took forever to walk from the vocal booth to the control room to hear the playbacks. On the road, when Ray, Robby, press agents, our manager, roadies, and I would be running to make a plane, Jim would refuse to quicken his pace. He usually walked unhurried onto the plane just as the door shut. Maybe he was psychic. Whatever it was, it was giving me an ulcer. "You can't be late for your own show," Jim would say.

While recording the vocal for the title track, we started the playback tape rolling just as Jim finished, to try to encourage him to move a little faster going from the vocal booth to the control room to hear what he'd just recorded. He still missed the first couple of lyrics . . .

When I was back there in seminary school
There was a person there who put forth the proposition . . .

Jim finally pushed through the control room door and leaned on the side of the console in the corner. Not in the center where the best sound is, but on the side, in front of the left speaker. He was still shy about hearing his voice. But the voice coming from the speakers was confident, sarcastic, and finally screaming from the bowels of his soul.

. . . That you can petition the Lord with prayer
Petition the Lord with prayer
Petition the Lord with prayer
YOU CANNOT PETITION THE LORD WITH PRAYER!

Jim's performance was so strong that the former little Catholic boy inside me thought we were blaspheming and would be punished.

Finding a way to complement Jim's lyrics through my drumming, or mixing the final product, still got me high as a kite. Knowing we were putting our music down for posterity gave me a quiet internal glow. It wasn't quite the instant gratification of live audience feedback, but it had its own subtle rewards.

I motioned to Rothchild to turn up Ray's harpsichord in the mix as it came in under Jim's vulnerable soft lament.

Can you give me sanctuary
I must find a place to hide
A place for me to hide

Can you find me soft asylum
I can't make it anymore
The man is at the door

If, at the time, I had really taken a closer look at these lyrics and seen how much Jim was hurting, maybe I *would* have quit; maybe we were cashing in on his pain. But I didn't take a closer look at those words, I just felt them.

It didn't occur to me how serious a price Jim was paying. Even with all the interpersonal problems, playing live had become my new religion. Our setup had evolved into a power center forming a diamond, with me in the back, usually on a riser (I wanted to be seen), and Ray and Robby on the sides. All the energy pushed forward through Jim at the forefront and out to the devotees. Jim was free to roam around, going over to Ray and encouraging him on during a solo, or walking the edge of the stage. Sometimes Jim would face me directly, with his back to the auditorium, and shout encouragement, or climb up behind me while I was playing and wave his arms, making the two of us look like some multilimbed animal.

We have assembled inside this ancient and insane theater
To propagate our lust for life
And flee the swarming wisdom of the streets

We were cast in the roles of the high priests in this drama. The audiences were our disciples. It was intoxicating. I concentrated so hard that I often put myself into a trance. In his poetry, Jim describes the primitive theater of the shaman, which comes close to explaining what happened when we peaked in concert.

> In the séance, the shaman led. A sensuous panic,
> deliberately evoked through drugs, chants, dancing,
> hurls the shaman into trance. Changed voice,
> convulsive movement. He acts like a madman. These
> professional hysterics, chosen precisely for their
> psychotic leaning, were once esteemed. They
> mediated between man and spirit-world. Their mental
> travels formed the crux of the religious life of
> the tribe.
>
> —Lords & New Creatures

George Harrison dropping by or not, the press killed us for changing our precious "Doors" sound. This didn't stop "Touch Me," a Krieger tune, from going to number one. The masses were with us more than ever. (Although rumors flew as to the intensity of some of Robby and Lynn's domestic squabbles, out of one of those fights had come "Come on, come on, come on, now, HIT me, babe!" Jim encountered no contest when he suggested to Robby changing the lyric to "Touch me, babe.")

The result of Jim and Robby's conflict over "Tell All the People" created a first for a Doors album. Individual songwriter credits were given to whoever had the first seed lyric or melody for a composition, whereas before all songs were credited as written by the Doors. The conflict was resolved, but the increasing Doors split was going public.

%

New York, January 21, 1969
The day before Madison Square Garden

It would be our first really big concert in New York. Sal Bonafette, our manager, had described our career as a big wave about to break. But there was a fatal flaw: Our singer was nuts. Sal had an idea: Because of Jim's increasing intake of alcohol, Sal's partner, Ash (who seemed more and more like a lush), should challenge Jim to a drinking contest the night before the concert. That way, he'd be completely burned out on booze and be too weak to do it again and in great shape for the performance the next night! What a concept! I was willing to try anything.

We all went to Max's Kansas City, and then to Steve Paul's The Scene on West 46th Street and Eighth Avenue. Jim was well on his way.

"Hey, John," Jim said, slurring at me, "Spencer Dryden from the Airplane says here that you're his favorite drummer."

"Let me see that," I responded, as Jim threw a paperback book on our table. Jim always had a book in tow, a literary security blanket that couldn't be taken away, like the friends Jim lost as his military family moved from base to base. This time it was Ralph Gleason's new one on rock music. He was a writer for *Rolling Stone* up in San Francisco and used to be a jazz critic for *Downbeat* magazine, a rag I pored over in the early sixties.

I thought back to when I saw Spencer out of the corner of my eye in Amsterdam when we played without Jim. This was a great compliment from a peer. I handed the book back to Jim as he headed for the stage.

Tiny Tim was "Tiptoeing Through the Tulips," when Jim arrived at the edge of the spotlight. Groveling around on his knees, fooling with the mike stand, it looked as if Jim were giving Tiny Tim head as Tim laughed nervously in his high voice. Tiny Tim told Jim that there is "nothing in the world like motherly love." Tiny was thirty-five and still lived with his mother. Considering that Jim had told the press that his parents were deceased (which they were not), it started out as a pretty funny scene.

Then it turned sour. Ash tried to get Jim off the stage, which he couldn't do, so a fight broke out. It was time for my exit. As I got to the door, I glanced back over my shoulder and saw the managers, Jim, and several other people rolling over tables.

It was a long walk, but I decided to hoof it back to the hotel in hopes that it would cool me out from worrying about the next night, our biggest and possibly most important gig yet. Walking up Eighth to 57th and across to the Manger Windsor Hotel on Sixth, I prayed all the way for Jim's sobriety.

The next morning I ran into Robby in the hotel's coffee shop.

"Jim called me last night at four A.M.!" Robby exclaimed while sipping fresh orange juice. "You know what he said? I was half asleep, mind you, and he said, 'This is God calling, and we've decided to kick you right out of the universe!' "

"What a card!"

"Yeah . . . I hope he's in good shape for tonight."

"Me too." After getting up from the counter, we left the hotel. I thought to myself how great it was to have an ally in the band. Robby and I never talked about it, but I sensed that he felt the same.

⁊

"Is that you, Ray?" I asked, hearing someone come into the stall next door to me.

"Yup," he responded in that deep, ponderous voice.

I could tell by the white buck shoes. We were sitting on toilets in the basement of Madison Square Garden.

"Having your preconcert shit?" I joked.

"Yup." Ray laughed. We could hear the crowd upstairs starting to stamp their feet.

"Boom-boom-BOOM-BOOM . . . Doors-Doors-DOORS . . . Jim-JIM-JIM!"

"Time to go," Ray and I said simultaneously.

Jim seemed in pretty good spirits. If his state of mind was in that delicate balance where he had a buzz, but not too much, my confidence was strong enough to reduce my preperformance nerves to small butterflies. I've always thought that if you aren't a little nervous, then you aren't risking enough.

We came out to the center boxing ring and twenty-four thousand people gave us the biggest roar I had ever heard. It was the ultimate in mass affection. How could this be topped? And the stage was still dark! Since there wasn't any curtain, we chose to be led out with flashlights and were tuning up in the dark—and they were already going crazy!

Ray lit a stick of incense that was preset on the organ, an idea we copped from Indian music. It had evolved into a ritual that signaled we were leaving the outside world behind, and the smell put us in a collective mood to play.

I started the beat to "Break On Through" in the dark, which drew more response, then after a few bars, when Ray and Robby came in with their respective organ and guitar lines, the lights came up. The combination of powerful electric instruments crashing in over primitive drums with simultaneous stage lights blasting in out of total blackness was very effective, an electronic coming of Christ. Or the Anti-Christ, to be more precise.

Then came Jim's voice, the voice of total belligerence, spouting out an improvised poem about "FAT CATS, DEAD RATS, suckin' on a soldier's sperm. CRAP—THAT'S CRAP!"

We settled down into the song's groove and built it up to its abrupt climax.

"Back Door Man" was next, not giving the audience a moment to breathe. The guitar started it, then Jim let out one of his blood-curdling screams. No one could scream like Jim.

"Whiskey Bar" followed as a change of pace. The lights were meticulously programmed to the mood of each song by Chip Monck, our new lighting designer. For "Whiskey Bar," Chip would bathe the band in blue light while giving Jim a yellow halo.

We argued in front of everybody about which song to play fourth. Harvey Brooks, our bass player, doubled over in laughter at the audience's response to our unprofessionalism. They loved it.

"You guys could take a crap onstage and they'd eat it up," Harvey whispered in my ear. "Incredible!" I was acutely tuned to not letting the ball drop for the audience, but by this point in our career we could do no wrong.

Jim, as usual, wanted to play "Little Red Rooster"; Robby was amenable to anything; Ray and I pushed for an original. We finally agreed on "Unknown Soldier." The execution section in the middle was terrifying. I would start the military drumming with Jim vocalizing "Hup-two-three-four;" Robby would go to his amp and turn a knob that made a siren sound.

"COMPANNYYY HALT!! Preessenntt ARMS."

Robby would aim his guitar at Jim like it was a gun; Ray would hold a fist in the air with one hand and pick up the top of his amplifier with the other, dropping it on cue. The sound blasted out like a gunshot.

This was the usual routine, but I could tell Jim was very concentrated tonight. When he got "shot," he slammed himself to the floor like never before. I stood up from my seat and looked down at him over the drums. He didn't move. Maybe he banged his head on the edge of the drum riser or on one of Robby's guitar pedals? He seemed unconscious and was all tangled up in the mike cord, a stillborn baby who'd just arrived with umbilical webs. Panic was setting in when finally, after a few long seconds, he started moving one of his legs. The shaman was returning from his seizure. All of a sudden, out of the PA, in slurred speech, came "make a grave for the unknown soldier, nestled in your hollow shoulder." Jim had the mike at his lips. I quickly sat down to play the accompanying cymbal splashes. We finished the song as usual, with Jim jumping up and ending the war lyrically. I thought to myself, The song really has evolved into a miniplay. The audience was so stunned it didn't know whether to keep quiet or applaud. I liked that response.

It was time for our anthem, "Light My Fire." As usual, the opening drum crack organ riff brought the house to its feet. We had played this number probably a thousand times already, but I always looked forward to it. The solo section in the middle allowed for long instrumental improvisation, which made it new each time. With improvisation there is danger. The chords we used were similar to Coltrane's version of "My Favorite Things," only stretched out and in 4/4.

Jazz.

I enjoyed spurring Ray and Robby on in their solos. It somehow evolved that I played the cue, two bars of fortissimo eighth notes on the snare, to signal the end of each of their solos. When Ray and I locked into a groove, it was unbounded joy. Robby floated on top, and Ray and I were the rhythm section, the bottom. At this particular gig, we were one.

When it was good, you wanted the groove to go on forever. Don't change to another set of chord progressions, don't go to the next section of the song; just stay right there and ride.

After twenty years, trips around the world, and two marriages, this is still one of the moments I miss the most.

Jim had to hang out sometimes for up to fifteen minutes waiting for us to finish. He loved to play his maraca, though, and dance like an American Indian. He would lift one leg and jump around in a circle as if he were at a campfire. This wasn't no James Brown dance imitation. Sometimes he would be so loose with his movements, I got inspiration for what I was playing from watching him. I drummed harder when Jim, Ray, or Robby were "into it." The groove got so deep, the mud splattered a third of the way up our pant legs.

Those inspired moments made me think that Jim's boyhood story about the American Indian shaman who possessed him in the desert was true. He said that when he was four years old, he and his parents were driving through New Mexico and passed a serious car accident. Jim said later that he felt the soul of the old Indian who was lying on the side of the road leap into him. A leap of faith if there ever was one.

At times like this it seemed that Jim was our puppet and we could take him, with our music, in any direction we wanted. He probably felt like he was doing the same to us, although he knew that music could hypnotize. And he allowed it to happen to himself, which one has to do in hypnotism.

He surrendered so totally some nights that we released the sorcerer inside him. We were caught in a ritual. Control seemed to be exchanged among the four of us until the ceremony was completed—three Apollos balanced by one intense Dionysus.

The last verse and chorus of "Light My Fire" was usually very strong, and the instrumental tag at the end left everyone sort of hanging. But they loved that song!

I had to take a deep breath and gather all my strength to play our last number. No wonder. "The End" was Jim's voyage into pain and death.

⁊.

. . . Your interview with Lizzie James, which was never released, is so brilliant, Jim. Unfortunately, I never read it while you were alive; it would have shown me the thoughts behind your words:

> *Pain is meant to wake us up. People try to hide their pain. But they're wrong. Pain is something to carry, like a radio. You feel your strength in the experience of pain. It's all in how you carry it. Pain is a feeling —your feelings are a part of you. Your own reality. If you feel ashamed of them, and hide them, you're letting society destroy your reality. You should stand up for your right to feel your pain. But people fear death even more than pain. It's strange that they fear death. Life hurts a lot more than death. At the point of death, the pain is over. I guess it is a friend.*

> *This is the end, beautiful friend,*
> *This is the end, my only friend, the end,*
> *It hurts to set you free*
> *But you'll never follow me*
> *The end of laughter and soft lies,*
> *The end of nights we tried to die.*
> *This is the end.*

. . . Technically, "The End" wasn't that difficult for me except at the finish, but the emotional concentration required to give it justice was

exhausting. Remember how many times the audience was right with us, patiently surrendering to Robby's hypnotic guitar and taking the trip? I was always surprised how tolerant the crowd was of the ten minutes of surrealistic poetry you read.

I don't think the recorded version ever equaled what happened some nights.

Too bad the intro that evolved between Robby and me isn't on record. . . . Remember the way he would turn the sound off with his guitar knob, strum some quick flamenco-style chords, and then turn the knob on and off, for an eerie wa-wa-wa-wa-wa effect? And how I would accompany it with bass drum and cymbal crashes? It was a great setup, a loud attention-getter, 'cause they knew the tuning from the record, and then Robby played those high, tinkly notes behind the bridge of his strings that sounded like individual hairs standing up on all of our necks, audience included.

Sometimes I was bored by the snake imagery you read before the double time and climax.

Ride the snake, ride the snake,
To the lake, the ancient lake.
The snake he's long; seven miles
Ride the snake, he's old,
And his skin is cold.

I occupied myself by filling in the gaps between poetry lines with 3/4 against 4/4, which I borrowed from Van Morrison's "Gloria." It worked in "Light My Fire," and I also got into squeezing the drum heads with my elbow, making them "talk" like primitive African drummers.

Remember that night at Madison Square Garden when you threw in some new verses about "Stop the CAR! The dead seal, the dull crucifix, I'm getting out of here"? Sounded like drug imagery to me. I loved that next line, "I can't live through each slow century of her moving."

Ray stopped playing! And started pounding on the keys in quick, expressive grunts: "UH-UH-UH-UH."

I immediately did the same thing, "BLAM-BLAM BLAM," and we

197

stopped the CAR, didn't we! It was free-form poetry and music. LIVE! No concern for chord changes or rhythm, just primeval grunts. When we sensed you were done, we slammed back into the rhythm. God, that was fun.

On to the double time, the finale. You always gave me a chill when you pounded your boots down on the stage while shouting "The killer awoke before dawn. He put his boots on." Method acting, huh, Oedipus! I liked the way you covered your eyes on the "Yes Son" section of "Father—yes, son—I want to kill you." It implied several characters as in Greek drama with masks. When Francis Coppola, a now-prominent movie director— you might remember him from film school—revived the song for his film Apocalypse Now, *he turned up the "fuck you, Mama, all night long, fuck, fuck fuck" part, which we had buried on the first album years ago for obvious reasons.*

I used to love to draw out the double time after the killer section as long as possible, milking every increase in tempo. The climax was orgasmic as ever at Madison Square Garden, and you sang the last chorus as tenderly as ever.

It seemed like the ultimate in appreciation when the audience quietly filed out. Drained. They had taken the trip and there was no more to give or receive. Mutual satisfaction. Everyone in attendance was cleansed— security guards included. What a show. A truly religious experience. Much better than church. Almost as good as sex. Better! A communion with twenty thousand people.

Jim, you were great that night. When you were on, boy, were you on. . . . I wish it had stayed like that forever. But it all started to slip. . . .

14

SHAMAN'S BLUES

The midwestern weekend tour in February of '69 that was crammed into one of the breaks in recording our fourth album was hectic. Running off to Cleveland, Pittsburgh, and Cincinnati Friday through Sunday and trying to record all bright and cheery on Monday was taking its toll. The next weekend road trip, Ann Arbor, Michigan, was a turning point. By now, everyone working for or with us knew that Jim couldn't go longer than three or four gigs before losing it. At the University of Michigan, he lost it. I grabbed Julia's arm in the airport and walked quickly to the baggage to get away from Jim 'cause he seemed nervous. There were two station wagons for transportation and only two seats left in opposite cars after everybody got in. I motioned for Julia to go in the car with Jim so that I wouldn't have to. We got to the hotel, checked in, and Julia had a surprised look on her face.

"I know Jim is crazy after that car ride!"

"What happened?"

"He rolled the window down, stuck half his body out, and started screaming all the way to the hotel."

"Great. Tonight should be interesting," I said sarcastically. Dread started creeping over me as the concert hour approached.

"I don't feel like going to the gig tonight," Julia said. "I'm tired from traveling."

"Okay. Wish me luck."

✗.

"Why don't we stop at that ice cream shop over there?" Robby said, pointing out the window from the jump seat of the limo.

"Good idea," Ray and I quickly responded.

"You guys are creeps. Do you have to stop for iicce ccrreeaammm? I wanna get to the gig," Jim growled.

"We've got plenty of time to stop," Bill Siddons volunteered from the front seat.

Jim frowned as we pulled up to the curb. "While the three of you are at the Dairy Queen, I'll just step into this liquor store down the street."

Uh-oh. Ice cream was a bad idea after all.

We all got back in the limo after making our purchases and headed toward the college. The only sounds that broke the tension were Jim knocking back Jack Daniel's from a brown paper bag and the rest of us slurping on our ice cream cones.

After arriving at the college gym, where the concert was to be held, Jim said he wanted to go on immediately. The opening act hadn't finished yet.

"Come on, let's play, man," Jim said to no one in particular. *"Now.* Goddamn, we're havin' some fun. Love my girl. Yeah, she's lookin' good." Ulcer time for John Boy. We were going onstage and our lead singer had turned into a Southern cracker asshole. I started walking around nervously, which I usually did, checking to make sure the drums were behind the amp line to protect my ears, peeking out to the crowd, seeing where they're at. They felt like a beer-drinking mob that wanted to boogie. I told everyone we should go on as soon as possible before things got worse.

By the middle of our set, Jim was blitzed. The whiskey had caught up with him. He was slurring lyrics, missing musical cues, swearing, and berating the students, which were Big Ten jock types: frat boys and pom pom girls. My heart was pounding double-time when I made the decision to leave the stage. And I did—in the middle of a song.

Robby followed suit after another number, and my whole being thanked him for siding with me. Ray picked up Robby's guitar and started playing the one blues lick he knew, and Jim began to sing something about Maggie M'Gill, who lived on a hill. The improv dribbled out after about five minutes, and Ray and Jim left the stage to the sound of boos.

The rest of the night I raged internally against Jim. As usual, no one said much of anything about the incident or how terrible the performance was, but it was eating me alive. Everyone was trying to pretend Jim's problems didn't exist. (After examining the rash on my legs and back, my dermatologist had asked me if I was nervous or under pressure. I'd said no. I, too, was hoping it would just go away.)

Ray tried to deal with Jim's deterioration by ignoring it. Robby occasionally admitted that Jim had a major problem.

When we arrived back in Los Angeles my old girlfriend Donna Port, who was housesitting for Robby, could see the stress coming off my face. She begged Robby to side with me and stop touring. We could still record, where we had control, and possibly tour later, when Jim seemed more grounded again. Robby agreed, but when I brought it up the next week at a rehearsal break when Jim stepped out, I lost my case. Temporarily.

"Let's continue a little while longer," Ray procrastinated. "We're booked the next few months."

"Robby?" I prodded.

"Let's see how it goes on these couple of tours we've got lined up."

My great friend Robby went back on his word. Or rather, he didn't want to give up playing live. To me, the hour onstage wasn't worth it anymore. The baby-sitting and the traveling. When we started out, we knocked 'em dead 90 percent of the time. Now we fucked up about 50 percent; 10 percent due to technical problems and 40 due to Jim. I couldn't stand to see perfection eroded. But my loyalty kept me in line. It would take another year to convince Ray and Robby to follow my advice.

Will you stop to think and wonder
Just what you'll see
Out on the train-yard
Nursing penitentiary
It's gone, I cry, out loud
Did you stop to consider
How it will feel
Cold grinding grizzly-bear jaws
Hot on your heels
Do you often stop and whisper
In Saturday's shore
That the whole world's a savior
Who could ever, ever, ever, ever
Ask for more

Do you remember
Will you stop
Will you stop
Will you stop
The pain . . .

٪

Elektra Records called and said Buick wanted to pay us seventy-five thousand dollars to use "Light My Fire" in a commercial. Jim was out of town, and there was a meeting about it at the record company. Ray, Robby, and I attended with our manager and met David Anderle from Elektra. David, who seemed like a cool guy, said Holzman thought it was okay and we rationalized that Jim wouldn't mind. We were becoming disciples in the number-one belief in America: $ is God. Older cultures had churches as the center of their cities. Today we seem to build our urban centers around banks. So it was the "Almighty Dollar" that focused the surfacing split between Jim and the rest of us. Jim was being deceived by the three soulmates with whom he had made a pact back in Venice, California, without any business people present.

٪

. . . *You were furious when you got back, weren't you? Mind you, you didn't write "Light My Fire," Robby did. All I can say is that, looking back, I am touched that you cared enough about one of our creations to stand up for it not being bastardized. We weren't businessmen when we got together in Venice, but we were on our way there. Me, Ray, and Robby, at least.*

You wouldn't believe all the sixties' songs that have been sold for commercials now, let alone the giant deals "artists" are now making for Pepsi or the like. Rock 'n' roll is incorporated now, selling jeans, perfume, and war. We were just ahead of our time! Ha ha. Seriously, it's a good lesson you taught me about greed. I've been adamantly opposed to the use of any of our songs for commercials ever since.

I remember that you didn't own a wallet. You kept your driver's license and American Express card between those two pieces of folded cardboard! What a rebel! I can remember swearing I'd never get a credit card, but we started doing so well, Robby's dad said we should now spend half our time worrying about how to keep the money we'd earned. Did you hear that one? So we got Stu Krieger's accountant, Bob Greene, to manage our money, and Bob said we should get credit cards so he could have better records of our expenses.

Of course, the difference between a successful artist and a nonsuccessful one is "business sense," which we all had. The more successful we got, the more we should have watched out not to forget the original, pure creative drive. You were right about that, Jim. Money allows you to do more of what you want, on your own time, but it also can seduce. The ultimate test of corruptibility. Viewed objectively, it's simply another form of energy, capable of making possible freedom and spiritual growth, as well as leading to corruption. That's objectively. Of course, when you earn large amounts of this energy, and we seemed destined to receive it, it's a real test to be highly conscious about using it.

You, of course, didn't say much of anything directly to any of the three of us about this incident, keeping in line with the Doors' unspoken credo not to confront each other. But your message was to confront! Maybe you were just too hurt. Fortunately, the commercial died an early death.

%

Jim came into rehearsal and said that he wanted to make some changes. He wanted to fire Sal and Ash. Ray joked about how Sal had said that he had been experiencing a headache on the top of his head for a couple of months. At that moment I realized that I had been experiencing the same thing, except for about a year, and Jim's comment intensified my headache immediately. He was uncontrollable; without managers, what were we going to do?

Jim suggested promoting our roadie, Bill Siddons, to the position of manager, and Ray seemed open to the idea. I was full of dread. Bill was a great guy, a peer as well as a good worker, but Jim was destroying himself, and who was going to stop it? I thought Sal and Ash would have wanted to curb Jim's descent, to at least have a long ride with his career.

Looking back now, I see the incident differently. It actually was a noble move on Jim's part, even though it came out of a not-so-noble impulse. A dialogue had started between Jim and Sal and Ash about Jim going solo. I think it originated from Jim complaining about how the Doors didn't feel like a group anymore, what with the three of us spending more time with our girlfriends, Jim having serious disputes with Pam, and everyone except Jim's new drinking buddies avoiding him a lot now that his self-destructive path seemed unstoppable.

Sal and Ash's reaction had been to support the star. "Yeah, we can get a new drummer, or a whole new band, whatever you want, Jim." They knew where their bread was buttered.

Jim had a change of heart and decided not to go solo, never even mentioning it to the band, even though his earlier romantic vision of a band of brothers, playing music, carousing, and drinking their way across the world hadn't panned out. Instead, we dumped our managers. We paid them fifty thousand dollars to terminate their contract; Ray found an office for rent, and Bill Siddons started answering the phones.

٪

In the studio, Rothchild was helpful in finding a framework for Jim's thrust. For vocals, Paul was an excellent producer. If Jim's live vocals in the recording studio weren't good enough, Paul always had several extra vocal tracks which had been put down as insurance to choose from. On the "Soft Parade" cut there were several vocals to choose from, and at the end of the song, just for fun, Paul turned them all on. It was beautiful chaos. Jim's vocals overlapped and commented on each other. One would say, "You gotta meet me at the crossroads," and another quickly retaliated, "TOO LATE, too late." And then a third vocal would take a positive overview: "We're goin' great! Yeah!" Schizophrenic multi-tracking. Rothchild and the studio had indeed become like the fifth Door.

During the fourth-album sessions, Robby did an interview that shed some light on the process: "Jim has so much energy it is as if he can't do it all alone. We use our musical structure to support Jim's lyrics. There are some people who go out on the edge—and Jim goes out into unknown territory. We keep his exploration of the chaos intact, by keeping his words to the chords and the rhythms."

On the ride out (the last series of chord progressions in a song) of "Shaman's Blues," we slid the vocal tracks in and out spontaneously and came up with spoken ad-lib bits that Jim had done on the various vocal takes.

He's sweatin', look at him . . . optical promise . . . YOU'LL BE DEAD AND IN HELL BEFORE I'M BORN . . . SURE thing . . .
Bride's maid . . . the only solution—ISN'T IT AMAZING!

Jamaican dub recording before its time.

Jim, however, found the studio work tedious. *The Soft Parade* took months to make, so Jim wouldn't come around until it was absolutely necessary. Eventually he left the final mixing process up to Rothchild and the rest of us. I thought Jim didn't care enough about recording, but in retrospect, I think he was only interested in the cathartic experience of creating, so he left the technical stuff to others.

✗.

"Our president, Tricky Dicky, is an asshole," I said to Julia while holding the morning papers. "Check out this statement: 'I'm aware of the Vietnam protesters but they will have no effect on my policy making.' Nixon conveniently forgot that because of the protesters, President Johnson quit."

"He was just elected, and already he isn't listening to the people," Julia commented.

"Maybe Richard should have given a call to the LBJ ranch," I quipped.

Julia surprised me by changing the subject. "When are we going to move in together?"

"Gee . . . I haven't given it much thought."

"Well . . . if we don't move in pretty soon, I might move out, interest-wise." I took note of Julia's comment, thinking I sure enjoyed her company and wanted to continue to enjoy it.

After breakfast I drove up Lookout Mountain Drive to Appian Way to look at this little Tudor house hanging over the edge of the hill with the most incredible view of L.A. When Robby and I were roommates on Lookout I used to walk up the street to check the view, the view from which Jim wrote "People Are Strange." There was a leaded glass window under the carport of the Tudor pad, and I would sneak up to it and stare in. I fantasized that if I ever had the money, I'd buy it.

Lo and behold, there was a "for sale" sign in front of the house! I called up the band's new accountant, Bob Greene, and dragged him up there immediately, and we found out the house was forty thousand dollars. A little expensive for me at the time, considering that Robby and I had been paying one hundred fifty dollars a month for a two-bedroom house in the canyon, but I didn't want to mess around bartering and risk losing it. Or losing Julia. Bob said that if the band's career kept going, I'd be fine. That seemed like a sure bet.

But what about Jim? UUUUUhhhhh. I decided to take the risk anyway.

A couple days later, I took Julia up to see the house and said, "You wanted to live somewhere together? . . . Here we are!"

She beamed.

Thinking back on those days, Jim, I wonder why I was such a control freak. It was nice to have a peer like Siddons manage us, but I was worried that he would have less control over you. Why did I torture myself into thinking anyone could control you? You were twenty-six years old, old enough to take care of yourself, but being in the same band, your fuckups reflected on me. Every time you got busted, the press would say "Jim Morrison of the rock band the Doors," and my family and friends would all give me funny looks and steal glances at me.

I was relieved when we got permission to have the limousines driven out to the bottom of the steps of the planes. It furthered our isolation from the public (and the real world), but avoided any possibility of a scene from you in a public place. Remember the time in the Minneapolis/St. Paul airport when you were asked for an autograph?

"Could you make it to Jill?" the fan said, pointing to his very shy girlfriend hiding behind him.

"You'd eat your own shit, wouldn't you!" you blurted out.

I checked out that sweet, vulnerable seventeen-year-old girl, and I felt outraged. The boyfriend's unintimidated response to you, Jim, pleased me as I headed to the newsstand for cover: "That's okay, man, whatever you gotta do to get through."

In retrospect, I can rationalize that you were again testing people's boundaries, or challenging their blind worship of you. But it felt like you were just plain rude.

You were beginning to hate your public image, which in a later interview you admitted to consciously and unconsciously creating. One of the lines in your "Celebration of the Lizard" marked the turning point, when you started to buy your own press image and lose your sense of humor about taking public admiration too seriously:

I AM THE LIZARD KING . . . I CAN DO ANYTHING!

207

Those lines certainly are the antithesis of what John Lennon wrote when he had a transition in his life: "I was the walrus, now I'm John."

Was it a case of you living out your myth, or of the myth turning on you? Buying that lizard skin suit might have been a clue. Our concerts had evolved into rituallike performances with you as the medicine man leading us all through the ceremony, but when asked in an interview if you were a shaman, you replied, "The shaman is not really interested in defining his role in society, he's just interested in pursuing his own fantasies." You went on to say that if one becomes too self-conscious of a function, then it might ruin one's inner trip.

It's too bad you didn't take your own advice. The audiences began to change with our growing notoriety, and instead of a few thousand people coming to surrender to the trancelike music, we had ten thousand specta-tors with a "show-me" attitude. You were egging them on, and they were egging you on. It became a vicious circle.

So there you were, the medicine man whose power should be secret, put up on a pedestal, envied for your fame and fortune (remember, in America this is God), when, in fact, you were becoming one of the more fucked-up people around.

The crowds swelled to twenty thousand people directing their screams and adulation to four guys! It reminded me of Hitler. You must have had the same thoughts when you improvised those new lyrics in the middle of "When the Music's Over" in Chicago:

Adolf Hitler is alive and well!
[audience squirms and starts booing and hissing]

I slept with her last night!
[audience cheers]

You favor life, she favors death . . .

And I'm on the fence and my balls hurt!
[BIG cheer from audience]

What a performer! Antagonizing us all and then releasing the hostility with a joke. It was ironic that while our mere presence onstage drove everyone nuts, from the inside it felt more and more isolated. I know you felt it from that acid trip you told us you had in which you fantasized going to your motel room after a gig and it was full of strange people having a party, and you weren't sure it was your room.

Remember Albert Goldman, the writer who was on tour with us for a while? He wrote a scathing book about Elvis, and now one on John Lennon. Both books dwelled on the self-destruction and missed the soul of the music, but he had some insights on us in an article in Crawdaddy. *I know you dug the paper, but did you see the "Unknown Soldier" article by Michael Horowitz containing this Goldman quote?*

The initial vision was essentially a vision of breakthrough. What they [The Doors] offered you was a coal with blue-black embers on the outside and a ferocious center leaping through. Occasionally they gash the outside of the ember and the real frenzy in the core breaks through.

That was the spirit of their first album. That's what got us all excited. That's what raised all the sunken continents in everybody's mind, you see.

They evangelically converted everyone. Then came the moment of truth. You've got the world on your side. But where are you at, baby? What are you going to do about it? You made the girl love you. Now do you love the girl? Do you want to marry her?

At that moment they really began to go into their problem. The flip side of breakthrough is estrangement. Once you've broken away, it's pretty bleak out there. The rebel cuts himself off. It's Christ in the garden.

Goldman used to be a good writer, huh? So here we were, with thousands of fans in the palm of our hands, going our separate ways. After a gig, Ray and Dorothy would retire, Robby and I would head off to a local club to hear some music, and you would go to the bar. Definitely a letdown after all the concert excitement.

I remember back in early '69, you started saying to Robby and me that

209

our career wasn't happening fast enough. Upon hearing this, Robby and I would glance at each other in disbelief.

"I think Jim had a sense of time, like Rothchild had said about him, that he wasn't going to live all that long and he had to do it in a certain space," Robby once said. Did you have an intuition about this? I wish you had let me in on it. All I knew was that success wasn't what it was cracked up to be. I wished we could go back a few steps somehow. . . .

15

TOUCH ME

The chaos actually began in L.A. a few days before the March '69 Miami concert. Bill Siddons received word that the promoter there had sold eight or nine thousand tickets at fifty cents or a dollar more than the agreed-upon price, so there were bad vibes before we even left town. If the promoters had been honest with us in the first place, the disaster might have been averted. If we had known that they had a history of not paying groups, or not paying them what was promised, maybe we wouldn't have boarded Delta Airlines for Florida. If, if, if.

Years later, Vince Treanor, our roadie, remembered it all like this: "At Miami International, we're met by this guy and this truck, and he takes the equipment. Of course this was the coming-out party, the debut of the new system that I had built for the Doors: the big amps. So the guy's got all his huskies, which turn out to be members of his karate club, and they hustle the equipment into the truck. I'm in ecstasy! Don't have to do anything. They take it all and promise to deliver it later. So Bill gets into it hot and heavy with the promoter and our New York agent, who has flown down to help straighten out the confusion. It seems that they've not only charged more than agreed upon, they've sold one to two thousand more tickets than agreed upon. They can't come to an agreement, so Siddons says, 'Fuck it, we're not going to play!' The promoter says, 'You're going to play.' Bill says, 'You

211

think so?' And the promoter responds with, 'You don't play, you don't get your equipment back.' Bill turns to me and says, 'Where's the equipment?' I point to the truck driving away and say, 'That was the arrangement.' And we had eighteen performances after Miami . . . all up the East Coast. Our first long tour."

⁒

"A message from Jim," Vince shouted out as he walked up the stairs and into our dressing room. "He's in New Orleans, he's missed another plane, and he'll be here around seven." It was five o'clock and we were supposed to go on at eight. Great, I thought. Waiting for Morrison.

"No sound check," I complained.

"Everything will be okay, John," Ray patronized.

Robby, of course, was practicing his guitar. His instrument was portable. No excuse. I wished he would show a little more emotion about things. Without a sound check, the first few numbers would be ragged.

As the audience filed in at seven o'clock and the opening act began their set, my anger toward Jim intensified. His unpredictability was affecting the live performances more and more, and it was making me nuts! Why did he want to ruin everything we'd created? I wondered as I took my usual peek at the crowd. Maybe it was a last, desperate attempt to fight the possession that was taking place. The vulnerable, shy college kid with his back to the audience was long gone. The Lizard King had won and Jim couldn't breathe with his new skin on.

"There's a point beyond which we cannot return. That is the point that must be reached," Kafka once wrote. Morrison had finally reached it. He had become the cockroach. He had metamorphosed into a monster that could still charm.

Until Miami. His charmed life ended in Miami.

What was it that drove Jim to the abyss and then made him jump that night, in his home state? He certainly had been born with some extra intensity or inner demons.

A vast radiant beach in a cool jeweled moon
Couples naked race down by its quiet side
And we laugh like soft, mad children
Smug in the wooly cotton brains of infancy.
The music and voices are all around us.

He was a precocious kid with a military upbringing. Travel City. Rumors of an aggressive mother, which were semiconfirmed when she came to see us play at the Washington Hilton back in '67. Jim hid from her the whole night, but she made herself ever-present, ordering the light crew to do a good job on her son's show.

Maybe Jim felt too much. I'd known he was different when we first became friends and fellow band members, but now we'd made it, and our dreams were coming true and it wasn't enough. For Jim, anyway.

Or maybe Jim was just working on Artaud's Theater of Cruelty:

This is what we want to arrive at: that each performance we take a grave risk. It is not to the mind or the senses of our audience that we address ourselves, but to their whole existence. Theirs and ours. So that ultimately the audience will go to the theatre as they go to the surgeon or the dentist; with a sense of dread but also of necessity. A real theatrical experience shakes the calm of the senses, liberates the compressed unconscious and drives towards a kind of potential revolt, which cannot realize its full value, unless it remains potential and imposes on the assembled crowd a difficult and heroic attitude.

The Dinner Key Auditorium in Miami was sweltering with all those extra people they stuffed in by taking out the seats. It was 8:15 P.M. We were supposed to go on *fifteen* minutes earlier, and there was still no sight of Jim. I was swearing at the fucker in my head.

"Should we go on without him?" Robby said.

"No!" I shouted, trying to stall for time. This weren't no sensitive European crowd. These people sounded rowdy, and I was sure they wanted the Doors with their hometown boy singing up front. I was livid. I busied myself with a drummer's stretching exercise: holding my arms straight out with the butt end of my sticks together in the palms of my hands and twisting my wrists upside-down.

Finally Vince came running up the stairs to the dressing room shouting "He's here!" I turned my back in order not to have eye contact as I felt the presence of someone coming into the room with an entirely different vibration from everyone else. You could literally feel the chaos. It's what the press people called "charisma." I call it psychosis.

I didn't look at Jim because I was afraid of him. I was so mad I wanted to punch him, and at the same time I was scared of saying anything hostile to him. When one gains so much power that others, friends as well as strangers, are afraid to comment on one's excesses, trouble lies ahead.

Robby frowned at Siddons, and Ray, usually the patient one, just mumbled, "Let's do it."

Jim was drunk on his ass.

> It feels like there's an elephant in the room but you don't mention it. You go around it . . . there's elephant shit everywhere . . . but you pretend it's not there.
>
> (Janet Woititz, *Adult Children of Alcoholics*)

"What do you guys want to play?" I said. "Let's start with 'Back Door Man,' okay?"

Everyone nodded, and we headed for the stage. I didn't push for more songs because there wasn't time. I usually couldn't get agreement past three songs anyway.

As we descended the stairs, it felt like entering a sauna. Dante's Inferno. Later I was to find out that there were over thirteen thousand people stuffed into the place meant to hold seven thousand. Vince had hired some locals to stand at the door with metal customer counters. As we stepped onto the stage, Vince warned us that it was poorly constructed. Ray sets the scene: "John, Robby, and I didn't know what Jim would do. We'd follow him into the jaws of the hell-hound itself, if we had to, 'cause this is Jim, this is our man, this is our main man—the poet."

We started "Back Door Man," and Jim sang a few lines and suddenly stopped. We vamped for a while but soon petered out. Then Jim went into a drunken rap:

"You're all a bunch of fuckin' idiots. You let people tell you what you're gonna do. Let people push you around. You love it, don't ya? Maybe you love gettin' your face shoved in shit . . . you're all a bunch of slaves. What are you going to do about it? What are you gonna do?"

I wanted to turn into liquid and dissolve into the spaces between my drums. I had never heard such rage directed at an audience.

He continued. "Hey, I'm not talkin' about revolution. I'm not talkin' about no demonstration. I'm talkin' about havin' some fun. I'm talkin' about dancin'. I'm talkin' about love your neighbor till it hurts. I'm talkin' about grab your friend. I'm talkin' about some love. Love, love, love, love, love, love, love. Grab yer friend . . . and love him. Come oooooaaaaann. Yeaaahhh!"

If only I could have melted down and hid behind my bass drum. I was small enough to fit down there. If I crouched. I didn't move. Jim's inspiration came from seeing Julian and Judith (Malina) Beck's Living Theatre a few nights previously at the University of Southern California. They were a confrontational performance group that got Jim's creative juices flowing again and scared the shit out of me. Jim had gotten tickets for everybody around our office. He really wanted us to see what they were up to. Bill Siddons recalls: "It was theater of confrontations, and Jim was profoundly affected by how real this made people become, because, in fact, it probably best reflected what Jim was really all about. He did things to provoke people because he felt you got

215

the person down to their nitty-gritty, and you dealt with it." At the Living Theatre performance, actors wore a minimal amount of clothing, g-strings and the like, and climbed up the aisles and over the audience shouting "No passports! No borders! Paradise now!" I was intimidated. Jim was elated.

"Hey, what are you all doing here? You want music. No, that's not what you really want. Awright, I want to see some action up here, I wanna see some people up here havin' some fun. I wanna see some dancin'. There are no rules, no limits, no laws, come on! Won't somebody come up here and love my ass. Come on. I'm lonely up here, I need some love . . ."

He bowed his head, and I thought of Pam. Now I felt sad and embarrassed for Jim. He shouldn't show that much vulnerability.

Miami was one of Jim's last attempts to get a new creative spark going and to quell the demons that had had him off center from birth. Demons, like Lenny Bruce's, that told of a sick world in need of a comedian or an exorcist.

Jim had intensified his quest with existential reading, psychedelics, and alcohol. Like his romantic idols Nietzsche and Rimbaud, he had glamorized death. Writing and performing seemed to be the only things that abated Jim's angst.

He who knows how to breathe in the air of my writings is conscious that it is the air of the heights, that it is bracing. A man must be built for it; otherwise it will kill him.

—Friedrich Nietzsche

Of course, neither the band nor the audience knew what Jim was up to. He hadn't told us about taking acid right before the Hollywood Bowl, and he hadn't mentioned how this night he was going to try to inject confrontational theater into our performance.

Musically, the concert was the worst ever. After several attempts at playing our songs, during which someone from the audience threw a gallon of orange fluorescent Day-Glo paint on us,

Robby and I got up from our instruments and started to leave. The left side of the stage made a cracking noise and dropped several inches.

Vince Treanor relives the next few moments: "Somebody jumped up and poured champagne on Jim, so he took his shirt off. He was soaking wet. 'Let's see a little skin, let's get naked,' said he, and the clothes started to come off. I'm referring to the audience."

At this point Jim lured many fans up onto the stage, forming a circle, locking arms and dancing. A policeman and Jim exchanged hats. The cop was wearing Jim's skull and crossbones hat, while Jim donned the cop's cap. Jim reached over and yanked his hat off the cop's head, flinging that hat to the audience. The policeman followed suit, taking his hat off Jim's head and throwing that hat to the audience.

Then Jim hinted that he was going to strip all the way. "You didn't come here for music. You came for something else. Something greater than you've ever seen." Ray yelled at Vince to stop him. Vince continues: "I went out past the hi-hat and John's snare, up behind Jim, and I put my fingers into his belt loops, twisting them, so he couldn't unbuckle or unsnap them."

I decided to bail. As I jumped off the stage and accidentally landed on the light board, which fell to the ground, a security guard flipped Jim like a black-belt karate expert, head over heels into the audience, thinking he was a fan.

Scared shitless, Robby and I ran up the stairs to get out of the chaos. Jim was now in the middle of the auditorium, leading a snake dance with ten thousand people following him. I looked down from the balcony, and the audience looked like a giant whirlpool with Jim at the center. As I went into the dressing room, Bill came racing out.

"Get him out of there!" I warned. "He could get hurt!"

"That's what I'm going to do!" Bill screamed.

Ten minutes later the Lizard King strolled in with a group of people laughing and talking. He was sober now; a concert being better for a hangover than drinking several cups of coffee!

My anger over the performance was subsiding as Ray and I looked out the window at the crowd driving away. "Do you feel the energy out there?" Ray remarked. I noticed that there was a higher sort of buzzing of conversation as the people drove away.

"They're pretty charged up out there, as if we gave them an energy jolt and they're going to take it out into the streets," Ray continued. Was he rationalizing?

"Yeah, I feel it," I replied, thinking that even though we'd played poorly, it had been theatrical. I looked over at Robby, who was pecking at the spread of food laid out for us. He seemed to have accepted what just went down onstage. There was one thought that I couldn't get out of my mind, though. How long were we going to get away with this? The ledge at the top of our pedestal was getting narrower.

⚡

On the plane from Miami to our Jamaican vacation, Jim told us that he had gotten out of New Orleans late because of a fight with Pam. Making a stab at a romantic vacation, he had rented an old Jamaican plantation house, but now he went there alone instead. It rested high atop a tropical hill, complete with slavery vibes. A few days later Jim showed up at our place. Robby and I and our respective mates, Lynn and Julia, had rented a big house on the water. Jim said his short stay up on the hill had been "spooky." He described sitting in the dining room at the end of a long table, eating, while the help sat in chairs along the walls, waiting to be called on. The bedrooms had lace curtains over the beds to keep the bugs out.

I felt sorry for Jim, alone up there, but I was bugged that he crashed our hideaway. He was drunk on rum, and his presence unnerved me. He knew that my bad vibes were directed toward his self-destruction, but it was clear to both of us that nothing was going to stop him. After a few days Jim left for the States, but not before Bill called and said warrants had been issued for Jim's arrest. He'd been charged with lewd and lascivious behavior, simulating oral copulation, and indecent exposure. I couldn't believe the charges! Yes, Jim had been drunk. But simulating oral copulation? They must have been alluding to Jim getting down on his knees to get a closer look at Robby's fingers as he played guitar. Since he didn't play an instrument, he was enamored with musicians. Later a photograph was used as evidence of this *obscene* act of fellatio on Robby, which was actually Jim honoring Robby's talent. No absence of malice in Miami. They insisted that Jim was giving Robby head.

If he had whipped *it* out, why hadn't they arrested him on the spot, and why had the police been so friendly after the concert?

Vince describes the next few days after the concert. "I went to the concert hall the next day with some helpers to pack up. There was no place you could step where there wasn't clothing. The sweepers who came in put all these clothes in a pile four or five feet high and ten feet around. There were bras, slips, skirts, dresses, blouses, sweaters, underpants, shoes, pants, socks, loafers, and sneakers. How did some kid go to a rock show and go home with no pants?

"We had one week before starting the whole East Coast tour, so I went home to Andover. The Doors had planned to go to the Caribbean. Nobody had made a secret of it. I'm in Andover and the fucking storm breaks. 'Lizard King Exposes Himself!' The long and short of it is: A) The warrant wasn't issued for nine days; B) It was a fugitive warrant—despite public knowledge of their planned vacation, the warrant claimed that Morrison left Miami to avoid prosecution; C) Political? You bet."

⅍

When the warrant was issued, Jim left Jamaica and returned to L.A. Our entire twenty-city tour was canceled. Paul Rothchild describes the scene at our office. "They couldn't get a job. Promoters all over the country were canceling the shows as fast as the Doors could answer the telephone. There was a horrible two weeks where the bottom fell out."

Vince adds: "We were ostracized. We were polluted. We were untouchables, contagious. The effect was that the media and public opinion shut us down."

Why did the world want to believe—so badly—that Jim had exposed himself? If one finds someone else to blame heavily, then one doesn't have to look closely at one's own neuroses. My theory is that some parents got curious about their kids coming home half clothed, called the local politicians, and they decided to use Jim as an example of moral decay. Or it was some right-wing bullshit plot. Fucking politics.

On the other hand, how could something horrendous *not* happen to Jim? In his smug, all-knowing way, Ray said in an interview that we'd been "concerned" about Jim's first bust in New Haven. Concerned? We knew there was an atomic bomb in the band! C'mon. We were like Slim Pickens in *Dr. Strangelove*, straddling the descending warhead—only we were pretending it wasn't happening.

I must have known all along it was going to end like this. I reacted schizophrenically: half of me hated him, like Ishmael hating Ahab, for taking us down; the other half said, "It could be for the better, all for the better." I was glad that he was tearing it all down, because I knew it was defective. As Billy James said under his breath while writing out our first bios for Elektra, "Too much power in Jim's hands could be dangerous." He must have sensed the chaos early.

٪.

Ocho Rios, Jamaica, was incredibly beautiful and romantic, but Julia seemed to be pulling away from me. The beautiful villa Robby and I had rented, with its own small private island, wasn't doing it for my mate. She was going through the motions of making love. No passion. My fantasy of an exotic holiday was crushed, but considering how much shit had hit the fan in Miami, I didn't have the desire to deal with it. More denial. I denied having a crazy person in the band; denied having stress rashes; now I was denying my girlfriend was pulling away. I couldn't face up to the music, so to speak. Keep those rose-colored glasses on. Thanks, Mom. Let the mud settle on the bottom of the glass and just meditate. Thanks, Maharishi.

The last few days in paradise were quiet and dreamlike as we prepared for the reality of life in Los Angeles and possible court appearances in Miami. I had just been through a fucking cyclone, and I wanted only to smoke herb, drink tropical rum, and watch the sunset.

And then, on the way back to L.A., Julia hit me with the news that she was pregnant! Everything was great with us, and now she was pregnant! I didn't want to be a husband yet, let alone a father! I could tell by the look in Julia's eyes that she was hoping I'd say "Let's have it." I couldn't believe it—I was numb.

I had asked now and then if Julia was using any kind of birth control, but in 1969, the assumption was that it was the girl's responsibility, and we had little dialogue on the subject.

⁂

Now we had a major problem. I was loaded with so much shame about sex, being raised a Catholic, I didn't inquire how it happened. Was it an accident? I didn't know. But I knew I was incensed. I didn't want a kid and I could tell she did. Julia didn't actually come out and say she wanted it, but . . . For the next month we went crazy with worry about what to do—abortions were illegal at the time. I was sweating bullets trying to find a doctor to do it. My chiropractor finally came through with a doctor, and Julia agreed.

16

PEOPLE ARE STRANGE

The fallout from the "flasher incident" in Miami was immediate and devastating to the band. The Concert Hall Managers Association had a confidential newsletter that circulated periodically. The next issue warned of the Doors' unprofessionalism and indicted Jim. The result was unequivocal. We were banned everywhere. The end of our live career, at least for a while. Secretly I was happy about it, since it meant we wouldn't have to deal with Jim's excesses. I didn't express this thought to anyone.

Jim was amused by the prospect of a courtroom scene: "There probably will be a big trial. I might even buy a suit. A conservative dark-blue suit. And a tie. Not one of those paisley ties, but a big fat tie, with a great big knot. Maybe I'll keep a diary and publish it in *Esquire*. My impressions of my hanging. We're the band you love to hate. But it's been that way from the beginning. We're universally despised. I kind of relish the whole situation."

Jim's smug anticipation was soon to change. I was not happy about having to go back to Miami to appear on the witness stand, especially after thirty thousand "Teens for Decency" filled the Orange Bowl in Florida two weeks after our concert.

At a Catholic youth group meeting, a guy named Mike Levesque got the idea for the decency rally.

"We were discussing about teenagers and things, and, uh, about

222

how the Doors, you know, had presented their show and everything," Levesque said in a *Rolling Stone* interview.

"The Miami presentation where Morrison is charged with having dropped his pants?" *Rolling Stone's* John Burks inquired.

"Yeah," responded Levesque, "and masturbated."

Thanks, Mike. Guilty until proven innocent?

"So I said, well, why don't we have the Silent Majority being heard instead of the 'loud minority,' the Jim Morrisons and the hippies and the demonstrators."

With the help of high school students, a local radio station, Archbishop Coleman F. Carol, and the Catholic hierarchy of Florida, the Rally for Decency was held on March 23. Original announcements for the rally stressed that "longhairs and weird dressers" would not be allowed in (long hair and weird clothes being the outer manifestation of inner indecency), but this violated regulations governing use of the city-owned stadium, so everyone was allowed.

Jackie Gleason, Anita Bryant, Kate Smith, the Lettermen, the Faculty (a Canadian band), and the Miami Drum and Bugle Corps were the performers.

President Nixon, who was now seeing red all over Southeast Asia, sent a letter of support to Levesque, and meanwhile, a pair of right-wing California politicians warned that rock (along with sex education) was a communist plot designed to eat away the minds of the nation's youth and cause them to revolt.

"The Beatles and their mimics use Pavlovian techniques to provoke neuroses in their listeners," warned Congressman James Utt (R) of Tustin. California State Superintendent of Public Instruction Max Rafferty said he "partly agreed." Which part, Max?

⁊.

Mexico City, June 1969

"The End" is not quite dinner-club Muzak, and watching people eat roast beef in a red velvet lizard lounge while we were onstage seemed surreal. In his black leather pants, Jim looked like he was from another planet. I could even hear the clanking of silverware right in the middle of the Oedipal section, where it was usually pin-drop time.

Father—yes, son—I want to kill you,
Mother, I want to . . .

Those homicidal lines stopped the diners in midchew. Jaws dropped. Mouths full of food gaped open. It must have driven Jim crazy, because he hated people who chewed gum, let alone crunched on dinner.

But Mexico was a place we could play, and a place to get an abortion. So early the next morning, Julia and I caught a cab to the doctor's office. It felt as if we were criminals making an illegal drug deal. The waiting room looked clean enough. The nurse seemed friendly as she invited us into the operating room. *Shit!* There was one of those tables with the stirrups at the end to hold up the patient's legs. Julia must have noticed them, 'cause she started crying. Before we came down to Mexico she'd agreed it was the best thing to do. Her tears were like daggers in my heart. The doctor, who was very nice, escorted me back to the waiting room. I nervously hoped for the best, while feeling like scum.

※

We were back in the cab going through the expensive residential neighborhood where our hotel was located. The doctor said everything had gone fine, but the silence in the car was deafening. It felt like we'd just left a funeral. I guess we had. Relief and depression. I thought we had done the right thing, because there was no way I was going to settle down and raise a family, but . . .

Believing in reincarnation, I rationalized that the soul has a life before conception and chooses its parents; therefore, if an abortion is performed, it's a risk the soul has willingly taken, because it knew of the personalities and circumstances of its chosen parents. Right? It's trying to get back into body form to do some further work . . . and takes a chance on a conception that might not be made in "Heaven." This all sounded great, but was I rationalizing? I felt terrible.

Awake
Shake dreams from your hair
My pretty child, my sweet one.
Choose the day and choose the sign of your day
The day's divinity
First thing you see.

Choose, they croon, the Ancient Ones
The time has come again.
Choose now, they croon,
Beneath the moon
Beside an ancient lake.
Enter again the sweet forest,
Enter the hot dream,
Come with us.
Everything is broken up and dances.

٪.

That night I told everyone that Julia was tired and didn't feel like coming to the show. The next night she came. And said she felt pretty good.

Thank God.

I couldn't stand the upper-class, Vegas-type club we had been suckered into, but the deal we'd made with the Mexican government was four nights in that sleazy hole in exchange for playing one night in the bullring for the masses at a price they could afford—a few pesos. I should have known from the Mexican press that it wasn't going to happen. *El Heraldo* called us "hippies" and "undesirables." We were denied accommodations in several large hotels, and we made sure that our plane didn't stop in Mazatlán on our way down to Mexico City. In Mazatlán, if you were a male and went through the airport, they cut your hair!

Two nights into the club gig we got the message: no concert in the bullring. Too much danger of a riot. Bullshit. Too much danger of our music riling up the peasants.

I began to hate the rich Mexicans who were filling up this club with their shirts unbuttoned to the waist. I couldn't understand what they were saying—not because of the language barrier, but because of the rattling of all the gold chains around their necks. We were constantly offered cocaine, which I put in the same category as heroin. Still do. But back then, just the mention of the word made everybody shiver. Everyone in our entourage partook of the coke except for me—I just fumed over not getting to play for the peasants. I felt helpless. It was city hall time. And Mexican, at that.

%.

A week later Julia and I were back in L.A., and the abortion seemed pretty much in the past. I was playing records when I noticed something odd about the gold album I had just received for *Waiting for the Sun*.

"Hey, this isn't our third album!"

"How can you tell?" Julia inquired.

"The number of songs on the label doesn't match up to the number of songs on the disk! Wait a minute . . . let me see . . . 'Love Street' is about three minutes long, and *there's no way it could fit into this tiny bandwidth!* This song looks like it's under two minutes."

"Can you open it?" Julia asked. Her eyes widened.

"I'll have to break the glass. It's sealed." I grinned at the prospect of smashing the front glass.

Julia nodded her encouragement.

After getting a hammer from the kitchen, I took the gold record outside to the trash cans. I leaned the frame over one of the cans and tapped hard on the glass. It broke and I carefully pulled out the record, making sure there wasn't any broken glass stuck to it. I brought it back inside to the turntable.

"This thing is really flimsy! It isn't a real record . . . some kind of pressing. . . . I wonder if it will play?" I put the needle down on the first cut, and through lots of audio crackling we could hear a large orchestra with someone reciting poetry.

"It's Rod McKuen! It's fucking Rod McKuen!"

"That's funny." Julia laughed. "Why do you think they did it?"

I laughed uproariously, yet at the same time I felt insulted. "I don't believe it. They're too cheap to spend five or six bucks on the real thing. So they just get an old $1.98 Thrifty Drug Store discount bin record and schlock it with fake gold, stick a new label on it and slam it into a frame! God damn."

Another myth shattered.

(Not long after firing our managers, I discovered that it was a smart decision, business-wise. Bill Siddons said we were popular enough that promoters would call us directly, and thus we could now avoid paying 10 percent to booking agents. It also must have been the right thing to do cosmically, because Sal and Ash now managed *Rod McKuen!*)

※

In August 1969, Julia and I flew east to catch Woodstock. Even after Jac Holzman, Bill Graham, and our manager bugged us to play, we turned down the invitation because Jim didn't want to perform outside anymore. Bad acoustics. Of course, no one knew that this weekend in upstate New York was going to define the decade.

Julia and I started driving up from NYC on Saturday morning. We missed Friday night, but most of the bands that night were playing L.A. in the near future, so we didn't mind.

When tents and campers in sleeping bags started appearing at the sides and in the center lane of the parkway, we could tell we were getting close.

"Wait a minute!" I exclaimed to Julia, "We're still seventeen miles from the place! This feels like the San Francisco be-in back in '67. Better. Or at least bigger."

We got to our room at Howard Johnson's, which Chip Monck, our lighting designer, had arranged for us. (Chip had built the stage for this one.) I was relieved to find that we had a reservation in light of the hordes of people. Helicopters were buzzing off all the time, as most of the artists were staying here.

"Have you been to the site?" was the main question going around. "Have you been to the site yet?" The site apparently was the stage and, more important, hundreds of thousands of people in front of it. No one had counted heads yet, but there was excitement in the air.

I ran into Chip at the motel. He said that there was no helicopter space right then so we should hop in one of the station wagons going to "the site."

We spent the next four hours in that station wagon trying to get to the stage five miles away. I felt like an officer in some war, crawling to the major hot spot.

"We might as well get out and walk," Julia said as the traffic came to a dead halt. There was only a mile left to go, so we trudged through a mud-covered country lane with thousands upon thousands of other "veterans."

The local people were out on their porches and lawns, amazed at the invasion. They seemed fairly tolerant, but there were some hassles. Hippies wanting to use bathrooms. Hundreds of hippies. Still, considering the number of people, the vibrations were mellow. Off to the right was a small lake with nude bathers. Yeah! You could hear the music rumbling up ahead.

Just as we got to the stage, a storm broke out and sent us under the scaffolding. We ran into Chip again, and he filled out stage passes while we waited out the rain.

We rode up in the elevator with Richie Havens to the center performing area. An elevator? All right, Chip!

Walking over to the side of the stage, I stole a glimpse of the audience. THIS WAS IT! A sea of faces cresting at the top of a hill about a quarter of a mile away. The biggest gig ever, and the Doors weren't playing! Oh, well. I was there.

I wanted to see the English singer who was up next. He had

recently done a cover record of the Beatles song, "With a Little Help From My Friends." We situated ourselves on top of some amplifier cases on the side of the stage as I was thinking of the rumor that this singer, Joe Cocker, was white. I didn't believe it. Chris Morse introduced him, and out comes this scraggly, tie-dye-shirted limey with bell-bottom jeans.

The Grease Band started the set and once again I heard a voice that didn't seem to match the body. I thought he and Janis should do a duet. The way he stuck his tongue out on the screams reminded me of Van Morrison.

Rolling Stone later voted Cocker best *guitar* player of 1970 for his spastic arm movements.

"God, is he great," Julia remarked as I was thinking that we were almost too close to the audience sitting on those cases on the edge of the stage. Every once in a while I glanced out at the hordes of people, making sure my eyes weren't deceiving me.

Crosby, Stills, and Nash were up next. They sang with just passable harmony compared with the record they had just put out. It was clear that in the studio they had doubled their voices over two or three times. Creedence Clearwater Revival followed, playing down-home farm-boy music.

We caught a green army helicopter back to the motel around 1 A.M. and Joan Baez was aboard. So was Bobby Neuwirth, a legendary sidekick of Bob Dylan. Neuwirth was pretending to throw hand grenades out the open door. I was watching Joan for any reaction, since she had just opened the Institute for Non-Violence. Nothing.

I wolfed down my HoJo's breakfast the next morning, afraid to miss anything at the site.

"Hungry?" Julia remarked.

"We're lucky they have food here!" I said.

"The crowds *are* amazing," Julia replied.

Janis Joplin played that day with her new band, which was okay, but they didn't have the soul Big Brother had had. Several

229

of the musicians were black, but the arrangements were too slick. Rumor was that Hendrix was going on last, but we bailed out around 2 A.M. I was dying to see him again, having gone through culture shock catching the Experience at the Whiskey right after they came over from England. They seemed from another planet, playing incredibly loud and using feedback as an instrument.

We were too tired, though. (As it turned out, Jimi closed the festival with his version of the national anthem around ten the next morning, a version that has since become legendary.)

*

Back in Miami in November 1969, for the trial, we checked into the Carillon Hotel. It was a quintessential Miami Beach hotel, complete with sunbathers holding cardboard reflectors up to their faces to get an overall tan. Suburbia on holiday. It depressed me.

Thinking about the trial, paranoia swept back over me. The thought that the local public would find out where we were staying and hassle the "Dirty Doors," as the *Miami Herald* labeled us, scared me. The local sentiment was summed up by Larry Mahoney, one of the *Herald* journalists who managed to work up the people of Dade County against us: "They'd crucify him [Morrison] if they could."

Meanwhile, the city of Miami tried to stop a three-day music festival starring the Grateful Dead, saying "they're the same type people and play the same type music as the Doors." I took offense to that.

We had lavish lunches between the trial sessions, with Max Fink, Jim's attorney, holding court at the restaurant. Jim seemed sobered by the ordeal. I was sobered by the fifty thousand dollars in attorneys' fees.

Following the prosecution's opening statement, our attorney moved for a mistrial, claiming that prosecutor Terry McWilliams had accused Jim of inciting a riot, though he was not charged with that offense. McWilliams had told the jury that Jim had called for a revolution among the spectators. Judge Murray Goodman, who was originally appointed to fill a vacancy on the court and was up for his first election in the fall, denied the motion.

When it was my turn to testify, Ray and Robby had to leave the courtroom because they were next. I felt as if I were on trial as I stepped up to the witness stand. Authority has always scared me. My voice meekly, instead of indignantly, answered "no" to the question of whether I, too, lived in Beverly Hills. I guess they thought they were onto something with Robby's post office address—rich musicians exploiting vulnerable teenagers and using the F word. Tsk, tsk. I could feel the judge glaring down at me as I thought of how a tour of Robby's messy hippie pad would force them to change their tactics.

A quick glance at Jim and back to the prosecutor. Jim seemed cocky sitting down there behind that table, busily taking notes on his pad. Why was I on the hot seat and not him?

"No, your honor, I did not see Mr. Morrison's organ." Grumblings from some hippies in the back row.

"But you're the drummer, you sit behind Mr. Morrison; you couldn't have seen anything," the prosecutor retorted.

"Well, it's not as if Jim doesn't move around any!" My voice was getting stronger.

"Witness excused."

UUUUhhhhhaaa. That's over with. Ray was up next. He was called in from the hallway and sworn in.

"Do you live in Beverly Hills?"

"No, I don't, your honor," Ray responded sarcastically. (He does now!)

"Did you see Mr. Morrison's organ?"

"No, I didn't, your honor, but I play organ!"

The courtroom audience burst out with a big laugh.

"ORDER! ORDER IN THE COURT!"

⁂

"That was very funny, Ray! Hysterical!" I complimented our "organist" as the two of us walked through the courtroom doors on our way to lunch.

"Just a minute, just a minute," yelled the group of hippies who were sitting in the back row. Oh, no . . . not autographs *now!*

"We know what you guys are doing up there. Lying on the witness stand!"

Ray and I glanced at each other in amazement.

"What are you talking about! I didn't see any . . . exposure!" I retorted.

"Did any of you see *it?*" Ray inquired.

"Morrison took the name of our Lord in vain in front of our women!" yelled what seemed to be their spokesman. Evading the question, he pointed to the two girls lurking behind their group. The confrontation was intense and felt weird. All the guys in this born-again Christian commune had hair down to their waists, and the two women looked as if they were carrying communicable diseases. Scuzzy hippies.

"Did you see Jim expose himself?" Ray continued to prod as we walked out into the hall. Lighten up, Ray, I thought to myself. These people are nuts!

They began following us and nodding their heads up and down in a vertical motion as if to say "yes." Pavlovian wooden puppets being obedient.

"Well, we'll see you later," I said as I motioned to Ray to split. We hurried down the hall and when we got out of ear range, I said with urgency, "What the fuck was that? Looks like acid casualties to me."

"Psychedelic Christians, or something," Ray decided.

"Yeah, psychedelic Christians. They said they saw Jim's cock! I saw him take his shirt off and pull his boxer shorts over his leathers, but that's all . . . and I watch him. You didn't see anything, did you?" Ray shook his head from side to side.

"That's right, you have your head down most of the time . . . Well, I'd *swear* he didn't do it . . . and I just *did! In court!*"

"I think those people had a mass hallucination," Ray concluded.

"God, we attract freaks!"

232

17

THE MORRISON HOTEL

After the first round of trials was over, we were back on Santa Monica Boulevard in our rehearsal room, where we wrote another album's worth of songs. I always got inspired when I thought of going into the studio and polishing new songs into gems. I didn't hear any hits, but it was another group of tightly arranged numbers with Ray's dependable trademark sound and Robby's risky guitar flights into failure and magic. The rehearsals weren't totally free of tension, though.

Jim and Robby got into a fight because Jim wanted to give credit to an old UCLA film school buddy for helping him pen a song.

"Paul Ferrara wrote that melody, Robby . . . the part where I sing 'At first flash of Eden, we raced down to the shore," Jim snapped.

"No, he didn't! That's my melody. I know you originally wrote those lyrics to one of Paul's melodies, but that was an old one. I know my melodies!" When it concerned his songs, Robby seemed to come alive. Jim finally gave in to Robby's insistence. All I could think about was how much fun it was going to be putting some Moog synthesizer on the track and making it "heavy." Heavy metal! I heard it in my head.

We moved ourselves and our equipment the half block to La

Cienega and Elektra Studios to begin the sessions for our fifth album.

Rothchild was right about going for a grittier sound than *Soft Parade*—a blues-based record. I thought twelve to fifteen takes was still too many, though. It was better than *Soft Parade*'s absurd thirty and above, but the energy still seemed to be lower than the versions we'd done a few takes earlier. I worked up a complicated skiffle beat to "Land Ho!"—Do, deda, dum, deda, dume, deda, da, deda—but I got tired doing take after take. Rothchild finally said we had it, and I went in the back to meditate. Next we recorded "The Spy," which was fun for me because I got a chance to show off my jazz brush technique. We tried to create a mood for the song to complement Jim's words. Putting heavy echo on Jim's vocal enhanced his lyrics.

I'm a spy, in the house of love
I know the dreams that you're dreamin' of
I know the word that you long to hear
I know your deepest secret fear

The song, which was later used in Brian DePalma's *Body Double*, showed a shrewd, voyeuristic side of Jim. Someone able to make love to a camera, perhaps. It was becoming easier to see the connection between our personalities and our music. Ray, with his professorial organ riffs; the lone wolf cowboy guitar howls of Robby; and me, blasting angry, coiled drum licks out of dead silence.

One day Rothchild arrived as excited as we had ever seen him. And he was always excited, but a little extra that day.

"I just saw Lonnie Mack, the guitar player, walking down the hall and asked him if he wanted to play bass on a blues since Ray Neapolitan called and is going to be late." We had used bass players on our albums since the second one, to get that punch.

Robby perked up and muttered, "Sounds good."

"What was his hit?" I asked, half impressed.

234

" 'Memphis.' "

"Yeah . . . that was cool!" I agreed.

؉

Half an hour later Lonnie arrived—ever so cool.

"Hey, how ya doin', man." Paul shook his hand and introduced him around.

"Nice to meet ya, man."

"So, what's happening?"

"Yeah, what we got here," Ray said, "is just a bluesy groove with a little turnaround. We call it 'Roadhouse Blues.' "

Lonnie grimaced for a second and took a long drag from his Sherman cigarette. "Well, I don't know man, I'm a guitar player, not a bass player."

"You can do it," Robby encouraged.

"It's just a shuffle," I supported, a little surprised by his humility. Maybe he's impressed by working with us, I mused. Far out.

"Okay, teach me the changes."

Lonnie sat down in front of the paisley baffles that soaked up the sound. A hefty guy with a pencil-thin beard, he had on a wide-brimmed, floppy leather hat that had become his trademark. Lonnie Mack epitomized the blues—not the rural blues, but city blues; he was *bad*.

"I'll sing the lyrics for you," Jim offered meekly. He was unusually shy. We all were, because to us, the guitar player we had asked to sit in with us was a living legend.

Three hours later we had gotten the track.

"Goddamn, Lonnie," I exclaimed. "You laid back as far as possible on the turnarounds, the 'let it roll' sections. You're in the back of the pocket, as far back as you can get."

"Is it okay?"

"It's great. Fantastic!" I countered. One beat is about a mile long, I thought to myself. Military music is on the front of the beat, black music on the back. This track we'd just laid down is *soo* far back it's as if we shifted down into second gear.

"Why don't we take a dinner break soon, and I'll call John

235

Sebastian to come down tonight and overdub some harp," Paul suggested.

"I want to give it a shot," Jim retorted. He had been honking on some of Robby's harps for a couple of years now, but he wasn't making much progress.

"Okay, Jim, go on out there and try it now," Paul responded.

I picked up the phone and called Julia.

"Hey, Robby," I yelled over the sound of Jim recording bad harmonica on "Roadhouse." "Lynn is over at our house . . . you wanna meet her and Julia at the Imperial Gardens for dinner?"

"Yeah," Robby quickly answered. "Hey, Paul, that's on a separate track, isn't it?"

"Of course."

"I can do better than that," Robby continued, referring to Jim's harp playing. In the folk days, Robby played pretty good blues harp and did a fair imitation of Bob Dylan.

"Let's give Sebastian a try," Paul countered.

The Lovin' Spoonful's lead singer came down around 8 P.M. and turned out to be a real friendly guy. He put some funky blues harmonica on "Roadhouse," and it sounded great. Everybody agreed, including Jim. I was relieved.

After Sebastian left, Paul spoke up.

"Is it okay if we give John double or triple scale?"

"Sure." "Definitely." "Yeah." We all responded in unison.

"John said he can't use his real name because of his commitment to Kama Sutra Records," Paul continued a little tentatively.

"But why doesn't he credit Kama Sutra?" Jim asked, still looking a little peeved about losing his chance to play harp.

"Sebastian wants to use the name 'G. Puglese'!" Paul said evasively.

"Ha ha. That's funny." Ray laughed. "Sounds like the name of a butcher in Little Italy."

Years later Rothchild confirmed my suspicions that back then John, like some of the public, was embarrassed by the Doors.

Sebastian didn't want to be associated publicly with the group. The backlash that had started with us changing our precious Doors sound by using an orchestra on our fourth album had escalated with the Miami incident, and it was still in force.

⁊.

He isn't real because he is a poster or a golden record or an idol or a picture to kiss at night under the covers, a doll, he is the ultimate Barbie doll, and Barbie speaks when we pull her string, that's what she's supposed to do, and she only says what we want her to say because you see on the other end of the string is a piece of tape, that's why she is our Barbie doll and that's why he is our Jim Morrison and that's why we want him to sing "Light My Fire" and stop Stop STOP all these other strange sentences that the doll didn't say when we bought her, these new words on the tape, she has no right to new words, just do her thing which is our thing because we own her/him/ the ticket/the poster/the record/the idol.

—Liza Williams, "The Doors at the Forum—
Morrison: The Ultimate Barbie Doll," *(L.A. Free Press)*

⁊.

In later interviews, I would say that we wouldn't have gotten back to our raw core on the fifth and sixth albums if we hadn't gone through experimentation. I wanted to say "fuck you" to our critics, but time has said it for me.

⁊.

Something good actually came from the terrible concert at the University of Michigan, the one where Jim was loaded—knocked-out loaded. On breaks during the *Morrison Hotel* rehearsals, I had encouraged Ray to pick up Robby's guitar and jam on the one blues lick he could play, the one he'd played at the University of Michigan. Jim joined in singing the Maggie M'Gill lyrics he had improvised at the aborted concert.

"I love the way Ray plays that lick, Robby. His Chicago roots show."

Robby smiled and nodded in agreement.

"You could play bottleneck," I suggested as a way for him not to feel left out. He opened his bottleneck guitar case and I picked up Ray's groove with a simple 4/4 snare-drum beat. Jim started throwing out short poems as verses.

Illegitimate son of a rock 'n' roll star
Illegitimate son of a rock 'n' roll star
Mom met Dad in the back of a rock 'n' roll car
I'm an old blues man
And I think you understand
Been singin' the blues
Ever since the world began

There is no greater vehicle for showing your pain than singing the blues. Through Jim's cool white trash imagery, he could *be* Howlin' Wolf.

Miss Maggie M'Gill, she lived on a hill;
Her daddy got drunk, and left her no will,
So she went down, down to "Tangie Town"
People down there, really like to get it on

In the studio, we got a real rural Southern country sound on the guitars, added fat-back drums, Lonnie Mack on bass, and heated it with a low to medium groove. Jim took us on down to "Tangie Town" with the old bluesman he had been looking like the last six months, with his full beard and a few extra pounds.

Now, if you're sad and you're—feelin' blue
Go out and buy a brand-new—pair of shoes,
And you go down, down to "Tangie Town."
The people down there, really like to—get it on,
Get it on . . .

Jim was literally going down, and I knew it. I didn't want him to be the old bluesman. Like his audience, I wanted him to stay the young prince.

⁀

He looks like a young Medici, his head back, that throat, that throat of exquisite muscles holding the face which hardly rises in prominence from the column of throat before it is swallowed in the cherubic curls, his heritage the wealth of the spoilers of the Orient.

— "The Doors at the Forum" (Liza Williams)

⁀

I loved his vocals, though. You could feel them, because he had packed seventy years of living into twenty-six. "We don't have long to go—no."

Well, I woke up this morning and got myself a beer
The future's uncertain and the end is always near.

⁀

In May of 1970, I came home early from the studio and I remember sitting in bed with Julia watching the eleven o'clock news. California governor Ronald Reagan had begun denouncing campus militants. He even called a press conference to exclaim chillingly "If it takes a bloodbath, let's get it over with. No more appeasements." Hundreds of thousands of young people attended prayer meetings, vigils, strikes, clashes, and hassles, culminating in four students being killed at Kent State, Ohio, by the National Guard. The total number of campuses closed nationally grew to 410 until Reagan, pleading for a cooling-off period, simply shut down all the colleges and universities in the California state system.

Looked like the people in power weren't ready for the "Age of Aquarius." I guess they missed the play, as well as the "harmony and understanding."

⁀

239

Bill Siddons talked us into doing the Isle of Wight festival in the fall of '70. We flew to London late Friday and played Saturday night, and then Jim had to appear at 9 A.M. in court in Florida, County of Dade, on Monday morning.

I was all for doing the festival even though it was expensive to fly over for one gig. It was clear that we wouldn't be playing live in the States for a long time, and we had equal billing with the Who. Jim, by his performance, was clearly against it. But he didn't say anything. Maybe he got depressed about his dilemma on the way over. Too bad nobody talked to each other in our organization.

Julia didn't want to come to England, so she stayed home and watched the house. We had been there almost a year now. I brought up the idea that it might be fun to be parents, but Julia didn't agree. She wasn't ready to make our relationship legal either. It seemed like the next step. Maybe I was being influenced by my parents too much. They had celebrated their thirtieth wedding anniversary, and I felt pressure to copy them as role models. They didn't say so, but I could feel that they were embarrassed that Julia and I were "living in sin." I liked that it challenged the old ways.

I was trying to spice up my relationship with Julia by having a kid. We weren't talking that much. I mean, we were talking, but not connecting on a deep level. I was out there on the road being the breadwinner, and she was back in L.A. being the housewife.

Our arguments were about trivial things, and we couldn't seem to get beneath them. Julia would push my buttons after a certain point, and my response would be to put the lid on my emotions until I couldn't stand it. Finally I would slam a closet door over and over real hard. Rage. It was a substitute for hitting her. Then Julia would comment that I was acting like Jim, which enraged me more.

✗

The band gets to this quaint little island off the coast of England that is still living in the thirties and is host to Europe's most famous rock music festival. The locals stiff-upper-lip it, tolerating the invading longhairs.

At the site, everyone is real friendly backstage except Jim. He is extremely introverted. Roger Daltrey, lead singer of the Who, offers Robby and me a hit of his peppermint schnapps after being coldly turned down—surprisingly—by Jim. Pete Townsend, the Who's mentor, seems like a friendly chap, and Donovan is here with his colorfully decorated tinker (gypsy) wagon. People are trying to have a communal, free-spirited time, but there is something ugly in the air.

Along one side of the grounds, the fans outside start pulling the fence down, yelling that the festival should be free. The promoters respond with guard dogs, which inspire the fans to rip the entire fence down.

Joni Mitchell goes onstage. Stopping in the middle of one of her songs, she jolts out of her mellow folk singer mode to criticize the audience for being so rowdy.

The promoter tells our manager that he doesn't know if he can pay us now that the gate has been crashed. He seems to be having a nervous breakdown and on the verge of tears. This feels like the last pop festival.

The time comes for our set, and I can tell Jim isn't going to give much. He is so quiet. And down.

"Ladies and gentlemen, I know this next group is one of the main reasons you came across the channel to the Isle of Wight Festival . . . the Doors!"

Jim isn't moving an inch and the whole set is almost over. His body language is matched by his emotional commitment to the singing—nothing. No energy.

The Who comes on next and blows us off the stage. They do the entire opera *Tommy*. I stand in the wings and scrutinize every beat that Keith Moon plays—"I'm your uncle Ernie and I welcome you to Tommy's Holiday Camp."

He is terrific. So fluid. It is as if his drum set is an entire orchestra and he is the conductor. A little fortissimo from the tom-toms, pianissimo from the cymbals.

Then the man with the guard dogs comes up on the side of the stage and I get the fuck out of the way. What a drag. The end of flower power.

⁂

Julia and I seemed to be getting closer again. I had asked her to tie the knot a few months before, and now she said she wanted to go ahead.

Our relationship now seemed easy. She certainly didn't mind the material side of my success, shopping with Robby's girlfriend, Lynn—which worried me a little. But finally Julia was willing to commit to the big commitment. I felt that every once in a while my Scottish purse strings needed to be pulled, and now I was inspired. I sprang for the ultimate hippie wedding.

⁂

October 1970

On a warm Saturday morning, after a three-month wait for a reservation, Julia and I exchanged rings on the lawn of the self-realization lake shrine in the Pacific Palisades. With the Gandhi Memorial behind us and a manmade lake complete with waterfalls and swans in front of us, a Unitarian minister recited lines from Kahlil Gibran's *The Prophet* as part of our vows.

Robby and Lynn were our best man and bridesmaid, and the pressure would soon be on for them to follow suit. Julia and I both wore white. We joked about how we looked like virgins. Several hundred folk showed up including Jimbo, our notorious lead singer.

I was pleased at that, even though he brought his newest entourage of drinking buddies. Babe Hill, Paul Ferrara, and Frank Lisciandro truly loved Jim, but they had him on a pedestal. Pam was fighting back by having her own affairs, which only intensified the growing split between them. Not that Jim was any saint. He had always been an example for me of pushing things too far with drugs, and now his relationship with Pam was a warning. It seemed they didn't want to work at making it work. Their constant fights had affected Jim's performances, and his lack of stability made me yearn for it.

My brother, Jim, whom I'd picked up a year before at Camarillo, seemed to be back to normal and was living in an apartment in Westwood. It made me feel good to have him at the wedding.

The reception was at a nearby hotel, the Santa Ynes Inn. The food was laid out around the pool, and the hotel piano player sang while everyone got soused. Julia's crazy Santa Barbara friend Lorenzo took off his clothes and jumped in the pool. It upset me. I had gone to some trouble to "produce" the perfect wedding as if it were a concert. I was nervous that something might ruin it. I looked over at my mother, hoping to God she wasn't offended, but she was off in a corner, jabbering away to anyone who would listen. Robby's mother, Marilyn, on the other hand, was on her tiptoes, trying to get a glimpse of the action.

After the Lorenzo incident, Julia and I decided it was time to make our exit, so we slipped out the front door. I heard later that Jim sang blues numbers to the older generation all night long. He was well received and didn't get too drunk.

Just before we left, Ray pleased me by asking if he and Dorothy could come up and watch us open gifts. An hour later they came by our Appian Way hilltop house.

"Perfect wedding, John," Ray said, shaking my hand. Dorothy hugged and kissed Julia. We opened the usual crockery from relatives and a beautiful Japanese print from Ray and Dorothy. Julia and I didn't consummate our marriage that night. After all, we had been living together for a couple of years. I rationalized that making love wasn't paramount. The price we paid for living together before marriage was a damper on our romance. Would marriage bring it back? I had purchased a water bed, thinking that nautical lovemaking would heat up our carnal contact. Unfortunately, every time one of us moved, there was a lot of slurping and rocking. Dramamine time.

⁊

On one of Ray's drives around obscure parts of L.A., he found a dingy hotel downtown called Morrison Hotel. Henry Diltz, our new photographer, said there was another great location near the hotel, a funky bar called the Hard Rock Café. We went down to these two locations to do a photo session for the cover of our fifth album. Unfortunately, the manager of the hotel wouldn't give us permission to shoot in the lobby. Money didn't swear this time, it didn't even talk. We went across the street and Henry suggested we quickly run into the lobby, look out the window, and he would shoot us from across the street with his telephoto lens. We did just that, and before the manager caught on and started walking over to throw us out, we had our shot.

On to the Hard Rock. We ordered beers, and the bartender said it was okay to shoot all the pictures we wanted as long as we kept ordering drinks.

The reviews of *Morrison Hotel* were very good. Bruce Harris of *Jazz & Pop* wrote, "A return to the tight fury of early Doors music, abounding with funk and guts and earth-energy. 'Morrison Hotel' is one of the major musical events of Rock 70." I felt that there were a couple of mediocre cuts on the record, though. "Queen of the Highway" had some nice autobiographical lyrics from Jim, but the track never settled into a good groove. It was the first time I ever thought we let Jim down in supporting his words. Not having enough material to fill out the album, like in the old days, we took a listen to "Indian Summer," the first song we ever recorded. It had been kept in the can because of a couple of bad notes from Robby and Jim, but among the *Morrison Hotel* songs, it felt like a breath of fresh air. Raga tuning with California lyrics.

"Peace Frog" was frustrating. Robby had this great rhythm guitar lick, but Jim wasn't coming up with anything lyrically to complement it. One day, when he was around the corner at the Palms

Bar with Frank and Babe, we went ahead and recorded an instrumental based on Robby's lick. The track smoked! Jim finally came in to do some vocals, and Rothchild asked him to bring his poetry notebooks the next day.

The following afternoon Paul and Jim performed a minor miracle. They superimposed two lyric poems, two lines of thought, on top of each other. One was a metaphor for Jim's life; the other, a metaphor for Pam.

There's blood in the streets
it's up to my ankles

Blood in the streets   *She came*
it's up to my knee

Blood in the streets   *She came*
the town of Chicago

Blood on the rise,   *She came*
it's following me

                     Just about the break of day

                     She came and then she drove
                          away
                     sunlight in her hair

Blood on the streets   *She came*
runs a river of sadness

Blood in the streets   *She came*
it's up to my thigh

The river runs red down   *She came*
the legs of the city

The women are cryin'   *She came*
and rivers a weepin'

                     She came in to town and then
                          she
                     drove away, sunlight in her hair

245

Blood in the streets
the town of New Haven

Blood stains the roofs
and the palm trees of Venice

Blood in my love
in the terrible summer;

Bloody red sun of fantastic
    L.A.

Blood screams the brain
that chop off the fingers

Blood will be born
in the birth of a nation

Blood is the rose of mysterious
    union

There's blood in the streets
it's up to my ankles

Blood in the streets
it's up to my knee

Blood in the streets
the town of Chicago

Blood on the rise,
it's following me

٪

Robby, Ray, and I, and our respective mates were enjoying our material success, while you continued to go down in spirit. Or, as you wrote in "Peace Frog," the blood continued to rise. A "spirit" was taking over your body, wasn't it? Alcohol. I went back to the strip club that was next door to our office a few years ago, before it closed, and the bartender told me that he'd never seen anyone drink as much as you, Jim. And he had been tending bar for ten years. You were a certified alcoholic. You had a patho-

246

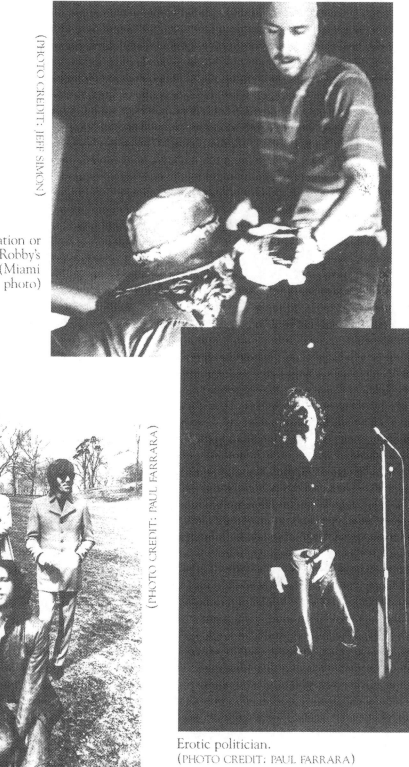

Oral copulation or
admiring Robby's
technique? (Miami
trial photo)

Erotic politician.

Can he breathe with his
new lizard-skin suit on?

A supper club, Mexico City.
(PHOTO CREDIT: JERRY HOPKINS)

The real Hard Rock Cafe.
(PHOTO CREDIT: HENRY DILTZ)

Me and my brother, Jim.
(PHOTO CREDIT: JOHN DENSMORE COLLECTION)

"I said, warden, won't you
break your lock and key?"
(PHOTO CREDIT: DOORS PHOTOS)

The end is always near.
(PHOTO CREDIT: ANDREW KENT)

"Skins."
(PHOTO CREDIT: BASIA)

The stories they could tell.
(PHOTO CREDIT: BOBBY KLEIN)

Dinner at The
New Grove, 1968.
(PHOTO CREDIT:
ROLLING STONE)

Jim and Pam in Paris, 1971.
(PHOTO CREDIT: HERVE MULLER)

"He's finally achieved peace."
(PHOTO CREDIT: PATRICIA KENNELY)

Moving forward.
(PHOTO CREDIT: LESLIE NEALE)

logical disease over which you no longer had control. I didn't know that back then.

Today there are a lot of clinics where people are detoxing. I don't think blaming it all on the sixties is right, though. We need detoxing from our high-pressured society. That's why I use drugs and alcohol moderately. Moderately.

Julia was being the dutiful housewife, making meals, and I was bringing home the bacon. We had a nice, warm home situation, and I know you and Pam had the same thing going. You reading and her working on clothes designing. When you were straight. With Julia's gregarious personality and love of animals, we adopted six cats. And you got six-packs. And cognac. That's when you would leave Pam and go stay at the Alta-Cienega Motel. The sleazy side of life attracts, doesn't it?

I was still amazed at how blue and dilated your eyes were. Remember when I kidded you that with all the acid maybe they were stuck! I was hoping you would reflect on the old psychedelic days and get out of this drinking. You responded with a half smile. Your sense of humor was on the wane.

Although, not totally. Pam told me that she asked you if you really exposed yourself in Miami, and she said you retreated into your little-boy look and nodded yes. She said she asked you why and you replied, "Honey, I just wanted to see how it looked in the spotlight." Pretty funny, Jimbo.

※

Jim went back to Miami on October 30 and was sentenced. The three-man, three-woman jury found Jim guilty of vulgar and indecent exposure and vulgar and indecent language. They decided Morrison was *not* guilty of gross lewdness and lascivious behavior (the only felony charges), or drunkenness. The jury got the whole thing backward. Jim was drunk as a skunk, but he did not pull his dick out. So much for justice.

Judge Murray Goodman knocked down Jim's sentence from eight to six months with a five-hundred-dollar fine. Where did this compassion come from all of a sudden? Maybe Goodman had

247

a premonition that he himself would be up for a bribery charge in a few years.

After exploiting the Miami exposure story at the start of the trial, national TV dropped the story before the sentencing, leaving the boring minor details to the local stations. It wasn't glamorous that the jury dropped most of the charges. To the press, Jim said that although legal costs had amounted to a "fortune," we would appeal the jury's decision. He also said he'd like to do a tour in someplace like Australia for a change. Small-town parish church halls rather than big auditoriums.

18

L.A. WOMAN

Los Angeles, 1981

I went to see *What Happened to Kerouac?*, a documentary on the legendary beat writer who inspired so many musicians, including our lead singer. During intermission, I decide to run across the street from "EZTV" video theater and take a look at the Doors' old office and rehearsal room. I cross the center divider on Santa Monica Boulevard with the obsolete railroad tracks and dart across the rest of the street. As I walk toward La Cienega, the old beige building comes into view. It's now a dump. Looks like it might be torn down soon. The outside stairs are broken off at the bottom, so I jump up to the fourth step, which is fairly stable. At the halfway platform I look over at the Fat Burger greasy spoon, which used to be the Topless Extension, a strip club where we took interviewers. It unnerved them having titties shake over their heads while we answered their questions.

Arriving at the top of the stairs, I hear some voices inside, where our office used to be. Must be bums crashing there. I carefully speak through the window.

"Hey, what's going on?"

"Nothin' . . . we live here," says a young street person in his mid-twenties. His voice is sloshy with rotgut wine.

"I heard the Doors used to practice in this building." I ask him, "Is that true?"

I don't usually prod people for their reactions to the band, but I'm feeling the power of pop culture after listening to Ginsberg, McClure, and others talk about Kerouac. I wonder if our myth has filtered down to the street.

"Yeah, the Doors," one of them says with awe in his voice.

The other one adds, "So what . . . the present owner is about to kick us out."

"Too bad," I respond. I slip them a twenty and say, "Well, good luck to you guys." Jumping down the last half flight of stairs, I think about how depressing Reaganomics is for street people. Where is the trickle-down for them? There are as many young homeless people now as there are old.

I wander over to the sliding glass doors downstairs and look into what used to be our rehearsal room. There is the doorway leading to the bathroom where Jim did his vocals. Bathroom echo! I turn around and glance at Monaco Liquors across the street. Memories of the *L.A. Woman* sessions back in the fall of 1970 flood in. . . .

Well, I just got into town about an hour ago
Took a look around, see which way the wind blows
Where the little girls in their Hollywood bungalows
Are you a lucky little lady in the city of light?
Or just another lost angel, city at night,
City at night, L.A. Woman, L.A. Woman

It felt good to be back at Sunset Sound, where we'd recorded our first two albums, but that was the only thing that felt good. We had been recording new songs for Paul Rothchild and there was a tense silence in the air, the same silence we encountered when Paul dropped in on our rehearsals. True, we didn't have enough songs, but Paul had a "show-me" attitude. He realized it would be another "pulling teeth" album, like *Waiting for the Sun*, which nearly killed all of us. We hadn't played the songs very well, and they weren't rehearsed enough, but I knew we had some good ones, even after all we'd been through. They were more blues-based, and the blues takes you to the root of your angst. As difficult as everything had become, when we got together to write new songs, all our problems outside of the music seemed to slip away. Rehearsing was the time when Jim was consistently straight and his demise faded into the background for the moment. Jim still respected the incubation state of creating new ideas.

Hey! There's something comin',
And there's nothin' you can do about it

"Watch this, Bruce. Did you ever see anyone walk away from a quarter of a million dollars!" Rothchild said to Botnick, the engineer, as he headed from the control room out into the recording room.

"What the hell are you talkin' about?" Botnick asked.

"I'm not into it anymore, guys. That one song about the killer on the road sounds like cocktail jazz to me. You should produce yourselves. You'll probably do fine."

Paul, who was usually articulate, was speaking meekly. He was taking big pauses between sentences. You could sense the wheels turning inside his head, as if he were thinking, No human being alive could pull another album out of these guys. They have to come together themselves.

Looking back, I don't think Paul had the enormous amount of energy it now took to pull—which is what he would have to do—the vocals out of Jim. The "fifth Door" was resigning. We were bummed.

L.A. Woman Sunday afternoon, L.A. Woman Sunday afternoon,
L.A. Woman Sunday afternoon, drive thru your suburbs
Into your blues, into your blues,
Into your blue, blue, blues, into your blues

That night we were sitting in the recording studio after Rothchild had left, and Botnick could sense the gloom.

"What are we going to do, Bruce?" Ray said.

"I'll produce you guys. We could coproduce. We could rent Wally Heider's mobile equipment and record in your rehearsal room, where you'd be real comfortable. Kind of like the old days."

He knew simplifying our recording process was the thing to do, and his suggestion sounded good. Less pressure. I started worrying, though, about who was going to control Jim from the control room if he got drunk. Bruce was fairly laid back about giving directions to other people. Could he direct Jim? Firing our managers had been a good move, and we gained more control, but we had to take on more of the burden of babysitting Jim.

We all agreed to go with Bruce's idea. I went home praying that it would work.

Botnick had all the equipment brought over to 8512 Santa Monica Boulevard, and we put the recording board upstairs in Bill Siddons's office. Bill: "In fact, the console was on my desk. I would work during the day, they would come in at night, move furniture, tack blankets to the walls, and use my office as the control room." We rigged a talk-back downstairs, but you couldn't see who you were talking to—no window. If you were doing overdubs it was especially eerie because you sat downstairs all alone talking to a speaker box. Everybody else was upstairs in the control room. Bruce's gentle nature created an easy atmosphere for recording, though.

"RAT, TAT, TAT, TAT," went my snare on the first day, as I hit single strokes with my sticks. After five or ten minutes, Bruce interrupted over the headphones, "Okay, let's move on to the bass drum."

"BOOM, BOOM, BOOM," went the big drum, responding to my foot pedal. Slow, single, monotonous strokes so Bruce could add treble, mid or bass to the sound. Another ten minutes passed.

"Now the tom-toms."

"I've loosely tuned the toms to the I, IV, V chords because we're going to work on 'Been Down So Long,' which is a blues. I didn't learn to tune the tympani in the high school orchestra for nothing!"

"Great. They sound good."

This is going quite fast, I thought.

"DUM, DOM, DUMP! DUM, DOM, DUMP!"

Forty-five minutes after starting, Bruce called me into the control room to hear the drum sounds.

"Sounds pretty good."

"I'm happy," Bruce countered.

"You mean that's it! We're done with the drum sound?"

"You like it, don't you?"

"Yeah, I love it, it's my sound, my jazz-oriented sound. So you mean we don't have to hack away at it for hours like we used to?" I was astounded.

"You guys know how to make records now, and I respect that."

"Great, Bruce, great."

٪

Bruce's brainstorm was to let us all assume more responsibility, including Jim, and it worked. It turned out that we didn't need to control Jim in the studio. He knew the reins were slackening, and he responded by taking more responsibility. Bruce never pushed us beyond a couple of takes; the vocals didn't have to be pulled out of Jim because most of them were live. We couldn't have gotten to this place without doing several albums with Rothchild. In an interview at the time, Jim exuded the confidence that Bruce allowed us to have: "We record right in our room. It's not that we don't like the Elektra studios, but we felt that we do a lot better when we're rehearsing. This will be the first record that we're actually doing without a producer. We're using the same engineer that we've used, Bruce Botnick. He will probably coproduce with the Doors. In the past, the producer . . . it's not that he was a bad influence or anything, but this will be a lot different without that fifth person there. So anyway we'll be by ourselves for better or worse."

We went for feeling. Fuck the mistakes.

It worked like a charm.

One afternoon I asked Ray, "Do you know that opening on 'So What' by Miles's *Live at Carnegie Hall*? Ba-de-da-do-da-de-da-de-damp . . . BLAAA-SCREECH-DUMP? There's that big, obvious bad note in the trumpet section?"

"Yeah."

"You know what Miles said about it? He said it doesn't matter because the *feeling*'s there. Screw the errors. I'd like to think we're doin' the same thing with *L.A. Woman*."

"I know what you mean, man," Ray confirmed. "That second take of 'Riders on the Storm' sounded good to me!"

"Exactly . . . I'll tell Bruce."

⅄

Michelangelo Antonioni, the famous Italian filmmaker, came to hear us during the *L.A. Woman* sessions. He was looking for music for *Zabriskie Point*, a story about America set in the sixties.

It was a terrible movie, as it turned out. But at the time, all we could think of was *Blow-Up*, his first English-language film, which we greatly admired. Antonioni had used the Yardbirds' music, which was a very hip thing to do. So Jim wrote some lyrics with the movie in mind, and we practiced our asses off before his arrival. He was standoffish. Possibly it was the language barrier; possibly he just didn't like our music.

Jim attempted to explain the title of "L'America," the song we thought would be good for his movie. "The apostrophe after *L* is short for Latin America . . . or Central America . . . or Mexico, for that matter. Anywhere south of the border."

During his monologue, I remember thinking how brilliant Jim was. God, I loved his mind. How did he continually come up with such original stuff? He still seemed creative and vibrant back then, even though he was on a downward spiral with his drinking.

Robby started the song for Antonioni, bending his guitar note very slowly as we began the tune. He was playing too loud, especially for someone not used to rock 'n' roll. Robby's playing was inconsistent. He took risks. Ray's sound was very dependable. That's why Robby was over the top with brilliant original licks, or occasionally not adjusting his level (volume) to the ensemble sound. At this moment I wanted to knock on his forehead and shout, "Hello!" I knew that five minutes later his pure musicianship and gentle nature would endear him to me all over again. But now my instinct told me that when Ray and I came in with our parts, the instruments would drown out Jim's vocal. Couldn't stop once we had started. Too unprofessional. I cringed as I sensed us losing Antonioni's attention. He looked more uncomfortable than when he'd first come in.

I took a trip down to L'America
To trade some beads for a pint of
Gold

The director certainly wasn't going to get our cryptic references to money (beads) and grass (gold—as in Acapulco). Jim's voice was in great form, but this song had dark, dissonant chords to it that would overshadow the singing. Robby sounded like cold steel on this one.

Oh well, our only hope now was to scare the shit out of Antonioni.

L'America, L'America, L'America

We built to the instrumental climax and . . . BAM! Yeah. That'll get the wax out of those Italian ears. He looked real confused. I was sure he was going to pass. The song was too much for him. It summarized his entire movie. No need to shoot the film!

He said good-bye, and we went back to recording our "cocktail jazz" song. I loved how it was evolving into a western ballad with a jazz feel to it. "Ghost Riders in the Sky" meets Vince Guaraldi!

Sixteen track had been invented, and in fact we'd used it on the album before, but Botnick suggested that we record *L.A. Woman* on portable eight-track machines. Bill Siddons reflects on the sessions for our last album: "*L.A. Woman* was a very visceral record. They intentionally made it closer to the bone. They had been high-teched out with *The Soft Parade* and 'take 35.'" It seemed crazy going backward in technology, but it forced us to put only genuinely great material on that tape. Our last record turned out like our first album: raw and simple. It was as if we had come full circle. Once again we were a garage band, which is where rock 'n' roll started. We even dropped the individual writer credits, just like on our first three albums: all songs written by the Doors.

In an interview to promote *L.A. Woman*, Jim said: "The first album we did in about ten days, and then each succeeding record took longer and longer until the last one *(Morrison Hotel)*, which took nine months. This one, we went in and got a song a day. It was amazing. Partly because we went back to the original instrumentation; just the four of us and a bass player."

Not that Jim wasn't still in trouble. On Sundays, when we were off, he would go to bars, get drunk, and crash his car. It was as if something started real early in Jim, got channeled into creativity temporarily, and was going to get him one way or another.

I began thinking that maybe some gigs would help him, but our rep was still sour. Jim wanted to play live again too: "It's just political football. They let us sign up for a concert, and then about two days before we show up, the mayor or sheriff, whoever wants to get his name in the paper, will try and cancel the show and get everybody outraged. Parents that wouldn't even know who we were, all of a sudden they hear that Sheriff Peabody says the Doors shouldn't be allowed to perform."

At least they couldn't ban our records. On a recording break one afternoon, Jim and Robby went across the street to Monaco Liquors to get some beers for themselves and cigarettes and apple juice for Ray and me.

"Do you know what 'Hyacinth House' means, Ray?" I asked while Jim was gone.

"Nope, but I see the bathroom is clear."

"Yeah, that's a funny line. It's almost pathetic in its paranoia. I love the feel, though. Folk rock is fun for me to play on drums . . . as a change of pace. It's loping and technically easy."

What are they doing in the Hyacinth House?
To please the lions this day?
I need a brand new friend who doesn't bother me.
I need someone who, who doesn't need me.
I see the bathroom is clear, I think somebody's near.
I'm sure that someone is following me, oh yeah.
Why did you throw the Jack of Hearts away?
It was the only card in the deck that I had left to play.
And I'll say it again, I need a brand new friend.

Edith Hamilton's book on Greek mythology illuminated the Hyacinth myth for me. She helped me realize that Jim's song, "Hyacinth House," was possibly the saddest one he ever wrote. Hamilton wrote:

Another flower that came into being through the death of a beautiful youth was the hyacinth.

The festival of Hyacinths
That lasts throughout the tranquil night.
In a contest with Apollo
He was slain.
Discus throwing they competed,
And the god's swift cast
Sped beyond the goal he aimed at

and struck Hyacinthus full in the forehead a terrible wound. He had been Apollo's dearest companion. There was no rivalry between them when they tried which could throw the discus the farthest; they were only playing a game. The god was horror-struck to see the blood gush forth and the lad, deathly pale fall to the ground. He turned as pale himself as he caught him in his arms and tried to stanch the wound. But it was too late. While he held him the boy's head fell back as a flower does when its stem is broken. He was dead and Apollo kneeling beside him wept for him, dying so young, so beautiful. He had killed him, although through no fault of his, and he cried, "Oh, if I could give my life for yours or die for you . . ." Even as he spoke, the bloodstained grass turned green again and there bloomed forth the wondrous flower that would make the lad's name known forever.

This passage is a very synchronistic metaphor for our band. Ray, who had "discovered" Jim, always refers to himself as an Apollonian. There was no rivalry between us when we wrote and arranged our songs; hence, we split the publishing. Jim forgot that life is a game, and self-destructed at a young age, although not so beautiful anymore. The Doors had killed him, through no fault of the band members, and Ray, sacrificing our individuality, never misses an opportunity to promote Jim. Our songs (flowers) have bloomed with wondrous longevity.

*

Robby and Jim returned with the beers, apple juice, and ciggies. I noticed that Jim was limping as he sauntered back into our rehearsal room. Cornering Robby in the back room, I asked him what had happened.

"He said he got it at the Chateau Marmont. He has a room there on the second floor, and he was playing Tarzan and tried to swing into his room off the rain gutter. He bounced off the roof of the shed attached to his cottage and hit his back on the railing."

"God, he never used to get hurt. I thought he was indestructible."

"Not anymore."

"Let's play 'Crawling King Snake' again," Jim suggested, coming out of the bathroom and giving me a wink. It looked like we were going to record it for our sixth album, four years after Jim and I first got excited over the song back in Venice. Jim knew I loved the groove, and in the middle I got a chance to give a nod to Art Blakey with a fast press roll. Jim got to give a nod to all those black blues singers he admired, just like his hero, Elvis Presley, once did—the two white singers from the South looking at their mentors with both prejudice and awe. Robby honored James Brown with a J.B. horn line on his guitar in "Changeling."

Another tip of the hat to Jim's roots was in the song "L.A. Woman." We had cut the tempo in half for the "change the mood from glad to sadness" middle section, and Jim came up with this phrase he wanted to repeat over and over. Since it contained the black slang word mojo (for sexual prowess), I got the idea to steadily increase the tempo back up to the original speed, a la orgasm. It was hard to estimate the original tempo after five minutes of slow music, but we got it on the second take. After getting the song down on tape, Jim called Ray, Robby, and me into the back room.

"Check this out."

He wrote: JIM MORRISON

"Watch this," he said with self-satisfaction.

He then proceeded to write each letter below in a different order, crossing each out in his name, one at a time. Jim the anagram man.

MR MOJO RISIN

The phrase we just recorded in "L.A. Woman"!

"God damn, Jim," I said. "That's cool!"

"Very nice," Ray added. Robby smiled.

※

The Miami hysteria had finally died down, and we started getting calls to play live. Bill Siddons told the press that we lost a million dollars' worth of gigs because of Miami, which I couldn't give a shit about. Jim's condition was deteriorating rapidly with more drinking, so I thought it was good to defuse the myth of invincibility a little. Cool down. In a later interview, Jim reflected on the

Miami concert, saying it put an end to the image that had been created around him, consciously and unconsciously, all in one glorious evening.

Regardless, we booked a tour of small five-thousand-seat halls, usually old Philharmonic ones with heavy velvet curtains to soak up the sound. They were certainly more fulfilling acoustically.

Unfortunately, the myth-busting was too little, too late.

٪.

New Orleans, December 1970

The limo picked us up at our hotel in the French Quarter. This city had a different feel from any other I had been to in the States. Ornate iron railings and the smell of gumbo. Before we got in the car, Jim and I ran into the corner bar for beers. A sign on the window said "No Coloreds Allowed."

Jim picked up the cue from the sign and started baiting our limo driver as soon as we jumped in.

"Shoulda seen the sign in that liquor store. Gotta keep those niggers where they belong."

"Yes sireee!" the white driver interjected without missing a beat. "Keeps 'em in their place."

Everyone in the limo cringed; real live racism right there before our ears. The driver went into a monologue, punctuated and spurred on by remarks from Jim, and it sounded like slavery was still in existence.

Jim had a big grin on his face, as he had provoked an incredible performance from the driver. Method acting. Of course, Jim was putting the driver on, but he sure knew the material well.

The gig was in a place known as the Warehouse. It was just that. A low ceiling with posts everywhere gave the place a claustrophobic feeling. It was heavily padded for acoustics.

There was an eerie mood that night—and it was coming from Jim. Someone must have been sticking pins in his psyche, because five years of bizarre vibes came to an abrupt halt. Rock had its origins here in New Orleans. Could it have been the voodoo revenge?

Strange eyes fill strange rooms,
Voices will signal their tired end
Bodies confused,
Memories misused,
As we run from the day
To a strange night of stone

As Ray and Robby glanced at me for the cutoff to end "Soul Kitchen," Jim started to tell this terrible joke.

"What did the blind man say as he passed the fish store?"

I cringed, knowing the punch line.

"Hi, girls!"

The audience groaned. Then Jim began his nonsensical story about the guy and girl holed up in a tree. He had first told us this "joke" in our rehearsal room, and the gag was that there was no punch line. He'd just rambled on and on. "The guy said to the girl, 'Hey, it's windy, isn't it . . .' " He told it because he loved to waste our time. An adolescent power game. This time he didn't have his tongue inserted in his cheek. He was just plain boring. It was pathetic—an artist on the skids. He droned on for another ten minutes as the three of us tried to get another song started. Jim didn't leave a space and the audience got more and more restless. No one was laughing. Finally I started "Break On Through," under Jim's rap, which jolted him out of his doldrums. We fumbled through the rest of the set without any spark.

Jim wasn't even drunk, but his energy was fading. Later Ray remarked that during the set he saw all of Jim's psychic energy go out the top of his head. I didn't quite see that, but it did seem that Jim's lifeforce was gone.

I knew the band's public life was over. I saw a sad, old blues singer who'd been great once but couldn't get it up anymore.

Cars hiss by my window, like the waves down on the beach
I got this girl beside me, but she's out of reach
Headlights thru my window, shining on the wall
Can't hear my baby, tho' I call and call

Rock 'n' roll's Dorian Gray was only twenty-seven.

The night before, in Dallas, I'd had hopes that we still had a future playing live, despite the steady decline in our stage ability. In Texas we played "Riders" for the first time in public, and it was received quite well. The song hadn't been released yet, so it was a pure response. Even Vince, our roadie, had a glow on his face in Dallas and said that "Riders" was a great new song. That night I thought our live performances could evolve into a subtler jazz format. Maybe we could recapture the magic in a different way, a more mature way. There are smaller peaks and valleys along the big career peak, and although we were on the down side, Dallas felt like a peak.

But New Orleans was the lowest note yet, especially after the tease of the night before.

I could smell death.

Well, I been down so goddamn long
That it looks like up to me
Now, why don't one of you people
C'mon and set me free
I said warden, warden, warden,
Won't you break your lock and key
Hey, come along here mister,
And let the poor boy be

The limo ride back to the Pontchartrain Hotel was ominous. It was like returning home from a burial. Jim made small talk, but the rest of us were dead silent. I knew Ray and Robby were finally ready to call it quits. It started drizzling as we pulled up to the curb in front of the hotel. Jim and Bill Siddons got out and went into the lobby. I hung back, giving Ray and Robby the eye to stay, implying I had something to talk about. After Bill and Jim were inside, I spoke up.

"Well?" I said. They knew what I was talking about. The gig had been so embarrassing they could read my mind.

"Okay, it's finished!" Ray retorted sadly.

Robby took a beat, digesting what Ray had just said, realizing that half of our quartet had just caved in. He nodded in agreement. It seemed that the black cloud that had been over my head for several years was starting to lift. The Jim who'd wanted to quit years ago now would play anywhere, at any time. It was the only thing left that he enjoyed doing besides drinking. *We* would have to be the ones to throw in the towel. And we just did. Three pallbearers, standing in the rain, had just put our live act in the ground. *Finally.*

In an ironic mood to celebrate or lament, we attempted a jazz-club crawl. Times had changed. Many music venues had turned into topless clubs. We chose one, and finally, after years of berating and chastizing Jim, I got drunk myself.

Secretly I was relieved that Jim's performance had been terrible. I was embarrassed for the couple thousand folks in New Orleans, but they didn't know what it meant to me. It meant that what we'd created wouldn't be dragged through the shit. We agreed to cancel the few gigs we had coming up.

The next day we had a pretty quiet flight returning to L.A. I buried my face in the local newspaper, not wanting to catch Jim's eyes. Actually, there were a couple of interesting articles. Nixon was bombing Cambodia (after being inspired by the film *Patton*), and Bill Graham was closing the Fillmores, East and West.

Something was in the air. Certainly the times were a-changin', and not for the better. Going back into the studio fairly soon for more work on our sixth album would delay any discussion about future gigs. At least I knew Ray and Robby were serious this time about ending the live phase of our career. I could tell it was hardest for Ray to let it go, but now even he knew it was for the best. Only time would tell how Robby would react. We were close friends, but he was hard to read. I could tell that he didn't want to talk about it, which meant he would miss the high of performing. He had the look of a lover about to be jilted.

I remembered back to a gig at the Seattle Pop Festival when Jim was scolding the audience more than I'd ever seen. After we finished playing and left the stage, he just stood there forlornly hanging on the mike stand, a tormented soul taking his grief out on his fans. Ed Jeffords, a Seattle journalist, saw the same thing: "Then the set was over. Manzarek switched off the bass accompaniment and left the stage. Krieger and Densmore followed. Morrison hung there, very still, bathed in a red flood, with head drooped, eyes closed and arms outstretched—Christ on the cross. After the performance he gave, it was difficult to accept his crucifixion gesture without feeling that he was doing it to himself."

Again the anger rose in me. I was so mad at him for insulting the audience mercilessly, I wouldn't get into the helicopter taking us back to the hotel. I was numb. I just sat on my haunches in the dirt, as Jim left with his disciples.

Jeffords continues: "I waited for him as he left the stage, flanked by several newsmen and some of his staff. 'It's going to be all right,' he was saying over and over. The groupies just lined the stage stairs and watched as Morrison climbed into his chartered helicopter and was lifted into the sky—a continuance, though unintellectual, of his Christ pose."

A fan, who had been observing us closely, came up to me sitting dejected by the stage. "What's happening?"

I looked up and could tell by the expression on his face that he sensed the years of accumulated tension. My eyes got a little teary and I quickly looked back down to the dirt so as not to be exposed. I knew in my heart then that it was almost over.

19

THE UNKNOWN SOLDIER

Make a grave for the unknown soldier
Nestled in your hollow shoulder

In the spring of 1971, the low-budget concept on the *L.A. Woman* album paid off. Our previous record had been a comeback for us, but there'd been no hit singles. Elektra prez Jac Holzman called a meeting to confer with us on picking a song to be released off what was to become our last album.

I was leaning against the Spanish fireplace in Jac's office, Jim and Ray sitting in the green velvet reupholstered antique chairs, when Jac made his pitch.

"I have a hunch about 'Love Her Madly.' "

I did too.

"Nah, it's too commercial," Robby responded quickly from the corner of the room.

It staggered me. Robby had written the song: didn't he want another shot at the big time ("Light My Fire" being his previous monster)?

"Isn't that what a single is supposed to be?" Jac retorted.

"Yeah . . . well," Robby said, walking up to the fireplace. "How about 'Riders' or 'Changeling'?"

" 'Riders' is too long, Robby," Ray chimed in.

Jim seemed ambivalent.

"I'd love to release 'L.A. Woman,' " I added, "but it would have to be cut at seven minutes, and I don't know where."

" 'Love Her Madly' is a top-five record," Jac negotiated. "Let's go with it, and if we get some action, then we can have a second single. 'Riders on the Storm' will get more FM airplay than any record in history. If 'Love Her Madly' is a hit first, then we release 'Riders.' "

"That sounds okay," I said, looking at Robby for approval. Ray and Jim nodded and Robby reluctantly confirmed. He knew that Jac had verbally committed to spending the money to release a second single. I still couldn't get over the fact that Robby was so protective of his version of the bad-boy Doors image that he would sacrifice having one of his babies on the air.

※

Song by song, Jac Holzman predicted exactly what happened. On April 24, 1971, "Love Her Madly" went to number four, and we were back on AM radio, hot and heavy. I didn't know yet that the lyrics predicted what was to come in my relationship with Julia.

Don't you love her madly
Want to be her daddy, Don't you love her face
Don't you love her as she's walking out the door

They aptly described my shaky inner world to come and our outer public life, which was getting increasingly stronger. Meanwhile, "Riders on the Storm" was receiving heavy airplay as was the single "Love Her Madly," and the pressure was on to put it out. But it was six minutes long and nobody knew how to cut it down. Except me. With my jazz background. I *heard* several sections in Ray's piano solo that could be lifted out, without sacrificing any soul. I called up Botnick, went over to his house, and we did the surgery. Bruce and I were very proud when Ray couldn't tell where the cuts were in the edited version. The piano solo still built melodically and logically, but it was condensed. Jac released

"Riders" on the heels of "Love Her Madly." Despite being our least commercial rock song, it too climbed the charts.

The Sunset Strip was now studded with billboards advertising record albums, a trend Holzman started with our first record. He forked out the bucks for our second billboard, with an image from the inner sleeve of the record jacket. It was a startling shot of a woman crucified to a telephone pole: the L.A. Woman.

Drivin' down your freeway
Midnight alleys roam
Cops in cars, the topless bars,
Never saw a woman, so alone,
So alone, so alone, so
Alone

What Jac didn't know was how prophetic it would prove to be. None of us knew. The sign was at the foot of the entrance to Laurel Canyon, facing the billboard where we'd had our first ad for the first record four years before. The entrance to Laurel was like a shrine to me. Where Jim, Robby, and I had lived. Bookends to our career. *The Doors*, our first album billboard, faced east—the rising sun, the occidental, a land we conquered. The *L.A. Woman* billboard, our last record, faced west—the setting sun, the end of Western civilization, and the end of our public life as a group.

Weird scenes inside the gold mine
Ride the king's highway west, baby

The west is the best
Get here and we'll do the rest

Laurel Canyon, January 1978

"John, you gotta come over here," my sister screams. "Your brother Jim is acting crazy . . . I was over here visiting and he grabbed Mom and Dad by the arm and wouldn't let go. He was saying 'We're a family now. A real family.' "

"Okay. Be right over." I slam the receiver down. Goddamn. What time is it? It's a long way from the Hollywood Hills to the Palisades. Sounds serious, though.

I race down Sunset toward the beach. No cops in sight at midnight, so I can wind out the Jag. Jaguar John. That's what Fritz Richmond, the assistant engineer at Elektra Studios, used to call me. I'm a sucker for these English cars that feel like a living room inside but mechanically are junk.

What is happening in my parents' living room right now? A few months back, I nearly choked while sitting in the backseat of my parents' car with my brother, when Mom turned around and joked that Jim was a mistake, birth control-wise. Dad just kept on driving. Too bad he never steps in.

Of course I never confronted Morrison. I wonder how much of that tight-lipped New England stoicism is in me? Jim sang about breaking on through and "Father . . . yes, son . . . I want to kill you," but I'm still shaking in my boots in the backseat of my parents' car, afraid to confront. Blood is thicker. Outwardly I've been the father to my parents for ten years now, buying them a house and helping with their bills, but inwardly Mom will always call me Johnny. They will always be my parents, I'll forever be their son. With the church dictating no birth control, and social pressures in the fifties saying have 3.2 children, I guess it was hard for Mom and Dad to be different. Sounds like I'm saying that I would prefer that my brother hadn't been born. I'm not. I was just real worried. Wishing he had an easier time. Maybe if he had an easier time we all would be able to lighten up a little. My psyche is working overtime.

I park in my parents' driveway and my sister hurries out with a worried look. "Your brother held your mother and father by the arm for half an hour!" And Jim was a big guy now. Not the little brother I used to tease and wrestle with. Six feet tall, 160 pounds . . . compared to my 130-pound, five-foot-eight-inch frame.

TM wasn't cooling him out either. I had encouraged Transcendental Meditation after his first Camarillo visit and later paid for his initiation. Meditation—sitting quietly for twenty minutes twice a day—was too hard for someone as antsy and nervous as my brother. Combustible contemplation.

I knew he wasn't into drugs, although some of his friends smoked dope.

Jim sat on the sofa as I walked into the tension-packed living room. He jumped up and greeted me. Too friendly.

"Hi!"

"Hi, Jim. Where's Ann?"

"Oh . . . she went home," Dad volunteers.

"And Mom?"

"She's in her room." Another quick answer from Dad.

We sit down on either side of my brother.

"I think we should go to UCLA," my father says bravely. "They have young people there and they care."

He was talking about NPI, UCLA's Neuropsychiatric Institute. Definitely a step above state hospitals.

"I don't know . . . maybe . . . wanna hear my new song? I think it's a hit," Jim mutters.

"Sure," I say, trying to pacify him.

His eyes are bulging, and it is hard to look at him. Just like Morrison.

The song was okay. The ones he had taped for me before had been better, but they all had one thing in common: a childlike innocence, a sweet world of fantasy. When I'd played them for Robby for feedback, he'd said my brother sounded like an American Donovan, who was now passé.

"It would be hard to get a record company interested in him," Robby had said, discouraging me from trying any further.

For the next three hours, my dad and I tried to get my brother out the front door and into my car. He would get up and start to leave with us, and then sit back down. Although my patience was wearing thin, I couldn't leave my brother sleeping at our parents' house.

Mom was probably quivering in her bedroom with her rosary beads.

We finally get him outside and into the backseat, but he won't let us close the door. He hangs a leg or arm out so we can't close it. He is scared. Of what? The hospital? Or the deeper recesses of his own mind? I think of my first acid trip and my hallucination of the giant abyss next to the couch.

The fear of losing it.

My dad and I are also afraid. Of my brother. It takes all the emotional strength we can muster to get him into that car.

I flash on being a merciless asshole trying to get him to go. I understand why he doesn't always want to take his medicine prescribed by his state psychiatrist. Maybe UCLA can get him on massive vitamin doses. It is the new thing, and they are the forerunners.

We get there, get him in the door, and of course the admissions procedure is taking its usual long time. And it's starting to get to Jim. Who wouldn't it get to? You would think they could speed it up for mental problems. They probably are trying to decide whether or not to admit him. My dad and I glanced at each other with the same worried look. What if they won't take him? It's 2:30 A.M., and we've had it.

The doctor comes out and Jim performs magnificently. As the doctor asks him questions and fills out a form, Jim starts babbling. It is pathetic. And so sad . . . and a relief. A great relief.

I climb into bed around 4 A.M., wondering what it all meant. Maybe praying is the only thing left to do.

20

The End

Los Angeles, 1981

. . . Well, I'm at it again. I thought I was through with conjuring you up, but I just came back from the newsstand, where I picked up the latest copy of Rolling Stone. *You're on the cover! The headline reads, "He's Hot, He's Sexy, And He's Dead!" Tasteless, but kind of funny.*

We have cut a lot of our old sixteen-millimeter footage into videos, and Ray is talking about it as a great vehicle for raising Doors' consciousness. Sounds like the Maharishi. Another quote from Father Manzarek: "I believe in the Doors. Our music was the appropriate vision for the second half of the twentieth century. I won't stop until everyone knows who Jim is. I might have to do a lot of talking, maybe the rest of my life."

Robby and I told Ray that it's for the audience and critics to say how important we are, but Ray continued to preach: "The Doors do what the Doors do, it has nothing to do with time periods. It has to do with the evolution of mankind." And finally: "You have to be intelligent to like the Doors." Amazing, huh! This is probably amusing to you, but down here the pomposity is embarrassing. The reason I'm riding Ray so hard comes from caring. I care so much I can't help getting emotional.

It's the same stuff that got stirred up over your performance at Miami. It's the stuff that was described as "bitterness turned into a knuckle-white grip" on my drumsticks. I describe it as love. Feeling and caring enough to express disappointment.

So Ray's crusading has worked, and there are a bunch of new born-

271

again Doors fans. The article in Rolling Stone *is written by a young woman who was in kindergarten when we were at our peak. One thing she says is right on the money: "The most important aspect of Morrison Resurrectus is the need today for kids—perhaps all of us—to have an idol who isn't squeaky clean." Permission to party. Well done, Dionysus.*

I went to the premiere of Apocalypse Now, *the film I mentioned by Coppola. There was some magical connection between the visuals in the beginning and our song, "The End," unlike what Ray had relayed when he saw the film in a screening. Knowing Coppola from film school, Ray was asked about the Doors doing music for the score. He didn't tell Robby and me about it, and even told Coppola that "The End" was cut wrong to the visuals of Martin Sheen sitting on the bed. Sheen sat down when the tempo sped up. I think Coppola didn't like being told how to make movies and dropped Ray.*

Remember Danny Sugerman? The kid who hung around our office and did the fan mail? The one everyone used to laugh at as I slammed doors in front of his fourteen-year-old face when he tried to get into private meetings in our back office? Well, his aggressiveness, which got him his first Doors job, has expanded into writing a book about you! And what a book it is. One of your poems from The Lords *comes to mind:*

Baths, bars, the indoor pool. Our injured leader prone on the sweating tile. Chlorine on his breath and in his long hair. Lithe, although crippled, body of a middle-weight contender. Near him the trusted journalist, confidant. He liked men near him with a large sense of life. But most of the press were vultures descending on the scene for curious America aplomb. Cameras inside the coffin interviewing worms.

First of all, it's called No One Here Gets Out Alive. *Familiar lyric, huh? A national best seller. Second, it is very factual, thanks to Jerry Hopkins's research. That's right . . . the old* Rolling Stone *writer you were friends with and suggested do a book on Elvis. Well, he did one on you, only his publisher, Simon & Schuster, rejected it. After five years of research, it came out with a very negative attitude toward you, and forty publishers passed on it. Enter Danny Sugerman, empire builder and num-*

ber-one disciple of St. James. The publisher called him the Doors' confidant, writing an intro proclaiming you a god, and with Manzarek crossing out a lot of the bad stuff, they got a deal with Warner Books, which had passed on it twice earlier. No One Here Gets Out Alive reads as if you were a complete asshole, ignoring the genius that went with it . . . and it made The New York Times Best Seller List, generating more album sales, so, Danny has an entire career, and I'm collecting more royalties than when we were touring! Danny as religious zealot and Ray as St. Paul, spreading the gospel according to you long after the messiah is dead. It's weird. I mean, I think the songs hold up, but your self-destruction has been glamorized. The French decadence movement of the nineteenth century —your heroes Baudelaire and Arthur "sacred disorder of the mind" Rimbaud—has arrived in Middle America.

Oh what a beautiful corpse I'll make.

I don't buy it; I never did. After you died, the three of us figured finding a replacement for you would be impossible, so Ray and Robby sang. We did two albums and then, with a lucrative record deal for three more albums (at a guarantee of $250,000 each), we realized that the front corner of our diamond was missing, so we called it quits. Looking back on that time, Robby says we should have let there be a space, a mourning period, before we continued. But we were so fired up to go on our own before you checked out that we didn't really acknowledge your death and grieve.

You were one of those people who have great excesses in their lives, but when it came to doing music, you were serious about it. As Ray recently said, "Jim always delivered." It was the excesses that killed you for us, and for the fans.

Vince said, "Kids would come up to me after the concerts the last two years of our career and say, 'Why did he do that?' They didn't want to see him so drunk he'd forget the words. They wanted Jim to be Jim Morrison the singer, and Robby to be Robby Krieger with the electric hair and the electric guitar, John Densmore to be this little guy who was an

273

amazingly adept drummer, and Ray Manzarek, who had the famous piano bass and the organ technique bordering on classics."

Well . . . ten years later, I've now realized that "of the Doors" is permanently etched on my forehead. I guess that's progress, considering that just after you died, I felt it was compromising our integrity and loyalty to you to keep the original band name. After all, we had started in Venice, four guys against the world, with no agents, managers, or fans.

"What the hell are we going to call ourselves?" I kept prodding Ray and Robby as we were rehearsing for our new album.

"We are 'the Doors,' with or without Jim," Ray said.

"I don't agree," Robby said.

"I'm on the fence." I squirmed.

Our first album after you died, Other Voices, *wasn't bad. Ray wrote a song, "Tightrope Ride," to you—post mortem. The only place he has expressed his anger over you not taking care of yourself is in those lyrics:*

Did you think, we were all together
Did you think, we were all the same
And you're all alone, like a Rolling Stone,
Like Brian Jones, On a tightrope ride, nobody
by your side, and we're goin' home.

In 1972, Nixon was reelected, and his vice president, Spiro T. Agnew, took on the "drug culture." He cited the movie Easy Rider *and lyrics to rock songs— "A Little Help from My Friends" by the Beatles, "White Rabbit" by the Jefferson Airplane, and "Eight Miles High" by the Byrds— as dangerous. "Rock lyrics brainwash young people into taking drugs. We may be accused of advocating song censorship but have you really heard the words of some of those songs? . . . Rock is anti-American," Agnew said to a congressional investigating committee. He never came out and advocated censorship of these songs, but . . .*

Between Other Voices *and* Full Circle, *our second album without you, Julia and I started having major trouble. It felt weird in the house, so I asked Julia if she was having an affair; she admitted that she was. I quickly put the lid on my anger, which immediately tightened the muscles in my neck.*

I moved my things into the side bedroom across the house, and then Julia's stomach began to show with the baby of the Allman Brothers' bass player, Berry Oakley. I was about to take the lid off my anger when the news came of his death in a motorcycle accident.

After that Julia was determined to have the kid. I impulsively said I would take care of it, feeling compassion for her and the baby, and hoping that she would now turn back to me.

She didn't.

She wanted to go back to the south, to Florida, during her pregnancy. I was considering taking my brother in for a while, so I paid for her trip. As Julia said, the timing seemed right.

My brother, Jim—you might remember him from the spaghetti dinners —was living in an apartment in Westwood (at that time they were very cheap) and going to a psychiatrist after several stints at mental hospitals. Once when I dropped him off for his hour-long appointment he was so nervous I was sure the doctor was going to admit him or give him extra medication or something. When I picked him up, he was still bouncing his leg up and down as if there were ants crawling all over it.

I took him to his apartment, but I didn't recognize the place. I had been there before, but this time it was a complete disaster. It was as if an atomic bomb had landed in his apartment. I had never seen a bigger mess. Dirty dishes in the sink piled to the ceiling, smelly clothing everywhere, and a bathroom where one was guaranteed to contract a disease.

"Do you ever clean your fish tank?" I asked cautiously. The glass was completely green and you could barely see the fish. Being in his apartment felt like being trapped in a limo with you.

"The fish are okay," my brother answered. He towered over my head now, and his black chest hair grew up out of the top of his T-shirt.

A man. I could feel his unbalanced energy as he constantly bounced his leg. I could feel from you a similar off-centeredness, only without any outward physical manifestations.

I told him to come and stay with me for a week, and we drove to my house. We talked for hours about how now he was more interested in music than in his painting. I loved his songs, but they weren't very accessible and I was worried that my public image was too big for a sibling to come out from behind. Why did he have to choose the same profession? Besides, his painting was unique.

We talked about his problems and it completely drained me. My intuition told me not to press him too much because it would be too intense for him to communicate calmly. When he got nervous, I got nervous. At that point, I felt, somehow, that I could get swallowed up in fear and panic as well. In John Perry's Far Side of Madness, it states that the only documented cure for schizophrenia has been someone dedicating his life (maybe ten years of intensive live-in work) to helping a specific person. It felt as if I were trying to keep someone above water who couldn't swim. I knew I wasn't going to be able to handle more than a few days of playing counselor. And he was my own brother.

I called Dad, and we got him into a halfway house before Julia came back.

Nothing was more depressing than going around to each room in the house with Julia and saying "I want that . . . that's mine, you take that . . . No, I want that. . . . Okay, but then I get this." The day I moved out, the Santa Ana winds were blowing, and I turned to her after packing everything and gave her a glance that said "Are you sure this is what you want?" She nodded her long brown hair up and down. I was on the verge of tears when I shut the front door. Good-bye to the American dream. And live happily ever after. Back on the street again, remembering when.

Maybe we took our wedding vows—"fill each other's cup but drink not from one cup, give one another of your bread but eat not from the same loaf"—too literally as a license for having affairs instead of as respect for each other's solitude within the structure of a marriage.

With all your spats, you and Pam never threw in the towel, did you? Of course, you never moved in together or got married. Maybe drugs took the place of more traditional rituals.

I checked into a plastic "cliffhanger" apartment one mountain away from, and with a slight view of, our Appian Way dream house. At least I still had Otto, my dog.

Don't you love her ways
Tell me what you say,
Don't you love her as she's walking out the door

For the next year, I dated and pursued girls I was physically attracted to—with a vengeance. Julia wasn't my ultimate physical fantasy, but something had attracted me to her soul. Now my eyes were working overtime. The carnal contact was short-term pleasure with long-term pain.

I was doing a lot of aimless driving around town and out into the country looking for girls, but really, I was looking for myself. I found myself when I had to pull over to the side of the road on the freeway because I was dizzy. The real me had lost its center.

I had reached the bottom of my downward spiral as a boy. It was time to grow up. And I had to do it alone. Everyone does—at some desperate point in his or her life. With the knowledge that, for me, nature heals, I nervously cruised Topanga Canyon as if it were Eden and found a house to buy. It was a risk, moving out in the middle of what most urban people would call "nowhere," but I was up against the wall of my sanity. I had had seven or eight years of rock 'n' roll and Hollywood, and depression was around the corner.

Why? I had everything people dream about, in the outer world. My inner world was something else. It was like a floor made out of Swiss cheese. Lots of holes around to fall into, like the one I had encountered at the beginning of my first acid trip. Time to go back to that rebellious little bohemian community where I had my first experience with "nonreality," as the shamans would say, and find my center again.

Our lawyers arranged an out-of-court settlement, and we filed for the big "D." California divorce law states that the spouse shall receive half of the conjoint income earned during the period of marriage. The size of the checks I have signed over to Julia twice a year at royalty time have shocked me, but they indicated that if she was doing well by me, I was doing obscenely well. The Doors myth marches on.

⅄

*Time heals. In retrospect, Julia was very supportive of me in my dealings
with you. Yes, you were difficult. . . . During the second album we did
after you died, Ray and Robby fought over musical direction. When it was
finished, we went to England to find a replacement for you. It was hard to
give up the musical synchronicity we had developed over six years. Maybe
we should have done instrumentals, as you had suggested for us if we
ever broke up.*

*We found some compatible musicians in England, but unfortunately,
Dorothy, who was pregnant at the time, started feeling shaky emotionally,
and Ray was forced to choose between our career and taking her back
home. He wasn't going to not support someone who had supported him
emotionally for so many years.*

*So here were Robby, his now-wife Lynn (you remember her!), and I
sitting in England wondering what to do.*

*Robby and I were determined to get something going after traveling to
what seemed like the other side of the globe. Not wanting to crawl back
home without some creative fulfillment, we formed a group called the
Butts Band and paid for recording half an album in England and the other
half on the way home, in Jamaica.*

*Blue Thumb Records, a jazz-oriented label, released the album, but the
group didn't take off. It was a reggae-jazz–influenced record before Bob
Marley and the Wailers ever got here. Oh yeah, you missed reggae.
Marley was the most important musical movement to happen in the
seventies. Not much else did.*

*David Geffen, now a big record mogul, was right. He listened to the
tapes from London and Jamaica and said we should go into the studio
here and record two more good songs and the album would be very
strong. We didn't take his advice because the new members had solo
careers in the back of their minds and returned to London. Made me think
of the dedication it takes to lay a foundation and launch a group, which
the Doors certainly had had.*

*"What you need is four or five guys that are equally talented," Robby
said in a later interview. "You can't have one guy who is a totally dedicated
musician, another guy who just is in it for the girls, and another who is just
learning music. The Doors were all pretty much in the same spot—*

psychically." Robby and I did enjoy a couple of good creative years playing music with those musicians, though.

In 1973 my divorce from Julia was finalized, as was the end of the Vietnam "conflict." That's what some politicians called it before escalation into the final U.S. expenditures of $109.5 billion and 360,000 dead or wounded, not to mention 3,250,000 dead or wounded soldiers and civilians in Vietnam.

In August 1974 Nixon resigned as president before being impeached for a large scandal called Watergate. The Republicans broke into the Democrats' campaign office and then tried to cover it up. Nixon was involved. He also had to pay a half-million dollars in back taxes! Almost a year before that, Spiro T. Agnew had pleaded nolo contendere *to one count of income tax evasion and quit his job as V.P.*

More important: One of the great swing drummers, Gene Krupa, died.

After just a few weeks of living in Topanga, I met a girl, Debbie Fife, who was house-sitting across the street from my new digs. "You're a tall one," I said sarcastically when I first met her. It was a cover for my insecurities with women. I figured that if I was rude, they wouldn't notice how shy I was. Does any of this ring a bell? After Debbie got to know me, she said I didn't seem to fit with the Doors' dark macho image. She was about to lose the house-sitting gig and move back to her mother's in the Valley when I asked her to move in with me.

Then I hit her with the idea of having a kid.

Out of wedlock! I guess I'm into shocking people.

Or afraid of commitment.

Deb didn't go for that, but she did enjoy quitting her job and not having to get up at six-thirty to drive downtown.

We had been living together for almost a year, and I still wasn't formally divorced. I encouraged Debbie to be friendly with Julia, trying to continue the sixties' ambiance, but when she invited Julia to a surprise birthday party for me, it felt weird. It was time to motivate the divorce lawyers, which I did, and then I found myself going out bar-hopping several nights a week, with Debbie staying home alone.

Where did this restlessness come from? A former life in the fast lane? I was supposed to be growing up. Living in Topanga, I had moved over to the right a couple lanes, but I wasn't ready to stop. I went to a girl's apartment, did "the bad thing," and then drove back to my house around 1 A.M. After a sleepless night I couldn't hold it any longer and told Deb in the morning. She was seriously shattered and it scared me. I knew that I had undermined our relationship.

It seemed like you and Pam had this sort of dialogue every few months. Must have been pretty rocky. Why is it so hard for men to commit? Something in the genes about sowing our seeds? We have to hurt ourselves and others to finally get it right. And then we still have doubts.

Deb seemed back to normal after about a week or so, and I hoped the lesson had reached me below the belt. I was having a dialogue with the lower half of my body, trying to get it to synchronize with my brain.

President Ford, who'd replaced Agnew and then replaced Nixon (talk about the Peter Principle concept of failing upward!), granted former President Nixon a full pardon for any criminal offenses committed while in office. Ford also granted limited amnesty to both Vietnam draft evaders and military deserters. I could have been one of them.

It was actually Debbie's prodding to get married that made me finally crack the whip under the terminally slow lawyers to get the divorce finished.

Did I want to get married again? Well . . . sort of. What about you? Didn't Pam ever pressure you to pop the question? In order to resolve your estate her side of the family produced a motel ledger from Phoenix indicating that you two slept together. Apparently cohabitation proves common-law marriage in Arizona. Then your parents came along and the Cursons decided to give them half. They were not required to, but I feel the two families splitting up the spoils is right.

Debbie had never been married, so . . . this time a small ceremony in our own backyard seemed appropriate to me, in light of my last marriage celebration being a big to-do and ultimately the wedding couple splitting up. We had been living in sin for a couple of years now at Feather Hill, the house in Topanga that helped ground me after years in Laurel Canyon. Built in the twenties, it sits atop a hill surrounded by oaks. The backyard patio has a shock of purple and white azaleas with a trellis of trumpet vines hanging down. Perfect spot for a wedding. The Smithers family, from whom I had bought the place, had named the backyard the Druid Circle, due to the feeling it gave off at twilight.

I, of course, wasn't supposed to see the bride before the ceremony, but I bumped into Deb in the hallway and she remarked that she was so nervous that she had taken a Valium. Was the ceremony going to mean as much with the edge taken off? I had done this ritual before so I knew what to expect, but this bothered me.

A cute little local minister married us, but I don't think he understood what we were trying to do with the ceremony. In retrospect, I don't think we knew what we were doing either. An edited version of "with this ring I thee wed . . ." was spoken with the "till death do us part" section struck out. At the time we thought it was corny. And morbid. How could we know what our relationship would be like ten years from now, anyway? It seemed like something old people would do. Too sentimental. We were young . . . and free!

Meanwhile Ray made two solo albums, The Golden Scarab being the first and most interesting. In it he professed his positive philosophy of life, with society heading toward the golden race. Remember those arguments you used to have with Ray? You fighting for individual cultures and Ray for homogenization? His solo career didn't take off, so he formed a band called Night City, which fashioned themselves after the Doors. It hurt my feelings. Did Ray think he could just replace us? I saw them at the Whiskey and they played a couple of our old songs and Iggy Pop (wearing a T-shirt with your head on the front) sang "Light My Fire." Ray motioned for me to come up onstage, but I stormed out of the club. The lead singer (Noa Somebody), strutted around like he was already God, without paying any dues. I wanted to yell at Ray, "This guy's a caricature of Jim!" They folded.

I got into acting and Robby did a couple of musical projects on his own. They were pretty good—jazz oriented. Robby was desperately trying to give the impression that his skin was darker than it actually was. Trying a little too hard. And you know how much I love jazz.

Our individual efforts may not have turned out to be earthshaking, but I still feel fulfilled creatively. And without that I s'pose I would feel like part of me was missing.

We are frustrated from time to time by the huge shadow cast by the Doors, but we're proud of it too. Frustrated and proud, frustrated and proud. It is bittersweet to have peaked back at twenty-six, but I've found a second wind through acting and writing. A different way of looking at things. Another creative avenue or two have opened a new door to my inner life.

My wife, Debbie, agreed to stop birth control, and we readied the sunny little bedroom at the end of the hall where, according to the previous owners, Hugh Lofting wrote The Voyages of Doctor Dolittle. *We both wanted a girl. And got one! I didn't care about passing on THE NAME, and I'm not into sports, either. This was a fairly happy time for me.*

In the fall of 1977, six years after you died, Ray, Robby, and I started listening to your poetry from the sessions you did on your birthday just before you passed over to the other side. A year and a half later, we finished An American Prayer, *the poetry album you dreamed of making.*

Our old producer, Paul Rothchild, said in the press that it was "a rape of Jim Morrison." Yes, you were originally thinking of an orchestral backing, motivated by striking out on your own, but unfortunately, your physical body gave out before the project could come to fruition. Ray, Robby, and I worked incredibly hard on the record, trying to make it a "movie for the ears," even though we knew that its concept wasn't commercial, and I'm very proud of it. I know *you* would love it.

To me, the poetry album was one of the few valid post-Morrison projects. We were honoring your words rather than exploiting them. Then we went on an interview tour of Europe to promote it.

⁊.

"I thought we were just going to sit in at a club!" I screamed at Danny Sugerman, now our press agent, as we rode in a crowded limo to the afternoon sound check. "You know, have a few drinks and then get called up onstage by the local band!" I was still screaming.

"Can't you guys cool it?" Ray's wife, Dorothy, surprisingly spoke up.

"It's a GODDAMN concert," I retorted.

"But we'll get a blurb in Rolling Stone's *'Random Notes,'" Danny and Ray said in harmony. Before you died, didn't we get press by just doing*

our thing? No manipulation. Although we couldn't duplicate American
Prayer *live, this was a publicity tour.*

*As we walked onto the Palace disco center stage in Paris, I couldn't
help complaining some more. "We haven't played together in three years
and we're playing a fucking concert, with* rented equipment!*" I was glad
to see Ray's face drop as he surveyed the large proscenium stage. He
was getting the idea that it was a* bad *idea.*

"Playing your own *drum set is like wearing a tight-fitting glove," I said
to no one in particular. Ray and Robby started trying to remember the
chords to some of our old songs.*

*That night, when the curtain rose, we got it up, but we were rusty.
Don't get me wrong. I agree with what you had said in that interview
about how our music had gotten progressively better, tighter, and that we
put out a lot of sound for just three guys. I think that the three of us
transcend our musicianship and reach something collective, something
more than the sum of its parts. But we were using borrowed equipment
and needed more rehearsal. We were doing it for the wrong reasons. I got
real drunk afterward, as I did in New Orleans after the shitty Warehouse
gig. I absolutely hate playing poorly, and we had played fair.*

*The car picked us up at 9 A.M. for our first visit to your grave. It was
hangover time.*

⁒.

*After several years of seemingly blissful times in Topanga, including one
touchy-feely encounter experiment with our dentist and his wife—made
easy by Quaaludes and the steady increase of herb smoking—Debbie and
I moved back to the city.*

Then she had an affair.

*She said it would help our relationship because she felt more open.
Now I was shattered. She saw the guy a couple more times and it was
over.*

Then Debbie had another affair. This time it was a marriage breaker.

*I give her credit for suggesting we go to a counselor, although at the
time I was against it. Therapy was for the* Bob & Carol & Ted & Alice
generation. We had acid, so we could take care of ourselves. She seemed

283

serious, so off we went to conjoint therapy. In retrospect, Debbie was still willing to fight for our relationship. At some point, she stopped.

You went to a shrink once, didn't you? I would love to have been a fly on the wall for that session. I heard you put him on, the whole hour. I now think they can be helpful. Like acid, or meditation, or music. These things are like guideposts, support systems that come up every so often in one's life, and if you're sensitive to their power, they can nourish you.

Back in '66, Maharishi told a small group of us that he was going to return to his cave in the Himalayas before 1970. He hasn't gone back yet; he's still traipsing around the world to his meditation centers and selling what has turned into the McDonald's of spirituality.

It makes me sad, because meditation is still good for the soul. Any technique. At least he didn't get into fifteen-year-old girls like another eastern guru, Swami Muktananda. It seems that the ultimate test for these sages is to come to the land of sex, power, and greed, and see if they can stay on their spiritual path.

I still can calm my mind with my mantra, though.

Take extra care not to lose what you feel
Careful your eating is simple and real
Water the flowers that grow at your heel
Guiding your visions to heaven
And heaven is in your mind

As to my new guidepost, the therapist's mere presence cuts through the bullshit and encourages you to be honest. Unless you're going solo and plan to put them on, like I heard you did.

I found out that with our kid well on her way at five years old, Debbie was having an identity crisis. She worked before we got married; she wanted to work again. Robby's wife, Lynn, thought Debbie was crazy, knowing that we didn't need the money. But Debbie needed something else.

The shrink, who was a woman, said that child rearing is possibly more important than a career, but that didn't help Deb. She wanted to do something again out in the marketplace, which was fine with me, but that wasn't enough either.

It was easy for me to focus on the thought that we did a good job of parenting, because I had already gotten lots of public acclaim. What was hard for me to say—or show—was extra warmth and support. I supported Debbie in her endeavors, but apparently not enough. My old streak of New England stubbornness seemed to stop me from giving special care. I didn't have the depth that was needed. I always thought she knew I loved her. I didn't know I had to show it that much.

My big public shadow didn't help either. Not that Deb and I were in competition, but thanks to what we started back in Venice when nobody was around, there's always something going on concerning the group that seems to be important.

I'm learning to enjoy my success more and feel less guilty about it. I went through Dante's Inferno with you. As Robby said, ". . . possibly part of the reason we've lasted is because other musicians would not have had the ability to withstand Jim's insanity."

And finally, I'm a good drummer. Not the fastest, but I seem to know how to play musically.

There's a price to pay in there somewhere.

Maybe she just fell out of love.

※

On April 25, 1978, a call came from the halfway house in Santa Monica where my brother had been in residence for several months.

"Is Ray Densmore there?"

"No."

"Are you John Densmore?"

"Yes."

"I've been unsuccessful in trying to reach Ray Densmore. Are you his son?"

"Yes." I knew something was coming.

"Would you give a message to Ray Densmore?"

I thought of saying "sure," but this sounded like an official call. "Yes."

"Jim Densmore has committed suicide."

"He has?"

285

"Yes. Can you pass this on to your father?"

"Yes."

"Thank you."

My brother. The phone call didn't really register. I didn't even bother to ask how it happened. As soon as I hung up I immediately dialed my dad's. But he wasn't home. I was in shock. I tried to make some breakfast and then called Dad again. When I finally reach him, the words came out mechanically.

"Hi, Dad. I've got some news. Are you sitting down? I think you should sit down, it's bad news." I could sense him getting nervous.

After exhaling deeply, I continued. "The halfway house called and Jim has committed suicide."

"What? What did you say? Are you sure? Are you sure you got the right message?"

"Yeah, Dad."

He asked me to repeat the message. Was I sure I'd got it right? His voice was getting shakier by the minute.

"Well, how did it happen?"

"I don't know. They didn't give me particulars and I didn't ask."

Take the highway to the end of the night
End of the night, end of the night
Take a journey to the bright midnight
End of the night, end of the night

My brother was cremated and buried at the Westwood Cemetery under a pepper tree. My sister, Ann, flew out from Boston with her second husband, a cancer surgeon. She was the one who finally got the family together to go out to the cemetery and honor my brother's death. Mom had said that she didn't want a funeral—that she couldn't take it— but the impromptu ceremony gave us all a much-needed sense of closure. As we gathered around the grave and held hands, I thought that there was definitely something to be said for some old traditions.

Who knows? If you were alive today, Jimbo, maybe you'd be having your parents over for dinner! I doubt it. You'd probably be a burned-out forty-seven-year-old drunk. The early part of our career was "sweet delight," but in the last years, you lived out your prophecy, the lines you "borrowed" from Blake:

Realms of bliss, realms of light
Some are born to sweet delight
Some are born to sweet delight
Some are born to the endless night

During the funeral, I looked around to the office where Debbie and my dad had heard the news from the undertaker how my brother did it. I was out at the burial spot when they found out. He apparently was in a good mood after lunch that day at the halfway house, as is often the case with suicides. I guess they have resolved the pain because they know it's going to end. He took one of the kitchen knives to his room and stabbed himself several times in the chest.

Seppuku.

Hari kari.

And you thought you were intense.

Debbie said my dad grabbed her hand upon hearing the news.

What rage. And pain. How do I assimilate this unbelievable act of violence my brother did to himself?

When I was a kid I never thought I would know anybody who died until I was old like my grandparents, but now peers—like you, Jimi, Janis, Brian Jones, Al Wilson, Bob Hite, Mike Bloomfield, Keith Moon, Paul Butterfield, Dennis Wilson, Richard Manuel, and my brother—are dropping like flies. The sixties started out with so much hope, symbolized by "Light My Fire."

The time to hesitate is through
No time to wallow in the mire
Try now we can only lose

Now everyone is burning out.

287

And our love become a funeral pyre
Come on, baby, light my fire
Try to set the night on fire

Right then, "The End" seemed like a death pact. Maybe it's just the curse of youthful success. When you don't have a slow, careful rise, taking two-thirds of your life to get there, the steep downside needs to be respected. Did you know about the Oriental poets who wouldn't publish before they reached the age of fifty? Wise men.

Reminds me of an early publicity photo we took on the Venice board-walk in front of a bench full of old Jewish women. I remember thinking at the time that if we knew their stories, we would probably be amazed. They've lived a lifetime and it's just their dopey old bodies that are falling apart. You didn't want to be around for the deterioration of your vessel, as Ray would say, did you? It is humbling. On the other hand, time becomes so valuable.

I wasn't always this grounded. For several months after my brother's death I was nervous about handling kitchen knives. I thought if I did it, too, it would somehow make it better. Atone for not saving him. Redeem something.

My dad scared the shit out of me a few days after the incident. We were in my kitchen, and I had never seen him cry. He cried buckets that day. My sister, Ann, was still back east, so the rest of us got together to grieve: Mom, Dad, and my wife, Debbie, who suggested the wake.

We all sat down in the living room and Dad started to get a little teary. Mom made a disapproving face, so Dad and I evacuated to the kitchen.

This was a Catholic family with a shy, introverted New England father and a mother who insisted we all wear rose-colored glasses.

"La Vie en Rose."

My brother had ripped them off of our faces.

"Jim said to me that I would be the last and only friend he'd have," my dad said, sobbing.

"That seems to have come true," I concurred. "The last time I visited him was months ago. I tried to lift his spirits, but the place was so filthy

288

that I left extremely depressed. And you, Dad, stood by him till the end, cleaning up after his tirades, helping with the laundry, and making sure he sent in his rent check."

My dad raised his head, opened his mouth, and let out a continuous, *moanful cry that scared me. Mother couldn't have stopped him even if she'd wanted to. It seemed he was crying from thirty years of bottled-up emotion. I couldn't believe the tears streaming down his face. After about ten minutes we returned to the living room. My mother was holding on as tight as possible, keeping everything in, but you could see pain in her eyes.*

"Your dad and I talked and we think he should be cremated," she volunteered. "How do you feel? You and he were sort of into Indian religion."

"That's fine with me. Fine. That feels right."

Aren't Catholics supposed to be against cremation? I thought.

"I'll help as much as I can with the arrangements," Debbie graciously offered.

"No funeral. I don't think I can take a funeral," my mom said.

No one responded.

⁊

. . . At the end of our little impromptu service we all dropped each other's hands and placed some flowers around the small box in the ground and I thought, goddamn . . . how can my brother be reduced to the size of a shoe box?

Your grave seemed small too. But I know, now, that you're in there. You definitely went downtown, didn't you? That wasn't in the press and it should have been. Did you know that Siddons's wife, Cheri, had a premonition about your death? Bill remembers: "I was woken up in the middle of the night by a call from Europe and my wife immediately sat bolt upright in bed and said, 'Something's happened to Jim. Jim's dead.' I got Pamela on the phone in Paris and she broke down and started to cry and said, 'You're right, okay, he died.' "

After burying you in Paris, Bill Siddons came back and told Ray, Robby, and me a very interesting story, which he strongly suggested we keep to ourselves. It was about being in Pam's apartment over there.

"The casket was right there in the bedroom, so you can imagine the

vibes in the place. I never thought to ask to see the body, as Pam was obviously shattered [hence the beginning of the fake-death rumors]. Once, while alone in the living room, I opened a carved box on the coffee table and found white powder in a clear envelope. Pam was in the kitchen, so I decided to try a little to see what it was. It wasn't coke. Soon afterward I became nauseous and felt very sick. It sure was something I'd never tried before."

Heroin.

I figure you took a big snort, had some Courvoisier, climbed into the tub . . . and good night. That's it, huh, Jim? A radio interview show I did in 1986 on Public Broadcasting shed more light:

DJ ROGER STEFFENS: Let us get to a crucial question which I have part of the answer to, and it shocked me when I finished reading the Doors' biography, No One Here Gets Out Alive, to see . . . back here, on page three eighty-one, the first line . . . 'The year following Jim Morrison's ALLEGED death' . . . and I think that's so harmful for people, to imply that perhaps Jim is still alive, because I know the people who found his body. One of them was Marianne Faithfull, and it's amazing to me that she has never come out in public and talked about it. To make a long story very short, I was living in Marrakesh at the time; a man who is mentioned in this book a great deal, a French count, his name was Jean de Breteuil, was one of Pamela's lovers—Morrison's old lady's lovers—and when they were all in Paris together, Pam called Jean and Marianne and said, 'Jim is in the bathroom, the door is locked, I can't get him out, will you come over immediately?' The story they told me two days later was that they had broken down the door and found Jim dead in the bathtub. They flew the next morning to Marrakesh where I was living and told me the story, and they were still shaking as they told it. I have no doubt that what they told me was the truth. Why does this myth persist? That Jim isn't really dead?

JD: First of all, thank you for that information. I didn't know about Marianne Faithfull. I knew there was this count that was hanging around Pamela.

RS: ·Who himself was dead within a year of a heroin OD.

JD: *Hmmm. Very interesting stuff. Well . . . Jim did die on a weekend and there was no autopsy. It was a closed casket and so Pamela was the last one to see him alive. And then she died a couple of years later . . . and so you can see how rumor and myth can get going. . . . Is he actually dead? You hope he isn't if you're seventeen because he represented breaking away and all of that. And then there also is . . . commerce.*

RS: *Hmmm.*

JD: *I didn't write the book.*

RS: *The myth-making machinery.*

JD: *ALLEGED was written by someone else.*

/.

. . . And the final nail in your coffin: Danny Sugerman recently said that he was around Pam after your death and she felt terribly guilty because it was her stash.

So there it is: another drug-related death. I consider alcohol (a drug) just as responsible. Now it's clear to me that you're alive only in all of our minds.

Robby and I knew what to expect when we visited Père Lachaise the second time and saw your small concrete rectangle. Ray was taken aback. He had finally gotten there to pay his respects after being too hung over from a Paris nightclub the first time we visited France. Or too scared. We walked up to your plot, which now has a bust of your head made by some Czechoslovakian who carved it behind the Iron Curtain and then snuck it across, and Ray froze and took a big three-second beat . . . then he regrouped, drinking wine with the fans, pouring it over your grave, and flicking his cigarette ashes on you. Robby and I looked at each other with raised eyebrows, but I know Ray loved you too much. Too much to assimilate your death. Yet. Those three seconds were flooded with too many feelings, and a wall was instantly erected. Walls have to be taken down carefully, step by step.

/.

So my brother committed suicide and you—another kind of brother—committed slow suicide. Before my family left the Westwood Cemetery I shakily took out a slip of paper with one of my brother's poems written in his own hand. I read it aloud.

Sitting in the middle of the room
Staring out the window
Someone knocking on my door again
Asking what has happened
So I told him I am made of tin
And I see a rainbow, and ask to be let in.

The last line was engraved on his marker.

⅄.

As you must know, a couple of years after you checked out, your mate Pam followed you down, with an OD. Paul Rothchild said that after Pam returned to the U.S. from Paris, she started coming over to his house at all hours of the night, offering him reds and skag. There was only one topic of conversation. You, Jimbo.

Every session ended the same. Talk of your death, accompanied by the most deep and tragic grieving Paul ever witnessed. I hope you and Pam are now together.

Speaking of tragedies, in 1980 we had a major one down here. Our first rock-'n'-roll assassination. Sometimes I still can't believe it; John Lennon's prophetic line "they gonna crucify me" came true. Some psycho shot him as he was returning to his apartment. I used to worry that a lunatic would take a potshot at you onstage. It's frightening when a fan makes the crossover to fan-atic. When I think about all the weirdos we used to attract, it's lucky nothing tragic ever happened (your self-destruction excluded).

Ray did get punched out in front of Elektra recording studios, didn't he. Did you hear the story behind that one? This guy was insulted that we were writing about him—he thought he was the Lizard King—so he slugged the first one of us to step outside. Of course, there was the inmate at Bellevue who wrote you every day with quotes like "You are the captain of my soul. You be the Christ," and you had to write a letter saying please don't write anymore, my girlfriend is jealous. Artists can't take responsibility for the individual psyches of all of their fans, but I could tell you were upset by the instability of these fans.

The classic weirdo was the guy we nicknamed Cigar-Pain, remember him? The young bum (and there weren't as many young ones then) who used to hang around our rehearsal studio and burn his tongue with a lit cigar in order to acquire a singing voice like you? Remember we couldn't concentrate on our rehearsal because he would sing through the air conditioning vent outside and it would reverberate throughout the building? Well . . . news came recently that he killed his mother and then himself . . . pretty scary. He got our lyrics all wrong; he was supposed to kill his father and fuck his mother! Don't people know that you're not supposed to take these things literally?

⁊.

This past winter, Debbie and I tried separate houses. I bought Debbie a condo, which she wanted, and the kid went back and forth. Joint custody and coparenting. It was initially confusing for the child and painful for me to watch, but better than the kid walking into our room crying because of all the noise and tension due to one of our fights. Soon she realized that we both were there for her. As parents we had planned her, and I definitely wanted her to continue receiving my half of the input. I was not going to be a weekend father.

Becoming a male mother instantly was an incredible test. I make a good salad and a mean grilled cheese, but kids don't like salads. I've got it down now, and a sense of accomplishment prevails. I can handle being totally responsible for another little person four days a week.

See what you've been missing? Your lyrics from "Universal Mind" thoroughly capture the male-female dynamic:

I was doing time in the universal mind
I was doin' alright.
Then you came along, with a suitcase and a song
Turned my head around.
Now I'm so alone,
Just lookin' for a home,
In every face I see . . .

293

I'm the freedom man
That's how lucky I am

﹡

Los Angeles, 1983

Another half a year of cutting through the bullshit with the therapist,
and this fall Debbie decided to stop the conjoint therapy. I was still holding
a candle for our relationship to work out, but "the future [was] uncertain
and the end [was] always near."

I continued analysis alone and made some interesting discoveries. Like I
could cry. Grieve over the death of my brother and what was happening in
my marriage.

"When you get married there are three contracts," my analyst said.
"One with the state you're getting married in, one with your spouse, and
one with your collective unconscious."

Right. A: the legal one, B: what you actually bring to the marriage—for
example, that we really didn't want it to last more than ten years; and C:
the contract with my collective, which is interested in my growth, and if I
have to move on, I have to move on. It all made sense in my head, but my
heart hurt.

We decided to make our separation official and permanent. The big
"D" number two. "Summer's almost gone" and good-bye to the "L.A.
woman."

Where will we be, when summer's gone?
Morning found us calmly unaware
Noon burnt gold into our hair,
At night we swam the laughing sea
When summer's gone, where will we be?

Around this same time, fall '83, the band's popularity continued to
increase, and as you know, there is not much in the way of unreleased
material. So we began listening to our old live material to see if anything
was there. I'm kind of glad that in the old days we didn't just turn the

recording machines on and jam. Avoids a lot of junk coming out post-mortem.

Rothchild was up for producing what was to become our second live album, Alive, She Cried, *so he gave me a call. He sort of apologized for the poetry album comments, and as you remember, he's the kind of guy you can't dislike for too long, so he joined the project.*

We didn't repeat any songs from the first live album, and we included "Gloria" from the sound check at the Aquarius Theater. It sounded great. Real raw.

Now I had something to say to the box boys at the supermarket who recognized me and would ask me over and over if there was anything new coming out. Or old. They weren't particular. They were only three or four years old when we were on the rampage. What did this mean? I was walking in Westwood when a thirteen-year-old boy came down the block the other way with a Doors T-shirt on. I wasn't in the mood for autographs so I made sure we didn't have eye contact. He didn't recognize me. There's a price for a high profile, as you know. Maybe the kid didn't realize that I was the same face as on his T-shirt because I had a six-year-old daughter in tow. And I'm the guy who used to hate anyone with kids! Maybe it was just the lack of a mustache and mutton chops. When my kid first heard our records around the house she asked me to take them off. I inquired why, and she said, "That guy's voice scares me." What does that mean? Something dark in those pipes of yours. Fate?

As the typical flower child, your aggression made me uncomfortable too. Was I the sensitive male the poet Robert Bly warns about who brought forth my feminine consciousness in the sixties but failed to expedite those new values with positive male energy? I think the seventies were a result of this. In the early eighties we saw aggression become popular again, and the Doors' resurgence began. We were new wave and punk before our time. These musicians have been gobbled up into different bands and fed to the great god of merchandising. What's left of the genuine revolutionary punk bands has eroded into narcissism, and they are dying out, as you died taking the dark male energy of Dionysus, Greek god of wine, too literally. The positive side of your dark nature was to eradicate the bullshit.

Reflecting on this today, I realize that you knew that Western man's quest for a better job, a house, and car was a substitute for his real quest: something sacred. That's why you weren't interested in material things. You also knew that the church was dead, that its symbols and rituals no longer had meaning for us, so you challenged the proselytizing of money-hungry preachers and lonely "sinners" in "PETITIONING THE LORD WITH PRAYER."

Now I'm going to preach to you for a second.

What you missed was that the need for the sacred must be transformed to an inner cathedral. Our songs contacted the Dionysian side of spiritual life through music, but "the God of Wine cheers and warms men's hearts; it also makes them drunk," according to Edith Hamilton's book on mythology, a book I know you were aware of. I'll refresh your memory some more. She goes on:

> The Greeks were a people who saw facts very clearly. They could not shut their eyes to the ugly and degrading side of wine drinking and see only the delightful side. They knew Dionysus was man's benefactor and he was man's destroyer.
>
> The momentary sense of exultant power wine-drinking can give was only a sign to show men that they had within them more than they knew; they could themselves become divine.

Maybe you are a god! Down here you are a media god. Back in the sixties I thought if our songs lasted ten years, that would be something. Well, we're going on twenty and there's no end in sight.

I wish we'd learned a little more about each other. Then maybe we would have been closer and ultimately wouldn't have traveled down such different paths. Or would we have? I'm trying to find out, even now. You certainly have made a mark. You've influenced me a lot. I've even been reading a little Nietzsche! A quote of his comes to mind. "A man's ancestors have paid the price of what he is."

You definitely are in me. And so I want to say thank you. And good-bye.

21

RIDERS ON THE STORM

Los Angeles, 1983

"You should check out Robert Bly. It might help your writing," Tony said. He was the director of my play, which we were about to take to New York and put on off-off Broadway. He had given me an article called "What Men Really Want," which was an interview with the American poet Bly. A National Book Award winner in 1968 for *Light Around the Body*, apparently Bly was now involved in men's consciousness.

There was a photograph on the front page of the article that caught my attention. It was a shot of the interviewer, Keith Thompson, with his arm around Bly, and Bly pointing a finger at Thompson. They were laughing and engaged in lively conversation. Something was going on that I wanted to know about. I could tell they weren't gay. I also could tell that they weren't macho guys who drank beer all the time and watched sports on TV. There was something slightly revolutionary happening in that photo and I wanted it.

New York, 1984

Is it you, dead?
If you are
Then why isn't there tears?

Is it you posing as dead?
Where are the mourners?
The grief?

The words come pouring out like lava. The rage is rising. La Mama Theater at last. Twenty-odd years of showcasing experimental theater on the Lower East Side. I feel naked and alone up here in front of these strangers. But goddamn, it's great not to be behind a group. I live or die on my own now: my acting and my words.

I pause for a moment and feel the audience's vibes. It's pin-drop time. I think they know *who* I'm talking about, even though this first act is Sam Shepard's words, his *Tongues*.

Did my friends show tonight? Did my publicist reach the critic from the *Voice*? I hope the music level is right—ah, the first thunderclap, the rain, the storm. The pain. Welling up inside me again.

Riders on the storm
Riders on the storm
Into this house we're born
Into this world we're thrown
Like a dog without a bone
An actor out on loan
Riders on the storm.

Now pull the track down. *Perfect* level for the next dialogue. Damn, these New York teckies are the best.

Is this really you appearing?
Again appearing?
Are you asking me to believe it?
What are you asking?

I can see you, you motherfucker! I scream to myself between stanzas. I've conjured you up again and there you are, with your

298

right leg cocked around the mike stand, one hand on the mike and the other brushing your long hair back from your face. The black-leather Lizard King still casting a giant shadow over me. I wonder if they can see you as vividly as I do.

Am I knowing you differently now?
Am I making you up?
Conjuring up this shape of you?
As I remember you once?
Putting you back together?
What are you asking? Can you tell me?
Can you say that you know you're not here
In this world
In this world I'm speaking from?

Down to a whisper. I'm drained. But I've been possessed with these images of you, of the band, since you died. For thirteen years I've been trying to crawl out from your—our—shadow and find who I was, who I am, who I can be, besides "John Densmore of the Doors."

The lights are down. Is that applause? Did it work?

Now I'm shaking backstage, thinking of all the letters, the journals, the new music, the relationships, the therapy, the pilgrimages, and now a play. Goddamn, that applause is sweet. I hang on to the curtain to steady myself.

⁄.

Hell's Kitchen. What in God's name am I doing here? More important . . . what am I trying to prove here? In this concrete jungle, as Bob Marley would say. I could be riding my horse in Ojai, California, right now. I have to believe I'm here to rekindle the creative juices with this writing and acting. I miss the passion of playing music, hitting the groove with the Doors, having an audience totally on edge. But I don't want to get into another band and try to make it again. So here I am. Moving on with my life.

299

I'm sitting in a friend's grungy two-bedroom apartment on 34th and Ninth. Nervous and unable to sleep after tonight's show. It's 12:30 A.M. I switch between two programs with my friend's cable selector. One show is a videotape of a lecture by Krishnamurti, the Indian sage. It is broadcast from Ojai.

The other program I'm watching is cable access, where the local citizenry can come down to the TV station and perform anything they want on the air. This particular show has a rather beautiful woman slowly taking off her clothes and masturbating. Krishnamurti has a magnetic glow emanating from his face. The woman has another kind of glow. It comes from being on the verge of orgasm.

On the one hand Krishnamurti talks of facing one's death—now, and living with it, making life fuller. The other program is about sex. In a few minutes the woman will reach a climax and die a little. Sex and death mirroring each other. Hand in hand. The woman is alone, masturbating, performing for other lonely people, like me. It turns me on. For a few moments I'm not so alone.

Back to Krishnamurti, and he is saying "Do it, do it, now. Live your life totally free from fear and be *truly* creative every day." The woman is writhing and about to come. I'm about to come, watching her.

The yin and yang of life, the culture of narcissism, the cult of sex and death, right here in NYC. And I keep switching back and forth like a video junkie between the two channels, faster and faster, insatiable.

Sex and death. Sex and death. Sex and death.

⅄

Mendocino, California, 1985
Bly Men's Conference

After driving on a dirt road for half an hour, I finally arrived at the Woodlands Camp. Lean-to cabins, surrounded by giant redwoods with only a small clearing, gave off a claustrophobic feeling.

I have always loved nature, but this place, with overcast skies and little light, was dark and cold. We were definitely in the forest.

The lodge had two fireplaces, one at each end. Thank God.

A large man of sixty, white-haired and jovial, walked to the center of the group. It was obviously Robert Bly.

"I want to welcome everyone and thank you for coming. It took courage to come up here with a bunch of men. As you know, my son, Sam, had an accident and was killed, so I've asked Jim Hillman to help out this year with the teaching, to lessen my load." A tear quickly ran down Bly's face as he spoke. "Jim's a wonderful Jungian analyst, writer, and thinker. Michael Meade is back with his drumming and Celtic stories, and as usual we will have contact and aikido movement as well as Indian sweats. Welcome."

⁂

"My brother went to 'Nam, got hooked on heroin, and OD'd." Joe was beginning his tale of "failure"; the theme Bly had chosen for the night. I sat erect in my chair, acutely attuned to every word.

A photo of Vietnamese monks burning themselves to death on the front page of the L.A. Times came to mind. It was a 1963 picture that captured the Buddhists protesting against America's increasing involvement in the war. Back then the image had jolted me into the decision that I wasn't going in the army. No matter what.

I wanted to put myself on the line and tell a story of failure. My two divorces came to mind. Objectively, the marriages were fairly long, four and eight years, but the feeling of failure still surrounded them. Possibly it was my parents having their fortieth wedding anniversary that heightened the sensation. My sister had gotten a second divorce as well. What had happened to the Densmore family? I thought we were "ordinary people."

I decided on my story and sat up shakily on the back of my folding chair. I wanted to be seen, but I was nervous over what I would say, which emotions might well up.

"I've integrated my feelings over failing to save my brother, but

301

a little bit of it will stay with me forever. I had two brothers . . . both named Jim . . . one was my blood brother . . . one was my band member . . . they're both dead . . . both died at the age of twenty-seven . . . I think I'm just about over my *real* brother—the guilt . . . saving or not saving him," I whispered.

"Louder . . . louder, John," the guys said cautiously.

"Uh? . . . YEAH. Uh . . . I feel like I'm JUST ABOUT OVER THE GUILT of not saving my brother Jim." I reiterated to the eighty sympathetic faces. "And, uh, Jim Morrison, I'm writing a book about . . . trying to get through all that . . . hanging on for years . . . ten years of stuff."

I let out a big sigh. This was my second conference and my courage was on the rise due to Bly's infectious openness. After about thirty seconds of silence, I started in again.

"When did *your* brother die?" I asked Robert.

"He died in '71."

"At what age?"

"In '71 . . . he was about . . . thirty-five."

"Mm . . . time helps," I offered.

"Mmmm," Robert agreed.

"Therapy . . . you guys . . . it all helps," I continued.

"Do you feel failure in both those two?" Robert asked.

"I did feel failure in my brother. . . ." I let out another big sigh. "I feel failure and I also know that if anyone's gonna change it's gotta be inside . . . you gotta go *snap.*"

"I feel your grief," one of the men said in support.

Silence.

"Morrison was an asshole most of the time." Then came an archetypal chill through me, and I found myself losing control of my facial features. I involuntarily lowered my head and a state-ment forced its way out of my mouth. I didn't know who was working my lips. "I miss creating [my voice began cracking and my eyes became red] music with him."

The eighty men groaned in support.

After that I couldn't speak. At that moment I realized how

important the creative act was to me. Especially with someone I felt simpatico with. How the public responds doesn't matter as much as the feeling while doing it; I missed the feeling.

I wept for about a minute and then continued.

"Boy, he was hard to live with." I spoke through the tears. "Life in hell; six years."

"Uuhh," Robert responded.

"I, uh . . . you know . . . I wanted to be in the Byrds, and be a puer." I sniffled. "And here I was in this band of darkness."

Pause. They understood the "puer" reference from Jim Hillman's *Puer Papers*, a controversial work on the eternal "boy in our culture."

"Interesting." I laughed, and everyone joined in.

"Fate," I whispered.

A long pause.

"Thanks," I concluded.

"Well, *thank you*, John," Robert replied.

There's a killer on the road
His brain is squirming like a toad
Take a long holiday
Let your children play
If you give this man a ride
Sweet family will die
Killer on the road . . . yeah . . .

I can't believe I'm standing here naked with a bunch of men, in the middle of the night, about to crawl into a small cramped hut to pretend we're American Indians! Or real men! . . . or something.

It's pitch black inside the sweat and the volcanic rocks, which were brought down from the recently exploded Mount Saint Helens in Washington, are glowing deep red in the center pit. They've been reheated in a huge bonfire we started for that purpose. A claustrophobic paranoia sweeps over me as I grab the aromatic mugwart that is provided to help breathing. The plant from the sage family helps . . . a little.

My bad drummer's back starts to ache, so I lie down between a couple of the guys and the walls of the lodge. It is real cramped, and we start sweating profusely, the dirt on the ground sticking to our skin.

What the fuck am I trying to prove here? I wonder. I guess it's the inquiring street scientist in me, which showed itself when I first took acid. Jim's quote about the early band days comes to mind: "Let's just say I was testing the bounds of reality. I was curious to see what would happen. That's all it was: just curiosity."

We go around the circle, passing a rattle, or truth stick, each man bringing into the sweat whoever or whatever he wants to work on. One of the guys says he's an alcoholic and would like to be healed.

"I bring in the spirit of Jim Morrison to help me understand his death," I say. "And to use his knowledge of alcohol, another 'spirit,' to help you." The confessor on the other side of the glowing rocks seems to get a jolt.

I don't think the Doors could have pulled back and rejuvenated. There was no such thing as "professional help" regarding chemical dependency, and we didn't communicate on a verbal level in the sixties.

Ray said that we never talked deeply to each other back then because writing music together was too delicate and fragile to risk getting into arguments.

Part of me doesn't buy that today. With our continuing success, the Doors has become like an empire, a multinational, and the corporation is always served. Members die off, but the corp remains. (The only purgatory for these gods is Chapter 11.)

It's been forty-five minutes, and we're crawling out of the sweat lodge. I feel cleansed. I thought I was going to lose it the first twenty minutes, but now a sense of accomplishment and power prevails. It certainly has been different from everyone in his Sunday best, sitting orderly in pews and listening to a sermon. I guess in these men's groups I've found not only the two brothers I lost, but a multitude of brothers sharing deep feelings.

22

WHEN THE MUSIC'S OVER

Los Angeles, 1989

My friend Jim Morrison got stuck. He didn't become president of the United States as Ray Manzarek had hoped, or continue to be the voice for Robby Krieger's music. Jim did become the voice of a generation. In Jim's words: "It's that old thing like a first novel, they usually give the cat a break, everybody kind of pats him on the back. And the second one, they really chop him up. Then if he does a few more, and shows he has staying power, they say welcome back to the fold, the family embraces you. I think it will be the same way with us. We just have to hold out for a while, and one day everyone will realize: 'they're just like old friends, they've been around for years now, they're part of our national psyche.' "

As long as there's young people, they can look to Jim to help them cut the umbilical cord. Good-bye, Mom and Dad.

Break on through
Break on through
Break on through, yeah

"Break On Through"—to what? What was the other side? After all those years I still only have a few hints, moments, reassurances that we did break on through. As the writer Tom Wolfe said, "The naivete that it could be achieved [nirvana] made the

306

sixties possible,'' but I don't think we were ready to "Have the world, and HAVE IT NOW!" Back then Robby and I were heavily influenced by the love generation, which was an evolving thing for males to do. We grew our hair long and integrated female values of sensitivity into our psyches.

So in the eighties, it's hard for former hippies to understand that ultimately, male energy comes from a deep male mode of feeling. The kind that goes out and gets things done. Zeus energy, but benevolent. The kind that women are experiencing right now in the marketplace. They are also experiencing "male" problems of overwork and stress.

The baby boomer's job now is to take the good intentions of the sixties and bring them into power areas. The discipline comes in the second half of the arc. We can't have the sexual freedoms, the rewards aren't as dramatic, but a sense of well-being pervades if we remember to pass it on.

"The students [in the sixties] never realized how much they had accomplished,'' says Robert Bly. "They didn't realize how much the antiwar protests really moved the bourgeoisie; they didn't pass a confidence in that down to the kids in school now.'' It's confusing when leaders such as President Reagan, speaking to the students at Moscow State University, reflects on the sixties as "a period in our country when there was a very great change for the worse. When I was governor of California, I could start a riot just by going to a campus. But that has all changed, and I could be looking out at an American student body as well as I'm looking out here and would not be able to tell the difference between you.''

Let's hope the nineties have some breakaway quality. Rock 'n' roll must continue to embrace this to remain vital. And I'm not talking about style. The original Hard Rock Café, which we're standing in front of on the back of our fifth album cover, was a skid-row bar on 5th Street in the homeless area of downtown L.A. Kids today just want the glory and glamour. Hamburgers and gold records. They take on the outer trappings of leather and long hair, and forget the inner thrust of creativity. Find your own uniqueness.

Ray has been quoted as saying that LSD helped create the Doors' communal mind. We never took acid together, but I suppose the fact that in the sixties the world was polarized into straights and hippies separated us from the common man. Dylan's "Ballad of a Thin Man" catches the feeling exactly. "Something is happening here, And you don't know what it is, Do you, Mr. Jones?"

We did feel camaraderie against the outside world, but I think what really developed our group spirit was our dedication to the music. Getting together every day for thirty months (weekends excepted) to rehearse, dissect, analyze, enjoy, and surrender to group compromises over our songs cemented the bond. We developed nuances and subtleties that could come only from time spent together, having a history together.

"The Doors were a real group," Robby said in an interview. Our mood in rehearsal was one of total freedom to say anything about a particular song or arrangement. Quoting Robby again: "People thought Jim was the leader but he was so scatterbrained he could never be a leader. Most bands there's one dictator and the rest followers. Our band was like no leaders." To the outside world we became Jim Morrison and the Doors, behind closed doors, four equal parts. In Cleveland, when a local DJ introduced us as "Jim Morrison and the Doors," Jim ran out immediately and grabbed the microphone and yelled, "HOLD IT, WAIT A MINUTE, WAIT A MINUTE . . . LADIES AND GENTLEMEN . . . THE DOORS."

Our roadie Vince reflected in an interview with a journalist, "I used to leave during rehearsal . . . if I was doing anything . . . making any noise, I would leave because it made Jim nervous to rehearse because it was raw. It wasn't polished. He used to throw Danny Sugerman out all the time. They felt best, and I think the juices flowed among the four of them, when they were alone and it was quiet."

Robby says that what kept us synchronous was the balance of power down at the end of the zodiac; I was born on the first of December, Jim on the eighth, Robby on the eighth of January, and Ray on the twelfth of February. Two Sags, a Capricorn, and an Aquarian all in a row.

Musically, we respected each other till the end.

No drum machine can tell you that your music is stiff, that it doesn't have that inherent sense of swing, or that you need to modulate or have a bridge or solo in a certain section.

I finally succumbed to electronic drums (have to keep up!), but synthesizers endanger drummers' musicianship. It's not from lack of gigs due to industrialization, but the player doesn't have to strive year after year to perfect his craft. The great jazz drummer Elvin Jones gave me my hands; I emulated his technique. Are today's drummers emulating Japanese electronics? When a drummer develops good time, it's like meditating; to be exactly in the groove is to chant an internal mantra. The product isn't hurting, as much as is the spiritual growth of the musician. Discipline does something for the soul.

I have been asked hundreds of times "Was it worth it?" "Why did you stay?" Philip Elwood from the *San Francisco Herald* helps me answer that question with his description of Jim's performance at the Winterland:

Morrison came on full steam at midnight and was still going strong well after one, when we departed. He throws out his excellent lyrics in tones ranging from strained whispers to bellowing, mike-swallowing roars. He does not just sing, he puts on a full dramatic performance. He sings "When the music's over, turn out the lights . . ." with such crescendo and dynamic force that one expects a dazzling ball of fire to light up the sky when the ten-minute tune ends. "Let's get it all together . . . one, more, TIME" . . . or "Rolll, rolll, e-rolly, all night long . . ." Morrison stretches out syllables, often making them theatrical incantations. A magnificent performer, no doubt.

309

That's why I stayed. I rode those crescendos musically with Jim, sometimes even leading them, and there was nothing like it. For all the pain Jim caused me over his demise, it was worth it for that "hour of magic" onstage, or recording, when we were playing our songs.

The late mythologist Joseph Campbell sums up the experience: "When you follow your bliss, and by bliss I mean the deep sense of being *in* it and doing what the push is out of your own existence, you follow that and doors will open where you would not have thought there were going to be doors. And where there wouldn't be a door for anybody else." I had always thought that a career in music was a total crap shoot: all or nothing. I considered it a hobby or avocation that paid for books at school. Bluffing my way out of the army was a turning point. I was afraid that if I ever wanted a government job, this rejection would haunt me, but I had to follow the push out of my existence: music. "The Doors" did open up; literally. I didn't know yet that I had just walked through the "Door" with my name above it.

But Jim burned out. Why? Because his childhood was one military base after another? Or was it just the program he came in with?

Jac Holzman says: "Jim sensed the distance between who he really was and his public persona."

In a rare moment of raw public candidness after a night of binging, Jim told the BBC that "Our music is like someone not quite at home, not quite relaxed. Aware of a lot of things, but not quite sure." He said he "would like to do a song, or a piece of music, that's a pure expression of joy, pure unbounded joy. Like the coming of spring, or a celebration of existence—a feeling of being totally at home."

At the end of our career Jim was quoted as saying "If I had it to do over again, I think I would have gone more for the quiet, undemonstrative little artist plodding away in his own garden trip." He never got to that place of contentment, that feeling of being totally at home. Until now. Jim wanted to go back to the good old club days, but they were just his metaphor for lost youth. As Robby said quietly to me when the news came about Jim's death, "He's finally at peace."

Jim knew that with a fast peak, the ledge at the top would be narrow. His response to the question of why creative people such as Janis Joplin and Jimi Hendrix were burning out was astute. Was it prophetic? "I guess that great creative burst of energy that happened three or four years ago [1967] was hard to sustain and for the sensitive, I guess they might be dissatisfied with anything, you know, except the heights."

What was his message?

Cancel my subscription
To the resurrection,
Send my credentials
To the house of detention,
I got some FRIENDS inside

In the sixties I took those lines as antiestablishment rhetoric. I felt a kinship with them. Now, with time and the fact that I have been able to shed a few tears over my bandmate's demise, these lyrics strike me as far more personal, a revelation of the true Jim Morrison, the one who identified with Rimbaud and Neal Cassidy, the ones who burned like Roman candles.

Twenty years ago I didn't want any tension in my life. Not that I seek it out now, but when it arrives, it can be useful. "Creative tension," psychologist Rollo May called it. Jim loved it. He describes it in an interview with *Rolling Stone* magazine in 1968.

"In a club with a small audience you feel free to do anything. You still feel an obligation to be good, so you can't get completely loose; there are people watching. So there's this beautiful tension."

Now, as an actor, I'm quite interested in it: drama is made of it. Julian Beck and Judith Malina recently came to a theater performance in Los Angeles that I was involved in, before Julian passed away, and I was thrilled. Times change, minds change. If I'd had Jim's consciousness in my early twenties, it wouldn't have worked. I wouldn't have been so innocent and open with suggestions. Jim knew I wasn't that aware of what he was trying to do, yet he also knew that I was the right drummer to bring out his words. Coming from the jazz improv background, I could spin off his word games.

As a sixties soft male, I didn't enjoy playing "The End," but intuitively I knew enough to take the snares off my drums for that number, getting the maximum darkness out of my tom-toms.

"BOOM-BOOM" came out of somewhere dark *in me* during the quiet parts in "The End." I knew it would jolt and scare people, and I knew that great music had dynamics. Hearing those drum shots from me must have convinced Jim that I was the right guy to "unleash the sorcerer" in him.

His respect felt good. I miss it madly.

I love the friends I've gathered together on this raft
We've erected pyramids in honor of our escaping.

To some extent, he loved us because we let him manipulate us. But he knew it was a thin raft. A few years after our initial climb toward success, he quickly became "a monster, black dressed in leather," to quote himself. The University of Michigan gig was the first leak, coming from some demon in Jim's psyche; the Buick ad tore a gaping hole that filled the raft with mistrust.

When I see Ringo doing a Schweppes commercial, or Michael Jackson and Lionel Richie making ten-million-dollar soft drink deals, I think of Jim. Friends have asked me if Jim was an asshole or really brilliant. He was both. He was foolish and destroyed himself, and he also had integrity.

I worry about the Kay-teling of the Doors, what with the incredible postmortem scrambling over very lucrative leftovers. Leftovers can be tasty, when heated up (digitally remastered) or with the right ingredient added. Technology has improved mastering equipment such that it was worth it to go in and add a little treble, bass, and/or midrange to the overall sound of our albums, which we've done. But the repackage jobs don't feel right. Back when the Stones put their first one out, *High Tide and Green Grass*, I just about died. I'm glad that the greatest hits albums inspire some to go back to the original records, because there was great care in programming.

CDs also worry me. The sound is incredible, but this obsession with technology says something about a lack of interest in what's really important: the actual songs. Michael Harner, in *The Way of the Shaman*, tells the results of the industrial revolution bypassing a culture: "The low technological level of 'primitive' cultures compelled them to develop the highest degree possible of the ability of the human mind to cope with problems."

Maybe it's just the covers of the compilation albums that bug me. They all have a head shot of Jim when he was in his prime, and I don't think he would approve. Not every shot. Jim even had regrets after approving the first album shot with his head covering the entire front. After our second album, *Strange Days*, came out, Jim was asked in an interview about the cover. "I hated the cover on the first album. *Strange Days* looks European. It's better than having our fucking faces on it."

Compared to *Strange Days* or even *Morrison Hotel*, our fifth album—with us looking like a road band of wanderers and drifters —these re-packaged records are selling sex again. The old album covers had more to do with the content, the music inside, not image. But I'm tired of fighting with Ray about these matters. It was Ray's Apollonian insistence that propagated the "Jim's-still-alive" rumors, not looking at the dark truth that Jim destroyed himself. As one rock publication said years ago, "Manzarek has a curious habit of referring to the group in the present tense, as if its singer's death and the eleven years apart are simply part of some long-range plan."

Jim's message was endarkenment, only Ray is so illumination-bound that he doesn't see his own darkness; the Apollonian shadow he casts as he faces the sun. Ray loved Jim as a son, and it's tough for a father to accept his son's demise. Actually, Ray has been a father figure to me, too. This book is one of many ways I've been struggling to prove myself. And separate myself. Like any other son, it's hard for me to say, but after all Ray and I have been through together, there is no way I can't say that I don't love him dearly. The thing I cherish about Ray is his commitment to art. When all the business bullshit is in the background, many's a time I've felt and shared Ray's love and excitement over creating something. In that area, we are totally connected. But like most sons, I want to love him from a distance.

It's easy for me to criticize when I'm collecting royalties from all this hullabaloo, but I just can't seem to forget back when these things were in their incubation stage and there was a sense of sacredness because it was small. Secret. We were taking drugs—psychedelics, not cocaine and smack—to expand our minds, not to escape.

Sometimes I think that if I'd had more integrity I would really have quit around the third album, in light of Jim's self-destruction. But then my creative side wouldn't have experienced the thrill of putting my drums down on the "L.A. Woman" track, one of my faves. My spirits are lifted when I hear that life-supporting groove.

Over the years there have been other fringe benefits far beyond royalties. The freedom to travel and experience other cultures has been an eye-opener. America is not the center of the world and doesn't necessarily do everything right. I always appreciate coming home, though. It is a great country.

I've been able to make contributions to charities and ecological groups, which gives me a sense of well-being. Money is an energy that can be used for good as well as greed.

The most fulfilling bonus of our career is positive feedback about the effect of the music. A few years ago I had a friend whose girlfriend worked with mentally disturbed kids. One in particular wore Doors T-shirts every day. This thirteen-year-old schizophrenic wouldn't talk—wouldn't open up to anyone. The girl-friend saw my face on his shirt and told him her boyfriend knew me. The kid "broke on through," spoke up, and has been getting better ever since.

This fills me to the brim. Through me, my brother in me, this kid has made a turn toward healing.

Vietnam vets were in an insane war, and Jim sang of being "lost in a Roman wilderness of pain, all the children are insane, desperately in need, of some stranger's hand, in a desperate land." This lyric section opened Francis Ford Coppola's film *Apocalypse Now*. Jim connected to people on the edge because they could sense that he, too, was on the edge.

Back in the sixties, I hated the guys who went to Southeast Asia. They were listening to "The Ballad of the Green Berets," and we hippies were turning on, tuning in, and dropping out of any establishment propaganda. After the war, when the vets started coming home and our government turned the other cheek, my compassion for them began. I realized that there were a lot of racial and economic minorities filling up the ranks and they hadn't had any choice in the matter. In the eighties, I worked with some Vietnam vets who wrote and acted in the play *Tracers*. My fear of these men turned to love. Getting to know the guys who had faced the heart of darkness broke my heart. The army had turned them on (which always seems to happen), the soldiers tuned into the bullshit, but couldn't drop out.

They had an intense experience, as I did. Not that mine was as heavy, but I, too, had survivor's guilt. They lost their buddies, I lost Jim.

I'm glad I didn't understand Jim's mentor Friedrich Nietzsche when I was twenty-one, or I too might have taken up the banner. Reading Nietzsche now, I can take only what I need. Nietzsche became "Zarathustra," and Morrison became "the Lizard King." Nietzsche was destroyed by the dark side because he went deeper into it than anyone until then. Explorers pay a price because they go farther than their mentors into unexplored territory. Nietzsche

315

held the candle up into one of the corners of darkness and then the flame went out.

"He is commanded who cannot obey himself," the German philosopher wrote. "To command is more difficult than to obey. And not only that, the commander beareth the burden of all who obey, and that this burden easily crusheth him—an effort and a jeopardy appeared to me to be contained in all commanding, and wherever living things command they risk themselves."

I know now that Jim read this. And took the risk. With the completion of this book, I have pretty much worked through my guilt over failing to save Jim. As the Beatles sang in "All You Need Is Love,"

No one you can save
That can't be saved

In recent years I have helped friends in trouble, with "tuff love" and interventions in response to their substance abuse, but I realized that these efforts are mostly for me. I couldn't live with myself if I didn't try, even though I know, as I knew in the sixties, that ultimately real change comes from the inside. And Jim knew it too. Salli Stevenson, an interviewer, asked Jim toward the end of his life if he thought of himself as a hero. His response: "I think of myself as an intelligent, sensitive human being with the soul of a clown which always forces me to blow it at the most important moments."

It was too late for Jim and Pam. They are no longer with us. Their tumultuous, volatile love affair ended tragically. It was clear they were deeply connected, though. Word came down that Pam slipped a photo of herself into Jim's casket before it was sealed.

I can't see your face in my mind.
I can't see your face in my mind.
Don't you cry, baby, please don't cry,
And don't look at me with your eyes.

316

I can't seem to find the right lie.
Insanity's horse adorns the sky,
I won't need your picture . . .
Until we say good-bye.

Writing isn't as much fun as playing in a band, but I can do it whenever I want and I don't have to depend on flaky musicians. The thrill of writing is a subtler high, but the obsession can be the same. Or more intense. Like Kerouac. He certainly was possessed. And Jim emulated him. A line from Carl Jung comes to mind: "Are you living the myth, or is the myth living you?"

Speaking of mythmaking, another one of Jim's quotes reverberates heavily. Hollywood has been courting us for years now, trying to turn us into "celluloid heroes."

Did you have a good world when you died?
Enough to base a movie on?

For ten years, Ray has been the one who's promoted the idea of making a movie, and now he's feeling the fear of turning it over to someone else. Robby was against it for a long time, but he's cautiously coming around. And now I'm getting scared as it comes to fruition. Finally it's in the hands of Oliver Stone. Even though he's an excellent filmmaker, I still worry that the film will use Jim's dark side to overshadow what he was really trying to say. As a friend of mine said, "They're going to take your six-year career and squash it down to two hours and then blow it up to the size of a two-story building . . . is that going to be reality?" I just hope when it's done, it has some sense of truth to it.

※

Jim's parents were recently asked how they felt about their son's original bio back in '67, which said they were deceased. The Admiral and Mrs. Morrison replied that Jim had done that for their protection and privacy. Personally I think the opposite is true, that Jim did it to proclaim independence and cut the umbilical cord once and for all, but a myth is something to live by.

When the music's over . . .

Like the myth I've orchestrated about my brother's death. I perceive it as courageous. Pills are easy. He must have felt inside like the Elephant Man looked outside, so . . .

When the music's over . . .

I try to view it as the courage of a samurai. I transform it into a gift that has made me cherish life. Now I know that suicide is not my route.

Turn out the lights . . .

I thought somehow I could redeem his death through imitation, but my way has been to learn from these tragedies.

There is life beyond the Doors. I've been a husband, a father, an actor, a writer, and a politically concerned American.

Music is your special friend . . .

I was worried about betraying myself. The only things I betrayed were my old world and the Catholic world of my mother. To my surprise, I recently realized that I first got exposed to music by going to church.

Dance on fire as it intends . . .

I now know the reason I stayed in the band through all the insanity was because music had become my new religion. It is a major theme through my life.

Music is your only friend . . .

Music is my closest friend, but not my only friend. Through journals, a play, and this book, I've been building an inner life— an inner peak to match the outer one the band had, only this one will take me on through to the other side.

Until the end

AFTERWORD

It has been the year of the Doors. Again. Resurgence number ten. People continually ask me why we've endured, and I sometimes give them a flippant reply—"It's the drumming!"—trying to defuse a question that can only be answered egotistically.

Then I hear my pat answer coming out of my mouth: "Jim had all the ingredients for perfect James Dean myth building—beautiful, brilliant, and dead at twenty-seven." "Twenty-seven forever," as an American TV commentator smugly said about Jim on a network morning show. If you examine the photos closely, or read my impressions of him at the end, you can see that Jim *looked* sixty-seven when he died.

I didn't realize that Jim was an alcoholic until a few years after his death. When I dropped into that bar near our old office, the one where we recorded *L.A. Woman,* Fred the bartender remembered Jim as someone who outdrank anyone in the place. Ever. And Fred was an elderly man who'd seen a lot of drunks. It was then that I realized that Jim had a disease. Back in the early seventies we didn't have substance-abuse clinics to explain this stuff to us.

So was it all worth it? What made us so special that Hollywood spent thirty million dollars to visualize the life of a drunk?

For what it is, I do think Oliver Stone's vision of Jim Morrison has integrity; however, it is a film about the myth of Jim Morrison (Oliver never met Jim; he missed the sixties while fighting as a marine in Vietnam). But you do get the impression that Jim died

321

for his beliefs, certainly muddled through the haze of the drink. Beliefs of "breaking on through" to a "cleaner realm" of consciousness. Inner work. Through outer techniques of "derangement of the senses" and "roads of excess."

I view William Blake's quote "The road of excess leads to the palace of wisdom" differently from Jim. For me, Blake meant lead one's life as fully as possible, getting the maximum out of each experience, but *not* splintered apart into the abyss.

I think there are a lot of people who grew up in the sixties who haven't splintered, and still retain, if only privately, a vision of the world that grew out of that time: a commitment to civil rights, gender equality, and peace in the world. I include myself as one of them.

So once again, what was it that made the band endure? I've received many fan letters since *Riders* has been published, letters that have warmed my heart, thanking us over and over for providing the soundtrack for important moments in people's lives. One letter stands out—"My parents were in a club when 'Hello, I Love You' was on the jukebox. The song gave my dad the courage to go over and introduce himself, saying 'Hello, I love you, won't you tell me your name?' If you guys hadn't written that song, I might not exist!"

Or, as Val Kilmer, the actor who miraculously re-created Jim in the movie, said to me at the end of the filming, "After all this hullabaloo is over, there will still be the music."

DOORS LYRICS

ALL OTHER LYRICS

Printed in the United States
by Baker & Taylor Publisher Services